Reader's Digest
Low Calorie Cookbook

Reader's Digest
Low Calorie Cookbook

Published by
The Reader's Digest Association Limited
London • New York • Sydney • Montreal

Contents

Introduction
pages 6 to 9

Breakfast
pages 10 to 35

Snacks
pages 36 to 61

Soups and starters
pages 62 to 95

Index
pages 252 to 255

Desserts
pages 218 to 251

Main meals
pages 96 to 185

Side dishes and breads
pages 186 to 217

Introduction

A healthy diet helps you to look good and feel great. *Low Calorie Cookbook* is packed with delicious calorie-counted dishes so you can make a daily choice to suit your tastes and energy needs. Nutrition fads come and go, but the key to eating well remains the same; enjoy a balance of varied foods that supply all the nutrients your body requires.

Getting it into proportion

Current guidelines are that most people in the UK should eat more starchy foods, more fruit and vegetables, and less fat, meat products and sugary foods. It is almost impossible to give exact amounts that you should eat, as every person's requirements vary, depending on size, age and the amount of energy expended during the day.

However, nutrition experts have suggested an ideal balance of the different foods that provide us with energy (calories) and the nutrients needed for health. The number of daily portions of each of the food groups will vary from person to person – for example, an active teenager might need to eat up to 14 portions of starchy carbohydrate foods every day, whereas a sedentary adult would only require 6 or 7 portions – but the proportions of the food groups in relation to each other should ideally stay the same.

Food on the plate

A simple way to get the balance right, however, is to imagine a daily 'plate' divided into the different food groups. On the imaginary 'plate', starchy carbohydrate foods fill at least a third of the space, thus constituting the main part of your meals. Fruit and vegetables fill the same amount of space. The remaining third of the 'plate' is divided mainly between protein foods and dairy foods, with just a little space allowed for foods containing fat and sugar. These are the proportions to aim for.

It isn't essential to eat the ideal proportions on the 'plate' at every meal, or even every day – balancing them over a week or two is just as good. This will ensure that the body receives the steady supply of vitamins, minerals and phytochemicals required to stay well. The healthiest diet for you and your family is one that is generally balanced and sustainable in the long term.

Daily energy requirements in adult life

Daily calorie needs vary according to age, sex and lifestyle. To maintain an ideal body weight, we need to balance the calories we consume with the energy we expend.

Men			Women		
18-34 years	sedentary	2510 kcal	18-54 years	sedentary	1940 kcal
	active	2900 kcal		active	2150 kcal
	very active	3350 kcal		very active	2500 kcal
35-64 years	sedentary	2400 kcal		pregnant	2400 kcal
	active	2750 kcal		breastfeeding	2750 kcal
	very active	3350 kcal	55-74 years	sedentary	1900 kcal
65-74 years	sedentary	2330 kcal		active	2000 kcal
75+ years	sedentary	2100 kcal	75+ years	sedentary	1810 kcal

Our daily plate

Fruit and vegetables:

eat at least 5 portions a day

Nutrition experts are unanimous that we would all benefit from eating more fruit and vegetables each day – a total of at least 400 g (14 oz) of fruit and vegetables (edible part) is the target. Fruit and vegetables provide vitamin C for immunity and healing, and other 'antioxidant' vitamins and minerals for protection against cardiovascular disease and cancer. They also offer several 'phytochemicals' that help protect against cancer, and B vitamins, especially folate, which is important for women planning a pregnancy, to prevent birth defects. All of these, plus other nutrients, work together to boost well-being.

Antioxidant nutrients (e.g. vitamins C and beta-carotene, which are mainly derived from fruit and vegetables) and vitamin E help to prevent harmful free radicals in the body initiating or accelerating cancer, heart disease, cataracts, arthritis, general ageing, sun damage to skin, and damage to sperm. Free radicals occur naturally as a by-product of normal cell function, but are also caused by pollutants such as tobacco smoke and over-exposure to sunlight.

What is a portion of fruit or vegetables?

Some examples are:

1 medium-sized portion of vegetables or salad
1 medium-sized piece of fresh fruit
6 tbsp (about 140 g/5 oz) stewed or canned fruit
1 small glass (100 ml/3½ fl oz) fruit juice

Starchy carbohydrate foods:

eat 6–14 portions a day

At least 50% of the calories in a healthy diet should come from carbohydrates, and most of that from starchy foods – bread, potatoes and other starchy vegetables, pasta, rice and cereals. For most people in the UK this means doubling current intake. Starchy carbohydrates are the best foods for energy. They also provide protein and essential vitamins and minerals, particularly those from the B group. Eat a variety of starchy foods, choosing wholemeal or wholegrain types whenever possible, because the fibre they contain helps to prevent constipation, bowel disease, heart disease and other health problems.

What is a portion of starchy food?

Some examples are:

3 tbsp breakfast cereal
2 tbsp muesli
1 slice of bread or toast
1 bread roll, bap or bun
1 small pitta bread, naan bread or chapatti
3 crackers or crispbreads
1 medium-sized potato
1 medium-sized plantain or small sweet potato
2 heaped tbsp boiled rice
2 heaped tbsp boiled pasta

Dairy foods:

eat 2–3 portions a day

Dairy foods, such as milk, cheese, yogurt and fromage frais, are the best source of calcium for strong bones and teeth, and important for the nervous system. They also provide some protein for growth and repair, vitamin B_{12}, and vitamin A for healthy eyes. They are particularly valuable foods for young children, who need full-fat versions at least up to age 2. Dairy foods are also especially important for adolescent girls to prevent the development of osteoporosis later in life, and for women throughout life generally.

To limit fat intake, wherever possible adults should choose lower-fat dairy foods, such as semi-skimmed milk and low-fat yogurt.

What is a portion of dairy food?

Some examples are:

1 medium-sized glass (200 ml/7 fl oz) milk
1 matchbox-sized piece (40 g/1½ oz) Cheddar cheese
1 small pot of yogurt
125 g (4½ oz) cottage cheese or fromage frais

Foods containing fat:

1–5 portions a day

Unlike fruit, vegetables and starchy carbohydrates, which can be eaten in abundance, fatty foods should not exceed 33% of the day's calories in a balanced diet, and only 10% of this should be from saturated fat. This quantity of fat may seem a lot, but it isn't – fat contains more than twice as many calories per gram as either carbohydrate or protein.

Overconsumption of fat is a major cause of weight and health problems. A healthy diet must contain a certain amount of fat to provide fat-soluble vitamins and essential fatty acids, needed for the development and function of the brain, eyes and nervous system, but we only need a small amount each day – just 25 g is required, which is much less than we consume in our Western diet. The current recommendations from the Department of Health are a maximum of 71 g fat (of this, 21.5 g saturated) for women each day and 93.5 g fat (28.5 g saturated) for men. The best sources of the essential fatty acids are natural fish oils and pure vegetable oils.

What is a portion of fatty food?

Some examples are:

1 tsp butter or margarine
2 tsp low-fat spread
1 tsp cooking oil
1 tbsp mayonnaise or vinaigrette (salad dressing)
1 tbsp cream
1 individual packet of crisps

Foods containing sugar:

0–2 portions a day

Although many foods naturally contain sugars (e.g. fruit contains fructose, milk lactose), health experts recommend that we limit 'added' sugars. Added sugars, such as table sugar, provide only calories – they contain no vitamins, minerals or fibre to contribute to health, and it is not necessary to eat them at all. But, as the old adage goes, 'a little of what you fancy does you good' and sugar is no exception. Denial of foods, or using them as rewards or punishment, is not a healthy attitude to eating, and can lead to cravings, binges and yo-yo dieting. Sweet foods are a pleasurable part of a well-balanced diet, but added sugars should account for no more than 11% of the total daily carbohydrate intake.

In assessing how much sugar you consume, don't forget that it is a major ingredient of many processed and ready-prepared foods.

What is a portion of sugary food?

Some examples are:

3 tsp sugar
1 heaped tsp jam or honey
2 biscuits
half a slice of cake
1 doughnut
1 Danish pastry
1 small bar of chocolate
1 small tube or bag of sweets

Protein foods:

eat 2–4 portions a day

Lean meat, fish, eggs and vegetarian alternatives provide protein for growth and cell repair, as well as iron to prevent anaemia. Meat also provides B vitamins for healthy nerves and digestion, especially vitamin B_{12}, and zinc for growth and healthy bones and skin. Only moderate amounts of these protein-rich foods are required. An adult woman needs about 45 g of protein a day and an adult man 55 g, which constitutes about 11% of a day's calories. This is less than the current average intake. For optimum health, we need to eat some protein every day.

What is a portion of protein-rich food?

Some examples are:

3 slices (85–100 g/3–3½ oz) of roast beef, pork, ham, lamb or chicken
about 100 g (3½ oz) grilled offal
115–140 g (4–5 oz) cooked fillet of white or oily fish (not fried in batter)
3 fish fingers
2 eggs (up to 7 a week)
about 140 g/5 oz baked beans
60 g (2¼ oz) nuts, peanut butter or other nut products.

Too salty

Salt (sodium chloride) is essential for a variety of body functions, but we tend to eat too much through consumption of salty processed foods, 'fast' foods and ready-prepared foods, and by adding salt in cooking and at the table. The end result can be rising blood pressure as we get older, which puts us at higher risk of heart disease and stroke. Eating more vegetables and fruit increases potassium intake, which can help to counteract the damaging effects of salt.

Alcohol in a healthy diet

In recent research, moderate drinking of alcohol has been linked with a reduced risk of heart disease and stroke among men and women over 45. However, because of other risks associated with alcohol, particularly in excessive quantities, no doctor would recommend taking up drinking if you are teetotal. The healthiest pattern of drinking is to enjoy small amounts of alcohol with food, to have alcohol-free days and always to avoid getting drunk. A well-balanced diet is vital because nutrients from food (vitamins and minerals) are needed to detoxify the alcohol.

Water – the best choice

Drinking plenty of non-alcoholic liquid each day is an often overlooked part of a well-balanced diet. A minimum of 8 glasses (which is about 2 litres/3½ pints) is the ideal. If possible, these should not all be tea or coffee, as these are stimulants and diuretics, which cause the body to lose liquids, taking with them water-soluble vitamins. Water is the best choice. Other good choices are fruit or herb teas or tisanes, fruit juices – diluted with water, if preferred – or semi-skimmed milk (full-fat milk for very young children). Fizzy sugary or acidic drinks such as cola are more likely to damage tooth enamel than other drinks.

As a guide to the vitamin and mineral content of foods and recipes in the book, we have used the following terms and symbols, based on the percentage of the daily RNI provided by one serving for the average adult man or woman aged 19–49 years:

✓✓✓ *or* excellent   at least 50% (half)

✓✓   *or* good   25–50% (one-quarter to one-half)

✓   *or* useful   10–25% (one-tenth to one-quarter)

Note that recipes contribute other nutrients, but the analyses only include those that provide at least 10% RNI per portion. Vitamins and minerals where deficiencies are rare are not included.

V denotes that a recipe is suitable for vegetarians.

Breakfast

A nourishing start sets you up for the day and should not be skipped. This chapter is packed with delicious ideas from the lightest Strawberry yogurt smoothie – a mere 55-calorie treat – to a little feast of Scrambled eggs with smoked salmon and dill – still quite acceptable at 363 calories. With healthy muesli, granola, scones, popovers, and brioches as well, you will find plenty of breakfasts to enjoy.

Banana and mango shake

A thick banana-flavoured milk shake with a tropical touch, this will appeal to children and adults alike. It is an ideal drink for busy breakfast times as it is packed with nourishment and very quick to prepare.

Serves 2

½ ripe mango

1 small ripe banana, sliced

150 ml (5 fl oz) semi-skimmed milk

120 ml (4 fl oz) orange juice

2 tsp lime juice

1 tsp caster sugar

2 heaped tbsp vanilla frozen yogurt

sprigs of fresh lemon balm to decorate
    (optional)

Preparation time: 5 minutes

1 Peel the skin from the mango and cut the flesh away from the stone. Chop the flesh roughly. Put into a blender with the banana.

2 Add the milk, orange juice, lime juice, sugar and frozen yogurt and blend on maximum speed for about 30 seconds or until mixed and frothy.

3 Pour into glasses and serve immediately, decorated with sprigs of lemon balm, if you like.

Some more ideas

● Use skimmed milk instead of semi-skimmed. Skimmed milk contains only 0.1% fat, as compared with 3.9% for full-cream milk and 1.6% for semi-skimmed milk, but still has similar levels of vitamins and minerals.

● Those who do not eat dairy products or who have a lactose (milk sugar) intolerance can substitute 300 ml (10 fl oz) soya milk for the cow's milk, and omit the frozen yogurt; or use 240 ml (8 fl oz) soya milk with 2 heaped tbsp soya ice-cream.

● Use a ripe peach instead of the mango half.

● For a shake rich in fibre, use 115 g (4 oz) stoned ready-to-eat prunes instead of the mango, with lemon juice instead of lime juice.

Plus points

● Milk is an excellent source of several important nutrients – protein, calcium and phosphorus (important for strong bones and teeth) and many of the B vitamins, particularly B_1, B_2, B_6 and B_{12}.

● Bananas are a useful source of the mineral potassium, a good intake of which may help to prevent high blood pressure.

● Mangoes are rich in vitamin C and carotenoid compounds, both antioxidants that protect the body against damage by free radicals.

Each serving provides Ⓥ

kcal 150, **protein** 5 g, **fat** 2 g (of which saturated fat 1 g), **carbohydrate** 30 g (of which sugars 29 g), **fibre** 1 g

✓✓✓ C

✓   A, B_1, B_6, B_{12}, niacin, calcium, potassium

Breakfast

Strawberry yogurt smoothie

This refreshing drink is perfect for summer when strawberries are plentiful and full of flavour. It provides a healthy start to the day, with its high vitamin C content and natural sweetness. Dilute it with extra orange juice for a variation.

Serves 4

450 g (1 lb) ripe strawberries, hulled

grated zest and juice of 1 large orange

150 g (5½ oz) plain low-fat yogurt

1 tbsp caster sugar, or to taste (optional)

To decorate (optional)

4 small strawberries

4 small slices of orange

Preparation time: 5 minutes

1 Tip the strawberries into a food processor or blender and add the grated orange zest, orange juice and yogurt. Blend to a smooth purée, scraping down the sides of the container once or twice. Taste the mixture and sweeten with the sugar, if necessary.

2 For a really smooth consistency, press through a nylon sieve to remove the strawberry pips, although this is not essential.

3 Pour into glasses. If you like, decorate with small strawberries and slices of orange, both split so they sit on the rim of the glass.

Some more ideas

● Add a sliced banana to the strawberries. This will thicken the texture of the smoothie and will also add natural sweetness, so be sure to taste before adding sugar – you may not need any.

● Swap the strawberries for dried apricots, to make a smoothie with a useful amount of beta-carotene and a good amount of soluble fibre. Gently simmer 200 g (7 oz) ready-to-eat dried apricots in 900 ml (1½ pints) strained Earl Grey tea for 30 minutes or until tender. Cool, then pour the apricots and liquid into a blender. Add the orange zest, juice and yogurt and blend until smooth. Taste and sweeten with sugar if required. Serve sprinkled with a little crunchy oat and pecan breakfast cereal or blueberry and cranberry granola (see page 22).

Plus points

● Strawberries are low in calories and are an excellent source of vitamin C.

● Most of the yogurt sold in the UK is 'live', which means that it contains high levels of beneficial live bacteria. Labelling does not always make it clear if yogurt is 'live', but if it is stored in the chiller cabinet of the supermarket you can be fairly confident that it is 'live' – that is, the yogurt has not been heat-treated after fermentation, a process that destroys the beneficial bacteria. The balance of bacteria in the gut is easily upset by stress, medication such as antibiotics, or a poor diet, but a regular intake of 'good' bacteria, such as that provided by 'live' yogurt, can help to maintain a healthy digestive tract.

Each serving provides Ⓥ

kcal 55, **protein** 3 g, **fat** 0.5 g (of which saturated fat 0.2 g), **carbohydrate** 11 g (of which sugars 11 g), **fibre** 1 g

✓✓✓ C

✓ folate, calcium

Breakfast

Mango, peach and apricot fizz

A luscious combination of fruit puréed together with fizzy ginger ale, or with tonic,
bitter lemon or sparkling mineral water, makes a wonderfully refreshing breakfast drink.
Choose perfectly ripe fruit for the smoothest low-calorie fizz.

Serves 4

1 ripe mango
1 ripe peach
2 large ripe apricots
500 ml (17 fl oz) ginger ale
fresh mint or lemon balm leaves to decorate
    (optional)

Preparation time: 5–10 minutes

1 Peel the mango and cut the flesh away from the central stone.
Roughly chop the flesh and put it into a blender or food processor. Alternatively, if you are using a hand blender, put the mango in a large tall jug.

2 Cover the peach and apricots with boiling water and leave for about 30 seconds, then drain and cool under cold running water. Slip off the skins. Roughly chop the flesh, discarding the stones, and add to the mango in the blender or food processor.

3 Pour over enough of the ginger ale just to cover the fruit, then process until completely smooth. Pour in the remaining ginger ale and process again.

4 Quickly pour into tall glasses, preferably over crushed ice.
Decorate with fresh mint or lemon balm leaves, if you like. Serve immediately with wide straws or swizzle sticks.

Some more ideas

● Use low-calorie ginger ale to reduce the calorie content.

● So many different fruit and fizz combinations are possible. Using about 450 g (1 lb) fruit in total, try: raspberry, peach and melon with bitter lemon; strawberry, banana and orange segments with tonic water.

● When soft fruit are not in season, use fruit canned in juice as a substitute. A delicious combination is fresh melon, banana and canned apricots with sparkling mineral water.

Plus points

● These golden fruits provide a feast of vitamins. Peaches are full of vitamin C (100 g/3½ oz gives 77% of the RNI); apricots are a good source of the B vitamins (B_1, B_6 and niacin); and mangoes are an excellent source of vitamin A – just 100 g (3½ oz) of mango provides half the RNI of this vitamin, which is important for vision and for the prevention of heart disease and cancer.

Each serving provides   Ⓥ
kcal 55, **protein** 1 g, **fat** 0 g, **carbohydrate** 14 g (of which sugars 13 g), **fibre** 2 g

✓✓✓ C
✓   A

Breakfast

Berry salad with passion fruit

Berries are the fresh healthy flavour of summer. Naturally tart, sweet and juicy, they range from delicate raspberries to fleshy strawberries, plump blueberries and rich blackberries. The passion fruit adds a fragrant edge to this breakfast dish.

Serves 6

450 g (1 lb) strawberries, cut in half
150 g (5½ oz) raspberries
100 g (3½ oz) blackberries
100 g (3½ oz) blueberries
100 g (3½ oz) mixed redcurrants and
    blackcurrants, removed from their stalks
2 passion fruit
1 tbsp caster sugar
juice of ½ lemon or lime

Preparation time: 10–15 minutes

1 Mix the strawberries, raspberries, blackberries, blueberries, redcurrants and blackcurrants together in a bowl.

2 Cut the passion fruit in half. Holding a sieve over the bowl of berries, spoon the passion fruit flesh and seeds into the sieve. Rub the flesh and seeds briskly to press all the juice through the sieve onto the berries. Reserve a few of the passion fruit seeds left in the sieve and discard the rest.

3 Add the sugar and lemon or lime juice to the berries. Gently toss together. Sprinkle over the reserved passion fruit seeds. Serve straightaway or cover and chill briefly.

Some more ideas

● Instead of passion fruit, add 3 tbsp crème de cassis. Chill until ready to serve.

● Omit the passion fruit and instead serve the berry salad with a peach and apricot sauce: peel and purée 2 ripe peaches and flavour with 2–3 tbsp caster sugar, the juice of ¼ lemon and a dash of pure almond extract. Finely dice 8 ready-to-eat dried apricots and add to the peach purée. Serve the berries on plates in a pool of the sauce.

● Serve the berry salad spooned over vanilla frozen yogurt.

Plus points

● Comparing the same weight of each fruit, blackcurrants come out top of the table for vitamin C, with 200 mg in each 100 g (3½ oz), while strawberries have 77 mg, raspberries 32 mg and blackberries 15 mg. These days vitamin C is recognised as essential for maintaining the immune system and as an antioxidant, preventing the damaging processes that can lead to heart disease and cancer.

● To this feast of summer fruit, rich in dietary fibre and vitamin C, passion fruit also adds vitamin A, which is essential for healthy skin and good vision, and blackberries add vitamin E, another important antioxidant. The effects of vitamin E are enhanced by other antioxidants like vitamin C, so this combination of fruits is particularly healthy.

Each serving provides ⓥ
kcal 55, **protein** 1 g, **fat** 0 g, **carbohydrate** 12 g (of which sugars 12 g), **fibre** 3 g

✓✓✓	C
✓	E, folate

Breakfast

Fruity Bircher muesli

This is an entire meal in one bowl. The original recipe for this nutritious breakfast cereal was developed over a century ago, by Dr Bircher-Benner at his clinic in Zurich. Soaking the cereal makes it easier to digest, and also easier to eat.

Serves 4

115 g (4 oz) rolled oats

115 g (4 oz) sultanas

250 ml (8½ fl oz) semi-skimmed milk

1 crisp dessert apple, such as Cox's

2 tsp lemon juice

30 g (1 oz) hazelnuts, roughly chopped

15 g (½ oz) pumpkin seeds

1 tbsp sesame seeds

100 g (3½ oz) strawberries, chopped

4 tbsp plain low-fat bio yogurt

4 tsp clear honey

Preparation time: 10 minutes, plus overnight soaking

1 Place the oats and sultanas in a large bowl and add the milk. Stir to mix evenly, then cover and place in the refrigerator. Leave to soak overnight.

2 The next day, just before eating, grate the apple, discarding the core. Toss the apple with the lemon juice to prevent browning.

3 Stir the hazelnuts, pumpkin seeds and sesame seeds into the oat mixture, then stir in the grated apple and strawberries.

4 To serve, divide the muesli among 4 cereal bowls, and top each with a spoonful of yogurt and honey.

Another idea

• To make a mixed grain muesli, soak 25 g (scant 1 oz) rolled oats, 45 g (1½ oz) malted wheat flakes, 30 g (1 oz) flaked rice and 115 g (4 oz) raisins in 250 ml (8½ fl oz) buttermilk. Just before eating, stir in 25 g (scant 1 oz) roughly chopped almonds and 20 g (¾ oz) sunflower seeds, then add 1 roughly mashed banana and 1 chopped mango. Serve topped with plain low-fat bio yogurt.

Plus points

• Yogurt is usually made by introducing 2 harmless bacteria into milk. Bio yogurts, which are made by using a slightly different bacterium, are believed to be more effective at keeping a healthier balance of bacteria in the gut than other yogurts.

• Oats have a low glycaemic index, which means they are digested and absorbed slowly and so produce a gentle, sustained rise in blood glucose levels.

• Hazelnuts are a particularly good source of vitamin E and most of the B vitamins, apart from B_{12}. Like most other nuts, they have a high fat content; however, this is mostly the more beneficial monounsaturated fat.

Each serving provides (V)

kcal 366, **protein** 11 g, **fat** 12 g (of which saturated fat 2 g), **carbohydrate** 56 g (of which sugars 37 g), **fibre** 4 g

✓✓ B_1, C, E, calcium, copper, zinc

✓ B_2, B_6, B_{12}, folate, niacin, iron, potassium

Breakfast

Blueberry and cranberry granola

A delicious toasted muesli, this is made from a mix of grains, nuts, seeds and colourful berries. Stirring maple syrup and orange juice into the mix helps to keep the oil content down, making this version much lower in fat than most ready-made 'crunchy' cereals.

Makes 500 g (1 lb 2 oz)

225 g (8 oz) rolled oats

45 g (1½ oz) wheatgerm

55 g (2 oz) millet flakes

1 tbsp sesame seeds

2 tbsp sunflower seeds

2 tbsp slivered almonds

50 g (1¾ oz) dried blueberries

50 g (1¾ oz) dried cranberries

15 g (½ oz) soft brown or demerara sugar

2 tbsp maple syrup

2 tbsp sunflower oil

2 tbsp orange juice

Preparation time: 40–50 minutes, plus cooling

1 Preheat the oven to 160°C (325°F, gas mark 3). In a large bowl, combine the oats, wheatgerm, millet flakes, sesame and sunflower seeds, almonds, dried berries and sugar. Stir until well mixed.

2 Put the maple syrup, oil and orange juice in a small jug and whisk together. Pour this mixture slowly into the dry ingredients, stirring to ensure that the liquid is evenly distributed and coats everything lightly.

3 Spread the mixture out evenly in a non-stick roasting tin. Bake for 30–40 minutes or until slightly crisp and lightly browned. Stir the mixture every 10 minutes to encourage even browning.

4 Remove from the oven and leave to cool. Store in an airtight container for up to 2 weeks. Serve with yogurt, milk or fruit juice.

Plus points

● This is a delicious way to get plenty of fibre, B vitamins and essential fatty acids. Wheatgerm is especially rich in B vitamins.

● A special feature of this recipe is the use of sunflower seeds, which not only add flavour but are also a rich source of nutrients. They are rich in healthy, polyunsaturated fat, and also provide plenty of magnesium, copper, iron and several B vitamins. Both sesame seeds and sunflower seeds can provide useful amounts of calcium, which is particularly important for people who do not include milk or cheese in their diet.

Some more ideas

● For a chunkier granola, replace the millet with barley flakes and the berries with a mixture of roughly chopped dried apples or apricots, prunes and dates. A little shredded coconut can also be added, if liked.

● The maple syrup can be replaced with clear honey, and the slivered almonds with chopped hazelnuts.

● If you prefer, use all dried blueberries or cranberries, or replace some or all of the berries with dried cherries.

A 60 g (2¼ oz) serving provides Ⓥ

kcal 250, **protein** 7 g, **fat** 11 g (of which saturated fat 0.8 g), **carbohydrate** 32 g (of which sugars 7 g), **fibre** 4 g

✓✓✓	E
✓✓	B₁
✓	B₂, B₆, folate, niacin

Apple and hazelnut drop scones

Drop scones are an almost instant sweet starter to the day. The batter is made by simply stirring together a few basic storecupboard ingredients, with hazelnuts and apples, in this case, for extra goodness. Top with a little maple syrup and enjoy warm from the pan.

Makes 16 scones

45 g (1½ oz) skinned hazelnuts, chopped

200 g (7 oz) plain flour

½ tsp bicarbonate of soda

pinch of salt

2 tbsp caster sugar

1 large egg

250 ml (8½ fl oz) buttermilk

1 dessert apple, about 150 g (5½ oz), cored and finely chopped

1 tbsp sunflower oil

4 tbsp maple syrup

Preparation time: 15 minutes

Cooking time: 20 minutes

1 Heat a small non-stick frying pan, add the hazelnuts and cook until golden brown, stirring and tossing constantly. Take care not to overcook the nuts as they burn easily. Tip them into a small bowl.

2 Sift the flour, bicarbonate of soda, salt and sugar into a large mixing bowl. Make a well in the centre. Lightly beat the egg with the buttermilk and pour into the well. Gradually whisk the flour mixture into the buttermilk mixture to make a smooth, thick batter. Add the apple and toasted hazelnuts, and stir in with a large metal spoon.

3 Lightly brush a griddle or heavy frying pan with a little of the sunflower oil, then heat over a moderate heat. Depending on the size of the griddle or pan, you can cook about 4 scones at the same time. For each one, drop a heaped tablespoon of batter onto the hot surface. Bubbles will rise to the surface and burst. Gently slip a small palette knife under the drop scone to loosen it, then cook for a further minute or until the underside is golden brown. Turn the scone over and cook the other side for 1–2 minutes or until golden.

4 Remove the scones from the griddle or frying pan and keep warm under a clean cloth. Cook the rest of the batter in the same way.

5 When all the drop scones are cooked, quickly heat the maple syrup in a small saucepan just to warm it. Drizzle the syrup over the warm drop scones and serve immediately.

Some more ideas

● For apricot and walnut or pecan drop scones, use 75 g (2½ oz) chopped ready-to-eat dried apricots instead of the apple, and 45 g (1½ oz) walnuts or pecans instead of the hazelnuts.

● Make fresh berry drop scones by adding 100 g (3½ oz) blackberries or raspberries to the batter in place of the apple, and seasoning with a good pinch of ground mixed spice. Omit the hazelnuts, if you prefer.

Plus points

● Buttermilk is the liquid left over after cream has been turned into butter by churning. Contrary to its name, buttermilk does not contain butterfat, but it does provide protein, minerals and milk sugar or lactose, as well as a delightfully piquant taste.

● Eating apples with their skins offers the maximum amount of fibre. Research has shown that apples also benefit the teeth as they appear to help to prevent gum disease.

● Hazelnuts are rich in the essential fatty acids, which are vital for normal tissue growth and development.

Each scone provides (V)

kcal 106, **protein** 3 g, **fat** 3 g (of which saturated fat 0.5 g), **carbohydrate** 18 g (of which sugars 8 g), **fibre** 1 g

✓✓ E

Breakfast

Blueberry popovers

Similar to Yorkshire puddings, popovers are a much-loved American classic, and this sweet version is perfect for breakfast or brunch. The batter is baked in deep muffin or Yorkshire pudding tins. Serve the popovers with sweet, fresh berries to add extra vitamin C.

Serves 4 (makes 8 popovers)
1 tsp butter
125 g (4½ oz) plain flour
pinch of salt
1 tsp caster sugar
2 eggs
250 ml (8½ fl oz) semi-skimmed milk
75 g (2½ oz) blueberries
1 tbsp icing sugar to dust
Mixed berry salad
150 g (5½ oz) raspberries
100 g (3½ oz) blueberries
200 g (7 oz) strawberries, thickly sliced
1 tbsp icing sugar, or to taste

Preparation time: 20 minutes
Cooking time: 25–30 minutes

Each serving provides Ⓥ
kcal 243, **protein** 10 g, **fat** 6 g (of which saturated fat 2 g), **carbohydrate** 40 g (of which sugars 16 g), **fibre** 3 g

✓✓✓	C
✓✓	B₁₂
✓	A, B₁, B₂, folate, niacin, calcium, copper, iron, potassium, zinc

1 Preheat the oven to 220°C (425°F, gas mark 7). Using a piece of crumpled kitchen paper and the butter, lightly grease 8 of the cups in a deep, non-stick muffin tray. Each cup should measure 6 cm (2½ in) across the top and be 2.5 cm (1 in) deep.

2 To make the popovers, sift the flour, salt and caster sugar into a mixing bowl and make a well in the centre. Break the eggs into the well, add the milk and beat together with a fork.

3 Using a wire whisk, gradually work the flour into the liquid to make a smooth batter that has the consistency of single cream. Pour into a large jug.

4 Divide the batter evenly among the prepared muffin cups – they should be about two-thirds full. With a spoon, drop a few blueberries into the batter in each cup, dividing them equally.

5 Bake in the middle of the oven for 25–30 minutes or until the popovers are golden brown, well risen and crisp around the edges.

6 Meanwhile, make the berry salad. Purée 100 g (3½ oz) of the raspberries by pressing them through a nylon sieve into a bowl. Add the remainder of the raspberries to the bowl, together with the blueberries and strawberries. Sift the icing sugar over the fruit and fold gently to ensure that everything is mixed together.

7 Unmould the popovers with the help of a round-bladed knife, and dust with the icing sugar. Serve hot, with the berry salad.

Some more ideas
● Use frozen blueberries, thawed and well drained. You can use thawed frozen raspberries and blueberries for the berry salad, too.
● For a baked sweet batter pudding, make the batter as in the main recipe, then add 4 tbsp fizzy mineral water or cold water. Pour into a 1.4–1.7 litre (2½–3 pint) shallow baking dish that has been lightly greased with butter (omit the blueberries). Bake for 30–35 minutes or until crisp and well risen. Spoon the berry salad into the centre of the hot pudding, scatter over 2 tbsp toasted flaked almonds, dust with the icing sugar and serve immediately.

Plus points
● Blueberries, like cranberries, contain antibacterial compounds called anthocyanins. These are effective against the *E. coli* bacteria that cause gastrointestinal disorders and urinary tract infections.
● Eating raspberries is believed by many to be beneficial in cleansing and detoxifying the digestive system. It is also thought to help with the discomfort of indigestion.

Apple and blackberry brioches

An irresistible start to the day – toasted brioche slices topped with caramelised apple rings and fresh blackberries, with a hint of cinnamon. Brioche has a slightly higher fat content than white bread, but it is still a deliciously healthy source of starchy carbohydrate.

Serves 4

25 g (scant 1 oz) butter
4 apples
½ tsp ground cinnamon
4 individual brioches
200 g (7 oz) fresh blackberries
4 tsp demerara sugar

Preparation and cooking time: 15 minutes

1 Preheat the grill. Line the grill pan with foil, put the butter on top and set it under the grill to melt. Meanwhile, core the apples and slice each one into 6 rings, discarding the outer edge pieces. Dip the apple rings in the melted butter to coat both sides, then lay them out in a single layer on the foil and sprinkle with the cinnamon.

2 Grill the apple rings for about 4 minutes or until they are starting to brown, turning them over once. Remove the apples on their foil from the grill pan and set aside.

3 Slice each brioche horizontally into 3 and spread out the slices in the grill pan. Toast lightly on both sides. Place 2 apple rings on top of each toasted brioche slice, add a few blackberries and sprinkle with the sugar. Put back under the grill and warm the berries for 2–3 minutes, then serve.

Some more ideas
• For a breakfast that is even higher in energy, make delicious banana and raspberry toasts. Toast 4 slices of white or wholemeal bread or Jewish challah bread. Arrange 2 large bananas, sliced, and 100 g (3½ oz) raspberries on top, covering the toast right up to the edges. Top with 25 g (scant 1 oz) butter, cut into little pieces, and sprinkle each with 1 tsp light soft brown sugar. Grill them until they start to brown and caramelise.

• Try orange and strawberry-topped muffins. Toast 4 split wholemeal muffins, then top with 2 oranges, divided into segments, and halved strawberries. Sprinkle each muffin with 2 tsp demerara sugar. Grill until the fruit sizzles.
• Drop scones or scotch pancakes can be topped with sliced kiwi fruit and orange, or strawberries and grapes.

Plus points
• Apples contribute pectin, a soluble fibre that helps to reduce the highs and lows in blood sugar levels and also helps to lower blood cholesterol. This makes apples a great start to the day.
• Blackberries are a useful source of the antioxidant vitamin E, which can help to protect against heart disease and keep the skin in good condition. They are also a good source of fibre and bioflavonoid compounds.
• A recent study of over 2500 middle-aged men living in the Caerphilly area of Wales found that those who ate 5 or more apples per week had stronger lungs than those men who ate no apples. Apples contain high levels of a flavonoid called quercetin (also found in onions, tea and red wine), which is thought to have a strong antioxidant effect and may help to protect the lungs from damage.

Each serving provides
kcal 280, protein 5 g, fat 10 g (of which saturated fat 6 g), carbohydrate 44 g (of which sugars 31 g), fibre 4 g

✓✓ C, E
✓ B₆

Breakfast

28

Breakfast muffins

American-style muffins are perfect for breakfast, providing the energy boost the body needs to get going. This particular recipe is packed full of good ingredients that add fibre, vitamins and minerals too, but still keep the muffins low in calories.

Makes 12 muffins

85 g (3 oz) plain wholemeal flour

150 g (5½ oz) plain white flour

2 tsp bicarbonate of soda

pinch of salt

¼ tsp ground cinnamon

55 g (2 oz) dark molasses sugar

30 g (1 oz) wheatgerm

170 g (6 oz) raisins

225 g (8 oz) plain low-fat yogurt

4 tbsp sunflower oil

1 egg

grated zest of ½ orange

3 tbsp orange juice

Preparation time: 15 minutes

Cooking time: 15–20 minutes

1 Preheat the oven to 200°C (400°F, gas mark 6). Grease a 12-cup deep muffin tray – each cup should measure 6–7.5 cm (2½–3 in) across the top and be 2.5–4 cm (1–1½ in) deep.

2 Sift the wholemeal and white flours, bicarbonate of soda, salt and cinnamon into a bowl, tipping in any bran left in the sieve. Stir in the sugar, wheatgerm and raisins, and make a well in the centre.

3 Lightly whisk together the yogurt, oil, egg, and orange zest and juice. Pour into the well in the dry ingredients and stir together, mixing only enough to moisten the dry ingredients. Do not beat or overmix.

4 Spoon the mixture into the muffin tray, dividing it equally among the cups. Bake for 15–20 minutes or until the muffins are well risen and just firm to the touch. Leave them to cool in the tray for 2–3 minutes, then turn out onto a wire rack. The muffins are best eaten freshly baked, preferably still slightly warm from the oven, but can be cooled completely and then kept in an airtight tin for up to 2 days.

Some more ideas

• Substitute chopped prunes or dried dates for the raisins.

• For carrot and spice muffins, replace the cinnamon with 1½ tsp mixed spice. Stir 100 g (3½ oz) grated carrot into the flour mixture with the wheatgerm, and reduce the amount of raisins to 115 g (4 oz).

• To make blueberry and walnut muffins, instead of raisins use 200 g (7 oz) blueberries, and add 100 g (3½ oz) chopped walnuts.

Plus points

• Breakfast is a good opportunity to top up the fibre intake for the day, which is why eating a high-fibre cereal is usually recommended. These muffins are another good choice, as they offer plenty of dietary fibre from the wholemeal flour, wheatgerm and raisins.

• Wheatgerm is the embryo of the wheat grain and as such contains a high concentration of nutrients, intended to nourish the growing plant. Just 1 tbsp of wheatgerm provides around 25% of the average daily requirement for vitamin B_6. Wheatgerm is also a good source of folate, vitamin E, zinc and magnesium.

Each muffin provides ⓥ

kcal 180, **protein** 4 g, **fat** 5 g (of which saturated fat 1 g), **carbohydrate** 31 g (of which sugars 17 g), **fibre** 2 g

✓ B_1, B_6, E, calcium, iron, selenium, zinc

Breakfast

Scrambled eggs with smoked salmon and dill

Here's a great new way to scramble eggs – cook in a double saucepan or in a bowl over simmering water, without any butter, then mix with crème fraîche. You will have a deliciously creamy result and, best of all, it is the lower calorie option.

Serves 4

6 eggs

3 tbsp semi-skimmed milk

6 plum tomatoes, halved lengthways

4 thick slices wholemeal bread

3 tbsp crème fraîche

75 g (2½ oz) sliced smoked salmon, cut into thin strips

1 tsp lemon juice

1 tbsp chopped fresh dill

salt and pepper

sprigs of fresh dill to garnish

Preparation time: 10 minutes
Cooking time: 10 minutes

Each serving provides

kcal 363, **protein** 22 g, **fat** 21 g (of which saturated fat 9 g), **carbohydrate** 24 g (of which sugars 6 g), **fibre** 4 g

✓✓✓	A, B$_{12}$
✓✓	C, E, niacin, selenium, zinc
✓	B$_1$, B$_2$, B$_6$, folate, calcium, copper, iron, potassium

1 Lightly beat the eggs together with the milk in a heatproof bowl or in the top of a double saucepan. Set over a saucepan containing barely simmering water – the base of the bowl or pan should just touch the water. Cook for 6–8 minutes or until the eggs begin to thicken, stirring frequently.

2 Preheat the grill to high. While the eggs are cooking, arrange the tomatoes cut side up on the rack of the grill pan, and sprinkle them with a little salt and pepper. Add the slices of bread to the rack. Grill for 4–5 minutes, turning the bread over halfway through, until the tomatoes are lightly browned and the bread is toasted on both sides.

3 Add the crème fraîche to the eggs, and season to taste with salt and pepper. Cook for a further 1 minute, stirring constantly, until the mixture is softly scrambled. Sprinkle the smoked salmon with the lemon juice, then add this to the eggs together with the chopped dill. Immediately remove the mixture from the heat.

4 Place the toast on warmed serving plates and divide the smoked salmon scramble among them. Garnish each with a sprig of dill. Add 3 grilled tomato halves to each plate, and serve.

Some more ideas

• Serve on slices of pumpernickel bread.

• For a ham and egg scramble, replace the salmon with smoked ham, and use chopped fresh flat-leaf parsley instead of dill.

• Make Parsee scrambled eggs, a spicy Indian version. Melt 15 g (½ oz) butter in a non-stick saucepan, and gently sauté 2 tsp grated fresh root ginger, 1 seeded and finely chopped fresh red chilli, and ¼ tsp each ground cumin and ground coriander for 1 minute. Stir in the egg and milk mixture, and cook over a low heat, stirring constantly, until softly scrambled. Stir in 3 tbsp Greek-style yogurt, 4 chopped tomatoes and 1 tbsp chopped fresh coriander. Serve hot, with warm naan bread.

Plus points

• Eggs are a highly nutritious food, and provide many essential nutrients in a very convenient package. In addition to high-quality protein, eggs contain useful amounts of vitamins A, B$_2$, B$_{12}$, E and niacin, and plenty of minerals.

• Salmon contains omega-3 fatty acids, a type of polyunsaturated fat that can help to protect against heart disease and strokes.

Herbed French toast

Give breakfast a twist with this savoury version of French toast. Triangles of bread are dipped into a herb-and-egg mixture, then pan-fried until golden. Serve with tasty 'meaty' mushrooms and lean bacon, both grilled to limit the calorie intake.

Serves 4

4 large eggs
4 tbsp semi-skimmed milk
1 tbsp finely chopped parsley
1 tbsp finely chopped fresh chives
½ tbsp chopped fresh thyme, or a pinch of dried thyme
pinch of paprika (optional)
4 large portobella mushrooms or large flat mushrooms, about 250 g (8½ oz) in total
3 tbsp sunflower oil
4 rashers lean back bacon, rinded and trimmed of fat
5 thick slices white bread
salt and pepper

Preparation and cooking time: about 25 minutes

Each serving provides

kcal 349, protein 19 g, fat 19 g (of which saturated fat 4 g), carbohydrate 28 g (of which sugars 2 g), fibre 2 g

✓✓✓	B$_{12}$, copper, selenium
✓✓	B$_1$, B$_2$, E, niacin, zinc
✓	A, B$_6$, folate, calcium, iron, potassium

---

1 Combine the eggs, milk, most of the parsley, the chives, thyme and paprika, if using, in a shallow dish. Season to taste. Set aside.

2 Preheat the grill to moderately high. Remove the stalks from the mushrooms. Using 1 tbsp of the oil, lightly brush the gill sides of the mushroom caps. Place them gill side up on the grill rack. Add the bacon rashers to the grill rack. Grill the mushrooms for 6–7 minutes and the bacon for about 10 minutes, turning the rashers over halfway through. When the mushrooms and bacon are cooked, remove from the grill pan and keep warm.

3 Meanwhile, cut each slice of bread into 4 triangles. Heat a large, non-stick frying pan over a moderate heat and add 1 tbsp of the remaining oil. Dip 6 or 7 of the bread triangles into the egg mixture to moisten on both sides, then put into the hot pan. Cook for 1–2 minutes or until golden brown on both sides. Remove from the pan and keep warm while you cook the rest of the bread in the same way, adding the remaining 1 tbsp oil as needed.

4 To serve, arrange 5 triangles of French toast on each plate. Cut the mushrooms into thick slices and add to the plates, together with the bacon. Sprinkle with the remaining parsley.

Another idea

● For sweet orange French toast, first make a fresh fruit compote to serve alongside, in place of the bacon and mushrooms. Combine 250 g (8½ oz) raspberries and 2 thinly sliced ripe peaches in a bowl. Cover and set aside. Gently whisk 3 large eggs with 3 tbsp semi-skimmed milk and the finely grated zest of 1 large orange. Cut 8 slices of brioche loaf, each about 5 mm (¼ in) thick, then cut each slice in half. Dip into the egg mixture and cook in batches as in the main recipe. Serve the hot French toast topped with the fruit compote and 1 tbsp Greek-style yogurt per serving.

Plus points

● This hearty breakfast dish contains fewer calories than the traditional version, which is often served with melting butter and maple or golden syrup.

● Wholemeal bread is considered to be healthier than white bread, but in fact all breads are important sources of starchy carbohydrate. Also, white bread has calcium added and subsequently contains more of this important mineral than wholemeal bread.

Snacks

Good news for snackers. A recent US study suggests that grazing may be healthy, as eating more frequently can lower blood cholesterol levels. So no need to feel guilty when sampling goodies, such as Ginger nuts or even Double chocolate chunk and nut cookies, provided you eat them within a balanced diet. Nutritious savoury treats include crispy Sesame cheese twists, Baked potato skins with smoked salmon and fresh dill, and Tuscan bean crostini.

Cereal bars

Naturally sweet and moist, these delicious bars will provide a great energy boost at any time of the day. They are also a good way of getting the family to try some more unusual grains and seeds, and adding new healthy ingredients to the diet.

Makes 14 bars

2 tbsp sunflower seeds

2 tbsp pumpkin seeds

2 tbsp linseeds

2 bananas, about 300 g (10½ oz) in total, weighed with their skins on

100 g (3½ oz) unsalted butter

3 tbsp golden syrup

50 g (1¾ oz) millet flakes

100 g (3½ oz) rolled oats

100 g (3½ oz) stoned dried dates, roughly chopped

Preparation time: 25 minutes

Cooking time: 30 minutes

1 Preheat the oven to 180°C (350°F, gas mark 4). Grease a 28 x 18 x 4 cm (11 x 7 x 1½ in) cake tin and line the bottom with baking parchment. Roughly chop the sunflower seeds, pumpkin seeds and linseeds. Peel and roughly mash the bananas.

2 Melt the butter in a saucepan and stir in the golden syrup. Add the chopped seeds and mashed bananas, together with the millet flakes, rolled oats and dates. Mix together well, then spoon the mixture into the prepared tin and level the surface.

3 Bake for about 30 minutes or until golden brown. Leave to cool in the tin for 5 minutes, then mark into 14 bars and leave to cool completely. The bars can be kept in an airtight tin for up to 2 days.

Some more ideas

• Instead of dates, use chopped ready-to-eat dried apricots or prunes or a mixture of chopped dried fruits.

• Replace the millet flakes with plain flour, either white or wholemeal.

• The cereal bars can be frozen and will keep for 2 months. Wrap them individually in freezer wrap or foil. Then, if you simply pack a frozen bar into a plastic container along with wrapped sandwiches, it will have thawed by lunchtime.

Plus points

• Naturally occurring fruit sugars found in bananas and dates are released more slowly into the blood stream by the body, giving a more sustained energy boost. Extrinsic or 'added' sugars (such as table sugar, honey and golden syrup), on the other hand, are quickly absorbed and burnt up by the body.

• Seeds are a rich source of protein and are particularly valuable for those following a vegetarian diet.

• Linseeds are an excellent source of omega-3 fatty acids, essential for brain and eye development in the foetus.

Each bar provides

Ⓥ

kcal 160, **protein** 3 g, **fat** 10 g (of which saturated fat 4 g), **carbohydrate** 17 g (of which sugars 8 g), **fibre** 1 g

✓ A, B$_1$, B$_6$, E, copper, zinc

Snacks

Ginger nuts

Here's a healthier, less fatty, version of a traditional favourite. Bake round biscuits,
or buy some fancy cutters and encourage children to have a go at making gingerbread
figures and shapes. Whatever the end result, these spicy, crunchy biscuits taste terrific.

Makes 12 biscuits

85 g (3 oz) plain white flour

85 g (3 oz) plain wholemeal flour

½ tsp bicarbonate of soda

2 tsp ground ginger

½ tsp ground cinnamon

50 g (1¾ oz) butter

4 tbsp golden syrup

Preparation time: 15 minutes

Cooking time: 8–10 minutes

1 Preheat the oven to 190ºC (375ºF, gas mark 5). Sift the white and wholemeal flours, bicarbonate of soda, ginger and cinnamon into a bowl, tipping in any bran left in the sieve.

2 Put the butter and golden syrup in a small pan and melt over a low heat, stirring occasionally. Pour the melted mixture onto the dry ingredients and stir to bind them together into a firm dough.

3 Break off a walnut-sized lump of dough and roll it into a ball on the palm of your hand. Press it flat into a thick biscuit, about 6 cm (2½ in) in diameter, and place on a greased baking sheet. Repeat with the remaining dough. (Or roll out the dough and stamp out decorative shapes; see Some more ideas, right.)

4 Bake the biscuits for 8–10 minutes or until they are slightly risen and browned. Leave to cool on the baking sheet for 2–3 minutes or until they are firm enough to lift without breaking, then transfer to a wire rack to cool completely. The biscuits can be kept in an airtight tin for up to 5 days.

Some more ideas

• Instead of shaping the biscuits by hand, roll out the dough on a lightly floured surface to 5 mm (¼ in) thick and use shaped cutters to stamp out biscuits. Bake for 5–7 minutes.

• For oat and orange ginger biscuits, instead of all wholemeal flour use 45 g (1½ oz) plain wholemeal flour and 45 g (1½ oz) rolled oats. Add the grated zest of 1 orange with the melted mixture, and use 1–2 tbsp orange juice to bind the mixture into a soft dough. Roll into balls, shape and bake as in the main recipe.

• For fruity ginger biscuits, peel, core and coarsely grate 1 dessert apple, and add to the flour mixture with 55 g (2 oz) sultanas and the grated zest of 1 lemon. Shape and bake as in the main recipe.

Plus points

• Making your own biscuits means you can include some wholemeal flour and control the amount of fat and sugar you use. Commercial biscuits are often very sugary and may also be high in hydrogenated fats.

• Ginger is a traditional remedy for nausea and can sometimes ease morning sickness in pregnancy. It is also known as an aid to digestion and circulatory problems.

Each biscuit provides

kcal 90, **protein** 1 g, **fat** 4 g (of which saturated fat 2 g), **carbohydrate** 14 g (of which sugars 4 g), **fibre** 1 g

Snacks

Apple and muesli rock cakes

A little diced apple makes these rock cakes moist and fruity, and a perfect replacement for shop-bought biscuits. Easy to prepare, they are ideal to cook with younger members of the family, who will enjoy making these nutritious treats as much as eating them.

Makes 24 cakes

225 g (8 oz) self-raising flour

100 g (3½ oz) unsalted butter, cut into small pieces

55 g (2 oz) light muscovado sugar, plus a little extra to sprinkle

1 tsp ground cinnamon

2 dessert apples, peeled and diced

75 g (2½ oz) sugar-free muesli

1 egg, beaten

4–5 tbsp semi-skimmed milk, as needed

Preparation time: 20 minutes
Cooking time: 15 minutes

1 Preheat the oven to 190°C (375°F, gas mark 5). Put the flour into a bowl, add the butter and rub it in with your fingertips until the mixture resembles fine breadcrumbs.

2 Stir in the sugar, cinnamon, diced apples and muesli. Add the egg and stir it in with enough milk to bind the mixture together roughly.

3 Drop dessertspoonfuls of the mixture onto 2 greased baking sheets, leaving space around each cake, and sprinkle with a little extra sugar. Bake for 15 minutes or until golden and firm to the touch.

4 Transfer to a wire rack to cool, and serve warm or cold. The rock cakes can be kept in an airtight tin for up to 2 days.

Some more ideas

● Replace the muesli with a mixture of 3 tbsp rolled oats, 2 tbsp sesame or sunflower seeds and 55 g (2 oz) roughly chopped hazelnuts or almonds.

● For apple and mincemeat rock cakes, use just 1 peeled and diced dessert apple with 150 g (5½ oz) mincemeat, and substitute 75 g (2½ oz) rolled oats for the muesli. Omit the cinnamon.

● For tropical rock cakes, replace the apples, muesli and cinnamon with 50 g (1¾ oz) desiccated coconut and 170 g (6 oz) chopped ready-to-eat exotic dried fruits, including pineapple, papaya and mango.

Plus points

● Apples are a good source of vitamin C and soluble fibre (in the form of pectin), as well as offering a flavonoid called quercetin, which is thought to have a potent antioxidant effect.

● Adding muesli to cakes and bakes is a good way to increase their fibre content.

● Children need healthy snacks to boost their energy and nutritional needs, and these little rock cakes are much better than sugar-laden commercial biscuits or salty crisps.

Each cake provides Ⓥ

kcal 90, **protein** 2 g, **fat** 4 g (of which saturated fat 2 g), **carbohydrate** 13 g (of which sugars 4 g), **fibre** 1 g

snacks

Orange and pecan biscuits

These are 'slice-and-bake' biscuits – the roll of dough can be prepared in advance and kept in the fridge. Then, whenever these energy-boosting biscuits are wanted, you simply slice the roll into rounds, top with pecan nuts and bake.

Makes 24 biscuits

55 g (2 oz) plain wholemeal flour, plus extra
for kneading

55 g (2 oz) self-raising white flour

85 g (3 oz) light muscovado sugar

55 g (2 oz) ground rice

30 g (1 oz) pecan nuts, chopped

grated zest of 1 orange

4 tbsp sunflower oil

1 large egg

24 pecan nut halves to decorate

Preparation time: 15 minutes, plus 2 hours
chilling

Cooking time: 8–10 minutes

1 Put the wholemeal and self-raising flours, sugar, ground rice, chopped pecan nuts and orange zest in a bowl, and stir until well combined.

2 In a small bowl, beat the oil and egg together with a fork. Add this mixture to the dry ingredients and mix with a fork until they come together to make a dough.

3 Knead the dough very lightly on a floured surface until smooth, then roll into a sausage shape about 30 cm (12 in) long. Wrap in cling film and chill for 2 hours. (The dough can be kept in the fridge for 2–3 days before slicing and baking.)

4 Preheat the oven to 180ºC (350ºF, gas mark 4). Unwrap the roll of dough and lightly reshape to a neat sausage, if necessary.

5 Cut the roll across into 24 slices using a sharp knife. Arrange the slices, spaced apart, on 2 large non-stick baking sheets. Top each slice with a pecan nut half, pressing it in slightly.

6 Bake for about 10 minutes or until firm to the touch and lightly golden. Transfer the biscuits to a wire rack to cool completely. They can be stored in an airtight tin for up to 5 days.

Some more ideas

● Instead of the sunflower oil, use 55 g (2 oz) melted butter.

● Chopped hazelnuts can be used in place of the pecans, with whole hazelnuts to decorate.

● To make almond polenta biscuits, mix 55 g (2 oz) instant polenta with 85 g (3 oz) icing sugar and 115 g (4 oz) self-raising flour. Rub in 55 g (2 oz) butter until the mixture resembles breadcrumbs. Beat 1 large egg with ½ tsp pure almond extract, add to the crumb mixture and mix to form a soft dough. Roll, wrap and chill as in the main recipe. Before baking, scatter 30 g (1 oz) flaked almonds over the slices.

Plus points

● Like other nuts, pecans are rich in fat – up to 70 g per 100 g (3½ oz) – but little of this is saturated fat, the majority being present as polyunsaturated fat. Pecans also provide generous amounts of vitamin E.

● Sunflower oil is one of the most widely used vegetable oils because of its mild flavour, and it works well in biscuits and other baked goods in place of saturated fats such as butter. It is a particularly good source of vitamin E, a powerful antioxidant. Polyunsaturated fats, such as are found in sunflower oil, are more susceptible to rancidity than saturated fats, but the vitamin E content helps to stop the oil going rancid.

Each biscuit provides

kcal 106, protein 2 g, fat 7 g (of which saturated fat 1 g), carbohydrate 9 g (of which sugars 4 g), fibre 1 g

✓✓	E
✓	copper

Snacks

Fruit and nut bread

This fruited German-style loaf is good at tea-time, served thickly sliced, or lightly toasted and buttered for breakfast. It contains no added fat (the fat present comes from the nuts), but the dried fruits give it a rich, moist texture and good keeping qualities.

Makes 1 round loaf (cuts into about 10 slices)

400 g (14 oz) strong white (bread) flour

½ tsp salt

grated zest of ½ lemon

1 sachet easy-blend dried yeast, about 7 g

85 g (3 oz) ready-to-eat dried apricots, roughly chopped

85 g (3 oz) ready-to-eat dried pears, roughly chopped

85 g (3 oz) stoned ready-to-eat prunes, roughly chopped

50 g (1¾ oz) ready-to-eat dried figs, roughly chopped

50 g (1¾ oz) chopped mixed nuts, such as almonds, hazelnuts and cashews

250 ml (8½ fl oz) tepid water

Preparation time: 50 minutes, plus 2½–3 hours rising

Cooking time: 30–40 minutes

Each slice provides Ⓥ

kcal 220, **protein** 6 g, **fat** 3 g (of which saturated fat 0.2 g), **carbohydrate** 44 g (of which sugars 14 g), **fibre** 3.5 g

✓ B_1, B_6, E, folate, copper, iron, potassium, zinc

1 Mix the flour with the salt, lemon zest and yeast in a large bowl. Add the chopped fruits and nuts and mix in well. Stir in the tepid water and work the mixture with your hand to make a soft-textured, heavy dough.

2 Turn the dough out onto a lightly floured work surface and knead for 10 minutes or until it feels pliable. Place the dough in a lightly greased bowl, cover with a damp tea-towel and leave to rise in a warm place for 1½–2 hours or until doubled in size.

3 Turn the risen dough out onto the floured work surface and knock it back with your knuckles to return it to its original size. Gently knead the dough into a neat ball shape, then set it on a well-greased baking sheet. Cover with a damp tea-towel and leave to rise in a warm place for about 1 hour or until doubled in size.

4 Towards the end of the rising time, preheat the oven to 200°C (400°F, gas mark 6). Uncover the loaf and bake for 30–40 minutes or until it is nicely browned and sounds hollow when tapped on the base. Cover with foil if it is becoming too brown. Transfer to a wire rack and leave to cool. This bread can be kept for up to 5 days.

Another idea

• To make spicy fruit buns, add 2 tsp ground mixed spice and ¼ tsp freshly grated nutmeg to the flour with the salt. Omit the lemon zest. After the first rising, divide the dough into 12 equal portions. Shape them into neat balls (see Basic loaf, Some more ideas, page 211), then set them, spaced well apart, on greased baking sheets and leave to rise for about 45 minutes or until doubled in size. Bake for about 25 minutes or until they sound hollow when tapped on the base.

Plus points

• Ready-to-eat dried apricots are an excellent ingredient to have on hand in the storecupboard, as they are very nutritious – an excellent source of beta-carotene and a useful source of calcium – and versatile. They can be used in cakes, biscuits, teabreads and sweet yeasted breads, as well as making a delicious addition to breakfast cereals, stews and casseroles. And they are ideal for a healthy snack.

• Like all nuts, cashews are rich in protein and unsaturated fats. Cashews also provide useful amounts of iron, zinc and folate.

Snacks

Double chocolate chunk and nut cookies

These American-style cookies are simply irresistible when eaten warm while the chocolate chunks are still soft and melting. Macadamia nuts, with their buttery flavour, add a crunchy texture. Like the chocolate, the nuts should be kept in fairly large pieces.

Makes 12 cookies

115 g (4 oz) unsalted butter, at room temperature

85 g (3 oz) light muscovado sugar

½ tsp pure vanilla extract

1 egg, beaten

85 g (3 oz) self-raising white flour

55 g (2 oz) plain wholemeal flour

20 g (¾ oz) cocoa powder

¼ tsp baking powder

¼ tsp salt

115 g (4 oz) good dark chocolate (at least 70% cocoa solids), roughly chopped

55 g (2 oz) macadamia nuts, roughly chopped

3 tbsp semi-skimmed milk

Preparation time: 20 minutes
Cooking time: 15 minutes

Each cookie provides Ⓥ

kcal 240, **protein** 3 g, **fat** 15 g (of which saturated fat 8 g), **carbohydrate** 22 g (of which sugars 13 g), **fibre** 1 g

✓ A, copper

1 Preheat the oven to 190°C (375°F, gas mark 5). Line 2 baking sheets with baking parchment.

2 Beat the butter with the sugar and vanilla extract in a large bowl until light and fluffy. Gradually add the egg, beating well after each addition.

3 Sift the white and wholemeal flours, cocoa powder, baking powder and salt over the creamed mixture, tipping in any bran left in the sieve. Add the chocolate, nuts and milk, and mix everything together.

4 Place tablespoons of the mixture on the prepared baking sheets, arranging the cookies well apart so there is space for them to spread during baking. Flatten the cookies slightly with the back of a fork, then bake for about 15 minutes or until they feel soft and springy.

5 Leave on the baking sheets for a few minutes, then transfer to a wire rack. Serve while still slightly warm or leave until cold. The cookies can be kept in an airtight container for up to 5 days.

Some more ideas

• Use walnuts or pecan nuts instead of macadamia nuts.

• For cherry and almond cookies, use plain white flour instead of the cocoa powder, and substitute 55 g (2 oz) dried sour cherries and 55 g (2 oz) flaked almonds for the chocolate chunks and macadamia nuts. If you want a pronounced almond flavour, use ¼ tsp pure almond extract instead of the vanilla.

Plus points

• Plain chocolate is a good source of copper and provides useful amounts of iron. The scientific name of the cocoa bean tree is Theobroma cacao, which means 'the food of the gods'. Casanova was reputed to drink hot chocolate before his nightly conquests – in fact, he was said to prefer chocolate to champagne.

• Butter contains useful amounts of the important fat-soluble vitamins A and D. Vitamin A is essential for healthy vision and skin, while vitamin D is needed for the formation of strong, healthy bones.

Snacks

Sesame cheese twists

These crisp cheese sticks are delicious served fresh from the oven. Enriched with egg yolks and well flavoured with Parmesan cheese, they are made with a combination of wholemeal and plain flour, so that they are substantial without being at all heavy.

Makes 40 sticks

85 g (3 oz) plain wholemeal flour, preferably stoneground

85 g (3 oz) plain white flour, plus extra for rolling

¼ tsp salt

45 g (1½ oz) butter

45 g (1½ oz) Parmesan cheese, freshly grated

1 large egg

2 tbsp semi-skimmed milk

1 tsp paprika

1 tbsp sesame seeds

Preparation time: 10–15 minutes
Cooking time: 15 minutes

1 Preheat the oven to 180°C (350°F, gas mark 4). Sift the flours and salt into a bowl, tipping in the bran left in the sieve. Rub in the butter until the mixture resembles fine breadcrumbs. Stir in the Parmesan cheese.

2 Whisk the egg and milk together. Reserve 1 tsp of this mixture, and stir the rest into the dry ingredients to make a firm dough. Knead on a lightly floured surface for a few seconds or until smooth.

3 Sprinkle the paprika over the floured surface, then roll out the dough on it to form a square slightly larger than 20 cm (8 in). Trim the edges to make them straight. Brush the dough with the reserved egg mixture and sprinkle over the sesame seeds. Cut the square of dough in half, then cut into 10 cm (4 in) sticks that are about 1 cm (½ in) wide.

4 Twist the sticks and place on a large baking sheet lined with baking parchment. Lightly press the ends of the sticks down so that they do not untwist during baking.

5 Bake for 15 minutes or until lightly browned and crisp. Cool on the baking sheets for a few minutes, then serve warm, or transfer to a wire rack to cool completely. The sticks can be kept in an airtight tin for up to 5 days.

Some more ideas

• Use finely grated mature Cheddar cheese instead of the Parmesan.

• For blue cheese and walnut biscuits, mash 30 g (1 oz) blue cheese, such as Gorgonzola, Stilton or Danish blue, with 55 g (2 oz) softened butter. Sift over 45 g (1½ oz) plain wholemeal flour, 30 g (1 oz) self-raising white flour and 30 g (1 oz) ground rice, tipping in the bran left in the sieve. Add 30 g (1 oz) chopped toasted walnuts. Rub together, then knead lightly to form a dough. Shape into a roll about 12 cm (5 in) long. Wrap in cling film and chill for about 30 minutes. Cut into thin slices, arrange on a baking sheet lined with baking parchment and bake in a preheated 190°C (375°F, gas mark 5) oven for 15 minutes. Transfer to a wire rack to cool. Makes about 16 biscuits.

Plus points

• Sesame seeds are a good source of calcium as well as providing iron and zinc.

• Wholemeal flour has a lot to offer: dietary fibre, B vitamins and vitamin E, together with iron, selenium and magnesium. Stoneground wholemeal flour has slightly more B vitamins than factory-milled wholemeal flour, because stonegrinding keeps the grain cool. Milling with metal rollers creates heat, which spoils some of the nutrients.

Each stick provides

Ⓥ

kcal 32, **protein** 1 g, **fat** 2 g (of which saturated fat 1 g), **carbohydrate** 3 g (of which sugars 0.1 g), **fibre** 0.3 g

Snacks

Crudités with three dips

Few foods can be healthier than raw vegetable sticks, so make the most of them by serving them with tempting low-fat dips for a snack. You could also offer a selection of fruit and warm pitta bread for dipping, as well as vegetables.

Serves 8

Pesto-yogurt dip

55 g (2 oz) fresh basil leaves

1 garlic clove, crushed

1 tbsp pine nuts

250 g (9 oz) plain low-fat bio yogurt

Fresh herb dip

170 g (6 oz) fromage frais

1 spring onion, finely chopped

2 tbsp finely chopped parsley

1 tbsp finely snipped fresh chives

1 tsp tarragon vinegar

Italian-style tomato dip

55 g (2 oz) sun-dried tomatoes (dry-packed)

85 g (3 oz) cottage cheese

85 g (3 oz) plain low-fat yogurt

30 g (1 oz) fresh basil leaves

salt and pepper

To serve

450 g (1 lb) mixed vegetable crudités, such as baby carrots, courgette sticks, baby sweetcorn (blanched in boiling water for 1 minute), green beans (blanched for 1 minute), pepper strips, chicory leaves and broccoli florets

Preparation time: 25 minutes, plus 30 minutes soaking

1 For the pesto-yogurt dip, use a pestle and mortar to crush the basil, garlic and pine nuts to a paste. Work in the yogurt a spoonful at a time, until thoroughly combined. Add seasoning to taste. Alternatively, purée all the ingredients together in a food processor or blender. Transfer to a bowl, cover and chill until required.

2 For the fresh herb dip, stir all the ingredients together in a bowl until well blended. Cover tightly and chill until required.

3 For the Italian-style tomato dip, place the sun-dried tomatoes in a heatproof bowl and pour over boiling water to cover them. Leave to soak for about 30 minutes or until the tomatoes are plump and tender. Drain the tomatoes well, then pat them dry and finely chop them.

4 Purée the cottage cheese with the yogurt in a food processor or blender. Alternatively, press the cheese through a sieve and stir in the yogurt. Transfer to a bowl and stir in the tomatoes. Cover and chill until required.

5 Just before serving the Italian-style tomato dip, finely shred the basil and stir in with seasoning to taste.

6 Serve the bowls of dips on a large platter with the crudités arranged around them.

Plus points

• Pine nuts are rich in a variety of minerals: magnesium, potassium, iron, zinc and copper.

• Dairy products such as yogurt, fromage frais and cottage cheese are valuable sources of calcium. This mineral is essential for the structure of bones and teeth, which contain 99% of all calcium in the body.

Some more ideas

• There is a wide choice of vegetables for making crunchy, delicious crudités. For example, try celery or cucumber sticks, whole radishes, baby plum tomatoes halved lengthways, small cauliflower florets (raw or briefly cooked) and baby new potatoes cooked until tender.

Each serving (3 dips alone) provides Ⓥ

kcal 115, **protein** 6 g, **fat** 8 g (of which saturated fat 2 g), **carbohydrate** 6 g (of which sugars 5 g), **fibre** 0.5 g

✓✓	B₁₂, E
✓	B₂, calcium

Cheese and watercress scones

The wonderful tastes of peppery watercress and mature Cheddar cheese flavour these tempting and nutritious savoury scones. Packed full of fibre, both soluble and insoluble, these scones also make a good protein contribution.

Makes 8 scones

140 g (5 oz) self-raising white flour

140 g (5 oz) self-raising wholemeal flour

1 tsp baking powder

50 g (1¾ oz) butter, cut into small pieces

50 g (1¾ oz) rolled oats

85 g (3 oz) watercress without coarse stalks, chopped

75 g (2½ oz) mature Cheddar cheese, grated

100 ml (3½ fl oz) semi-skimmed milk, plus a little extra to glaze

salt and pepper

Preparation time: 20 minutes

Cooking time: 10–15 minutes

1 Preheat the oven to 230ºC (450ºF, gas mark 8). Sift the white and wholemeal flours and the baking powder into a bowl, then tip in any bran left in the sieve. Rub in the butter with your fingertips until the mixture resembles fine breadcrumbs.

2 Add the rolled oats, watercress, about three-quarters of the cheese, and a little salt and pepper. Use a fork to stir in the milk. Scrape the dough together with a spatula and turn out onto a well-floured surface. Pat together into a smooth, soft ball. It will be a little softer than a standard scone dough.

3 Pat or roll out the dough until it is about 2 cm (¾ in) thick. Using a 7.5 cm (3 in) round cutter, stamp out the scones. Press the trimmings together lightly, re-roll and stamp out as many more scones as possible.

4 Place the scones on a greased baking sheet, arranging them so they are not touching. Brush the tops lightly with milk and sprinkle with the remaining grated cheese. Bake for 10–15 minutes or until risen and golden brown. Cool on a wire rack. These scones are at their best eaten on the day they are made, but will still be good the next day; store in an airtight tin.

Some more ideas

● To make a scone round, place the smooth ball of dough on a greased baking tray and press it out into a flat round 2–2.5 cm (¾–1 in) thick. Use a sharp knife to cut the dough into 8 wedges, leaving them in place. Bake for about 15 minutes or until risen and golden.

● For cheese and celery scones, replace the watercress with 2 celery sticks, finely chopped.

● To make carrot and poppy seed scones, instead of watercress and cheese, add 50 g (1¾ oz) finely grated carrot and 1 tbsp poppy seeds with the oats. Before baking, sprinkle the top of the scones with 1 tbsp poppy seeds instead of cheese.

Plus points

● These scones are a good source of fibre – both the insoluble type found in wholemeal flour and soluble fibre from the oats.

● Cheddar cheese is a good source of protein and a valuable source of calcium, phosphorus and the B vitamins B_{12} and niacin.

● Watercress provides beta-carotene, vitamin C and vitamin E, nutrients that act as protective antioxidants. It also contains a compound that has been shown to have antibiotic properties.

Each scone provides

kcal 230, **protein** 8 g, **fat** 10 g (of which saturated fat 5 g), **carbohydrate** 30 g (of which sugars 1 g), **fibre** 3 g

✓✓	A
✓	B_1, B_6, B_{12}, C, folate, calcium, copper, iron, selenium, zinc

Snacks

Pissaladière

The Provençal relative of Italian pizza, Pissaladière has a thick bread base, enriched with olive oil, topped with a tomato and onion mixture, then decorated with a lattice of anchovies and olives. Serve warm or cool for a snack high on flavour but low in calories.

Makes 64 bite-sized squares

Dough

450 g (1 lb) strong (bread) flour, plus extra for kneading

1 tsp salt

1 sachet easy-blend dried yeast, about 7 g

3 tbsp extra virgin olive oil

300 ml (10 fl oz) hand-hot water

Topping

3 tbsp extra virgin olive oil

4 onions, about 750 g (1 lb 10 oz) in total, thinly sliced

2 garlic cloves, crushed

1 can chopped tomatoes in rich tomato juice, about 400 g

2 tbsp tomato purée

1 tbsp chopped fresh oregano

2 cans anchovy fillets, about 50 g each, drained and halved lengthways

16 stoned black olives, about 55 g (2 oz) in total, quartered

pepper

Preparation time: 1½ hours, plus 1 hour rising
Cooking time: 40 minutes

Each square provides

kcal 44, **protein** 1.5 g, **fat** 1.5 g (of which saturated fat 0.2 g), **carbohydrate** 6.5 g (of which sugars 1 g), **fibre** 0.5 g

1 For the dough, sift the flour and salt into a bowl, then stir in the yeast. Make a well in the centre and pour in the oil and water. Gradually mix the dry ingredients into the liquids, using a spoon at first and then your hand, to make a soft, slightly sticky dough.

2 Turn the dough out onto a lightly floured surface and knead for 10 minutes or until the dough is smooth and springy. Place in a lightly oiled bowl, cover with cling film and leave in a warm place to rise for about 45 minutes or until doubled in size.

3 Meanwhile, make the topping. Heat the oil in a large saucepan, add the onions and garlic, and cook over a low heat for about 40 minutes or until very soft and lightly golden but not browned. Add the tomatoes with their juice, the tomato purée, oregano and pepper to taste, and cook gently for a further 10 minutes, stirring occasionally. Remove from the heat and leave to cool.

4 When the dough has risen, knock it back and knead again gently. Roll it out on a floured surface to a 30 cm (12 in) square and place on a lightly oiled baking sheet.

5 Preheat the oven to 200°C (400°F, gas mark 6). Spread the onion mixture evenly over the dough square, then make a criss-cross pattern on top with the anchovy fillets. Place the olive

quarters in the squares. Leave the pissaladière to rise at room temperature for about 15 minutes.

6 Bake the pissaladière for about 30 minutes or until the crust is golden and firm, then reduce the oven temperature to 190°C (375°F, gas mark 5) and bake for a further 10 minutes. Allow to cool slightly before cutting into squares for serving.

Plus points

• This pissaladière is made with a thick bread base, providing generous starchy carbohydrate. As white flour by law must contain added iron, calcium, vitamin B_1 and niacin, the bread base can also make a contribution to the intake of these nutrients.

• Canned tomatoes are a nutritious storecupboard ingredient as the canning process does not destroy the lycopene content but rather enhances it. Lycopene is a phytochemical with powerful antioxidant properties.

Some more ideas

● For an onion and pancetta pissaladière, leave the tomatoes and tomato purée out of the onion mixture. Cut 100 g (3½ oz) thin slices of smoked pancetta in half lengthways, twist them and lay them on top of the onion mixture in a criss-cross pattern. Place whole capers in the squares in between.

● Make a tomato and red pepper pissaladière. Cover the dough base with a thin layer of passata, then arrange a mixture of sliced fresh tomatoes, strips of sun-dried tomatoes and coarsely chopped, grilled and peeled red peppers over the top. Brush with a little extra virgin olive oil, sprinkle over some freshly ground black pepper and bake as in the main recipe. Serve garnished with fresh basil leaves scattered over the top.

Baked potato skins with smoked salmon and fresh dill

Potato skins are usually deep-fried, but brushing with a mixture of olive oil and butter and then baking gives just as good a flavour and crisp texture. Here the potato skins are topped with a herby low-fat fromage frais, smoked salmon and dill filling.

Serves 8

8 small baking potatoes, about
　　200 g (7 oz) each
2 tbsp extra virgin olive oil
20 g (¾ oz) butter
125 g (4½ oz) smoked salmon
1 tbsp lemon juice
150 g (5½ oz) fromage frais
1 tbsp capers, drained and chopped
2 tbsp chopped fresh dill
salt and pepper
small sprigs of fresh dill to garnish

Preparation and cooking time: 1¾–2 hours

1 Preheat the oven to 200°C (400°F, gas mark 6). Scrub the potatoes and dry them with kitchen paper. Thread them onto metal skewers – this helps them to cook more quickly. Brush the skin of the potatoes with 1 tbsp of the oil, then sprinkle with a little salt. Arrange on a baking tray and bake for 1–1¼ hours or until tender.

2 Remove the potatoes from the skewers and cut them in half lengthways. Scoop out the flesh, leaving a layer of potato next to the skin about 1 cm (½ in) thick. (Use the scooped-out flesh for fish cakes or mash to make a savoury pie topping.) Cut each piece in half lengthways again, and place flesh side up on a large, clean baking tray.

3 Melt the butter with the remaining 1 tbsp oil and season with salt and pepper to taste. Lightly brush this mixture over the flesh side of the potato skins. Return to the oven and bake for a further 12–15 minutes or until golden and crisp.

4 Meanwhile, cut the smoked salmon into fine strips and sprinkle with the lemon juice. Mix together the fromage frais, capers and chopped dill in a bowl, and stir in the salmon.

5 Allow the potato skins to cool for 1–2 minutes, then top each with a little of the salmon and fromage frais mixture. Garnish each with a small sprig of dill, and serve while the potato skins are still warm.

Each serving provides
kcal 162, **protein** 7 g, **fat** 7 g (of which saturated fat 3 g), **carbohydrate** 18 g (of which sugars 2 g), **fibre** 2.5 g

✓　B₁, B₆, B₁₂, C, folate, niacin, potassium

Plus points
- Baking potatoes in their skins helps to retain their vitamins and minerals – many nutrients are found just beneath the skin. Eating the skins also boosts the intake of dietary fibre.
- Salmon is an oily fish and a rich source of essential omega-3 fatty acids, a type of polyunsaturated fat that is thought to help protect against heart disease. Smoking the salmon doesn't destroy the beneficial oils.
- Capers, the pickled buds of a shrub mostly grown in southern Europe, are commonly used to add a salt-sour taste, and can reduce the need for salt in a dish.

Snacks

Some more ideas

● For a salmon and tomato topping, mix together 2 cans salmon, about 105 g each, well drained, 350 g (12½ oz) diced ripe tomatoes, ½ diced cucumber, 6 sliced spring onions and 12 chopped black olives. Whisk 2 tbsp extra virgin olive oil with 2 tsp red wine vinegar, 1 tsp Dijon mustard, and salt and pepper to taste. Add to the salmon mixture.

● For a chunky guacamole topping, peel and dice 2 ripe avocados, and mix with 3 tbsp lime juice, 3 tbsp Greek-style yogurt, 4 finely chopped ripe tomatoes, 1 seeded and finely chopped fresh red chilli or a dash of Tabasco sauce, and salt and pepper to taste.

● Instead of making potato skins, bake 12 small potatoes, about 125 g (4½ oz) each, for about 50 minutes or until tender. Halve the potatoes and scoop out most of the flesh, then fill with the smoked salmon and fromage frais mixture or one of the other toppings.

Tuscan bean crostini

Here's an appetising snack to be enjoyed hot or cold – toasted slices of baguette topped with a creamy white bean purée flavoured with garlic and thyme, and finished with slices of tomato and leaves of rocket. Pretty, and low in calories, these are a real treat.

Makes 22 crostini

2 tsp extra virgin olive oil
1 small onion, finely chopped
1 garlic clove, crushed
1 can cannellini beans, about 400 g, drained
   and rinsed
2 tbsp crème fraîche
1 tbsp chopped fresh thyme
1 thin baguette, about 250 g (8½ oz)
3 plum tomatoes, thinly sliced
salt and pepper
rocket or sprigs of fresh herbs to garnish

Preparation and cooking time: about 25 minutes

1 Heat the oil in a small frying pan, add the onion and garlic, and cook gently for about 10 minutes or until softened, stirring occasionally.

2 Meanwhile, place the cannellini beans in a bowl and mash with a potato masher or fork. Remove the pan of onion and garlic from the heat and stir in the mashed beans, crème fraîche and thyme. Season with salt and pepper to taste and mix well. Keep warm while preparing the toasts.

3 Preheat the grill to high. Cut the crusty ends off the baguette and discard, then cut the loaf into 22 equal slices, each about 1.5 cm (¾ in) thick. Toast the bread slices on both sides under the grill. (The toasts can be left to cool and then kept in an airtight tin; when ready to serve, top with the bean mixture, cooled to room temperature, and garnish.)

4 Thickly spread some bean mixture over each slice of toast, top with a tomato slice and garnish with rocket or fresh herb sprigs.

Some more ideas

● Instead of cannellini beans, use other canned pulses, such as flageolet or butter beans or chickpeas.
● Top the bean mixture with grilled courgette slices, lightly cooked button mushrooms or halved cherry tomatoes.

● Herbs such as fresh basil, oregano, sage or parsley can be used in place of the thyme.
● Use different types of bread, such as ciabatta, pugliese, wholemeal or Granary.
● Make tuna crostini. Drain and flake 1 can tuna in spring water, about 400 g. Mix with 1½ tbsp each mayonnaise and plain low-fat yogurt, 2 tbsp chopped fresh chives and pepper to taste. Spread each slice of toast with ½ tsp tomato relish or chutney, top with the tuna mixture and garnish with tiny watercress sprigs or rocket leaves.

Plus points

● Cannellini beans, popular in Italian cooking, belong to the same family as the haricot bean and have a similar floury texture when they are cooked. Though an excellent source of dietary fibre, beans can produce side effects such as bloating and wind. These can be minimised by ensuring that canned beans are thoroughly rinsed before use.
● Crème fraîche is a cream that has been allowed to mature and ferment so that it thickens slightly and develops a tangy taste. Because of its rich texture, only a little is needed to give a creamy finish.

Each crostini provides Ⓥ
kcal 62, **protein** 2 g, **fat** 2 g (of which saturated fat 1 g), **carbohydrate** 9 g (of which sugars 1 g), **fibre** 1 g

Snacks

Soups and starters

From light broths to thick pottages packed with nutritious ingredients, soups are a very versatile food. Classic gazpacho, Celeriac and spinach soup or King prawn bisque, for instance, are excellent to start a meal, as none are high in calories, while Hearty mussel soup or Borscht with crunchy mash can be meals in themselves, with a little bread. The light and varied starters here include Goat's cheese toasts, Tiger prawns with pepper salsa, and Dolmades (Greek rice-stuffed vine leaves).

Classic gazpacho

This traditional Spanish soup is full of fresh flavours and packed with vitamins as all the vegetables are raw. Cool and refreshing, it is ideal for a simple lunch or supper, with some crusty country-style bread or as a delicious first course in an evening meal.

Serves 4

500 g (1 lb 2 oz) full-flavoured tomatoes, quartered and seeded

¼ cucumber, peeled and coarsely chopped

1 red pepper, seeded and coarsely chopped

2 garlic cloves

1 small onion, quartered

1 slice of bread, about 30 g (1 oz), torn into pieces

2 tbsp red wine vinegar

½ tsp salt

2 tbsp extra virgin olive oil

500 ml (17 fl oz) tomato juice

1 tbsp tomato purée

To serve

1 red pepper

4 spring onions

¼ cucumber

2 slices of bread, made into croutons

Preparation time: 20 minutes, plus 2 hours chilling

1 Mix all the ingredients in a large bowl. Ladle batches of the mixture into a blender and purée until smooth. Pour the soup into a large clean bowl, cover and chill for 2 hours.

2 Prepare the vegetables to serve with the soup towards the end of the chilling time. Seed and finely dice the red pepper; thinly slice the spring onions; and finely dice the cucumber. Place these vegetables and the croutons in separate serving dishes.

3 Taste the soup and adjust the seasoning, then ladle it into bowls. Serve at once, offering the accompaniments so that they can be added to taste as the soup is eaten.

Some more ideas

• For a milder flavour, use 2 shallots instead of the small onion.

• In very hot weather, add a few ice cubes to the soup just before serving, to keep it well chilled. This will also slightly dilute it.

• To make a fresh green soup, use 500 g (1 lb 2 oz) courgettes instead of tomatoes and cucumber. Add 450 ml (15 fl oz) vegetable stock, preferably homemade, instead of the tomato juice. Use a green pepper instead of a red one. Add 15 g (½ oz) fresh basil leaves and 85 g (3 oz) pitted green olives. Mix, purée and chill the soup as above. Serve with a diced green pepper instead of red.

Plus points

• Up to 70% of the water-soluble vitamins – B and C – can be lost in cooking. In this classic soup the vegetables are eaten raw, which means they retain maximum levels of vitamins and minerals.

• Peppers have a naturally waxy skin that helps to protect them against oxidation and prevents loss of vitamin C during storage. As a result their vitamin C content remains high even several weeks after harvesting.

Each serving provides ⓥ

kcal 215, **protein** 6 g, **fat** 9 g (of which saturated fat 1.5 g), **carbohydrate** 30 g (of which sugars 17 g), **fibre** 5 g

✓✓✓ A, B₁, B₆, C, niacin, potassium

Soups and starters

Celeriac and spinach soup

With celeriac you can create a rich soup with lots of character and a creamy texture, so there is no need for other calorie-rich thickeners. Young leaf spinach complements the celeriac beautifully, bringing colour and a light, fresh taste in the final minutes of cooking.

Serves 4

2 tbsp extra virgin olive oil

1 large onion, thinly sliced

1 garlic clove, crushed

1 celeriac, about 600 g (1 lb 5 oz), peeled and grated

1 litre (1¾ pints) boiling water

1 vegetable stock cube, crumbled, or 2 tsp vegetable bouillon powder or paste

500 g (1 lb 2 oz) young leaf spinach

grated nutmeg

salt and pepper

To garnish

4 tbsp single cream

fresh chives

Preparation time: 10 minutes

Cooking time: about 20 minutes

1 Heat the oil in a large saucepan. Add the onion and garlic, and cook for about 5 minutes or until the onion is softened but not browned. Add the celeriac. Pour in the boiling water and stir in the stock cube, powder or paste. Bring to the boil over a high heat, then reduce the heat and cover the pan. Cook the soup gently for 10 minutes or until the celeriac is tender.

2 Add the spinach to the soup and stir well. Increase the heat and bring the soup to the boil, then remove the pan from the heat. Leave the soup to cool slightly before puréeing it, in batches, in a blender or food processor until smooth. Alternatively, you can purée it in the pan using a hand-held blender. The soup will be fairly thick.

3 Reheat the soup, if necessary, then stir in a little grated nutmeg, salt and pepper to taste. Ladle the soup into warm bowls. Swirl a tablespoon of cream into each portion and garnish with fresh chives, then serve at once.

Some more ideas

● For a hearty winter soup substitute shredded spring greens for the spinach.

● Crispy bacon makes a delicious garnish for the soup. While the soup is cooking, grill 4 rinded lean back bacon rashers until crisp and golden. Drain on kitchen paper, then crumble or chop the rashers into small pieces.

● For a more substantial dish, add a poached egg to each bowl of soup.

● To make a delicious potato and watercress version of this soup, use peeled, diced potatoes instead of celeriac, and watercress instead of spinach. Add extra stock or semi-skimmed milk if the puréed soup is too thick.

● For a vegetarian main course soup, top with grilled tofu. While the soup is cooking, cook a 200 g (7 oz) block of tofu under the grill preheated to moderate. Allow about 3 minutes on each side or until browned. Cut the tofu into small dice and set aside. Toast 2 tbsp sesame seeds in a dry, heavy frying pan, stirring frequently, until golden. Ladle the soup into bowls, divide the tofu among the bowls and sprinkle with the sesame seeds.

Plus points

● Celeriac, a relative of celery, complements both the flavour and texture of spinach, making the most of the modest amount of cream used to enrich the soup. It also provides potassium.

● Onions have many health benefits. They contain sulphur compounds, which give onions their characteristic smell and make your eyes water. These compounds transport cholesterol away from the artery walls.

Each serving provides Ⓥ

kcal 150, **protein** 6 g, **fat** 10 g (of which saturated fat 3 g), **carbohydrate** 9 g (of which sugars 7 g), **fibre** 9 g

✓✓✓	A, folate
✓✓	C, B$_6$, calcium, iron
✓	E

Soups and starters

King prawn bisque

This classic seafood soup is ideal for impressing guests. A last-minute addition of chopped red pepper brings a delightful flourish of flavour, texture and extra vitamins instead of the fat found in the traditional swirl of cream.

Serves 6

450 g (1 lb) raw king prawns, without heads

4 tbsp dry white wine

4 slices of lemon

4 black peppercorns, lightly crushed

2 sprigs of parsley, stalks bruised

1 bulb of fennel

1 tsp lemon juice

15 g (½ oz) butter

1 tbsp sunflower oil

1 shallot, finely chopped

45 g (1½ oz) fine white breadcrumbs, made from day-old slices of bread

pinch of paprika

1 red pepper, seeded and finely diced

salt and pepper

chopped leaves from the fennel bulb, or herb fennel, to garnish

Preparation time: about 45 minutes, plus cooling

Cooking time: about 35 minutes

Each serving provides

kcal 165, **protein** 8 g, **fat** 6 g (of which saturated fat 2 g), **carbohydrate** 9 g (of which sugars 3 g), **fibre** 1 g

✓✓✓	A, B$_6$, B$_{12}$, C, phosphorus, selenium
✓✓	copper, iron, zinc
✓	B$_2$, folate, calcium, potassium

1 Peel the prawns and set them aside. Place the shells in a large saucepan. Pour in 1.2 litres (2 pints) cold water and add the white wine, lemon slices, peppercorns and parsley. Bring to the boil, then reduce the heat and simmer for 20 minutes. Skim off any scum that rises to the surface during cooking.

2 Use a small sharp knife to make a shallow slit along the curved back of each prawn. With the tip of the knife remove the black vein and discard it. Cover and chill the prawns until they are required.

3 Allow the prawn-shell stock to cool slightly, then pick out and discard the lemon slices. Line a sieve with muslin and place it over a large bowl or measuring jug. Process the stock in a blender or food processor until the shells are finely ground, then strain the stock through the muslin-lined sieve. Discard the residue from the shells.

4 Coarsely chop 85 g (3 oz) of the fennel, and finely chop the remainder of the bulb. Place the finely chopped fennel in a bowl, add the lemon juice and toss well, then cover closely with cling film and set aside.

5 Melt the butter with the oil in the rinsed-out saucepan. Add the coarsely chopped fennel and the shallot. Cook, stirring frequently, over a moderate heat for about 8 minutes or until the vegetables are soft but not browned. Stir in the breadcrumbs, paprika and stock. Bring slowly to the boil, then reduce the heat so that the soup simmers. Add the prawns and continue simmering for 3 minutes.

6 Use tongs or a draining spoon to remove 6 prawns for garnishing the soup. Set them aside. Season the soup with salt and pepper to taste and simmer for a further 15 minutes.

7 Purée the soup in a blender or food processor until smooth. Return to the pan and add the finely chopped fennel and the red pepper. Reheat the soup until piping hot. Serve garnished with the reserved prawns and chopped fennel leaves.

Plus points

• Prawns are a good source of low-fat protein. They are an excellent source of vitamin B$_{12}$, selenium and phosphorus.

• Making the stock with the prawn shells gives the bisque a full flavour, and at the same time boosts its calcium content.

Some more ideas

● To add extra fibre, sprinkle the soup with garlic-flavoured rye bread croutons just before serving. Cut 55 g (2 oz) light rye bread into 1 cm (½ in) cubes and toss these with 1 tbsp garlic-flavoured olive oil. Transfer to a baking tray and bake at 180°C (350°F, gas mark 4) for 10 minutes or until crisp.

● To serve the soup as a filling main course, make the stock with 1.3 litres (2¼ pints) water and add 250 g (8½ oz) frozen sweetcorn with the red pepper and fennel. Serve with a simple side salad of mixed leaves, cucumber and green pepper, and plenty of crusty bread.

● A variety of other vegetables can be added with or instead of the red pepper. For example, try a mixture of small broccoli florets, finely chopped celery and frozen peas.

Golden lentil soup

This velvety-smooth soup owes its rich colour to a combination of lentils, parsnips and carrots. The sherry and a horseradish-flavoured cream adds a piquant taste and a luxurious touch. Serve with crunchy melba toast or oatcakes.

Serves 6

30 g (1 oz) butter

1 large onion, finely chopped

450 g (1 lb) parsnips, cut into small cubes

340 g (12 oz) carrots, cut into small cubes

150 ml (5 fl oz) dry sherry

85 g (3 oz) red lentils

1.2 litres (2 pints) vegetable stock, preferably homemade light or rich

salt and pepper

fresh chives to garnish

To serve

2 tsp grated horseradish

6 tbsp crème fraîche

Preparation time: about 15 minutes

Cooking time: about 1¼ hours

1 Melt the butter in a large saucepan. Add the onion, stir well and cover the pan. Sweat the onion over a gentle heat for 10 minutes or until softened. Stir in the parsnips, carrots and sherry. Bring to the boil, then cover the pan again and leave to simmer very gently for 40 minutes.

2 Add the lentils, stock, and salt and pepper to taste. Bring to the boil, then reduce the heat and cover the pan. Simmer for a further 15–20 minutes or until the lentils are tender. Purée the soup in a blender until smooth or use a hand-held blender to purée the soup in the pan. Return the soup to the pan if necessary, and reheat it gently until boiling. If it seems a bit thick, add a little stock or water.

3 Stir the grated horseradish into the crème fraîche. Snip some of the chives for the garnish and leave a few whole. Ladle the soup into warm bowls and top each portion with a tablespoon of the horseradish cream. Scatter snipped chives over the top and add a few lengths of whole chive across the top of each bowl. Serve at once.

Some more ideas

• Use celeriac instead of parsnips, and swede instead of carrots. Prepare and cook the soup as in the main recipe. Dry white vermouth or white wine can be added in place of the sherry for a lighter flavour.

• For a lower-fat version, top each portion with 1 tsp creamed horseradish instead of the horseradish and crème fraîche mixture, and scatter chopped parsley over the soup.

Plus points

• Lentils are a good source of protein and an excellent source of fibre. High-fibre foods are bulky and make you feel full for longer, so are very satisfying. A diet high in fibre and low in fat is good for weight control.

• Root vegetables have long been enjoyed as an excellent source of vitamins and minerals during the winter months.

• Children who are reluctant to sample plain cooked vegetables will not even realise they are eating them in this tasty, colourful soup.

Each serving provides

kcal 250, **protein** 6 g, **fat** 11 g (of which saturated fat 3 g), **carbohydrate** 25 g (of which sugars 11 g), **fibre** 6 g

✓✓✓	A
✓✓	B₁, B₆, folate, potassium
✓	calcium, iron

Salmon and tomato chowder

A chowder is a classic American meal-in-a-bowl soup. This delicious version is flavoured with lean bacon, leeks and tomatoes and thickened with potatoes, all of which provide the perfect background for the protein-packed salmon. Try it with sourdough bread.

Serves 4

200 g (7 oz) piece of skinless salmon fillet

1 bay leaf

300 ml (10 fl oz) fish or vegetable stock

600 ml (1 pint) semi-skimmed milk

15 g (½ oz) unsalted butter

1 tsp sunflower oil

1 large onion, finely chopped

1 leek, chopped

1 thick rasher back bacon, about 30 g (1 oz), derinded and chopped

340 g (12 oz) potatoes, peeled and diced

340 g (12 oz) tomatoes, skinned, seeded and diced

3 tbsp chopped parsley

4 tbsp Greek-style yogurt

salt and pepper

Preparation time: 15 minutes

Cooking time: 30 minutes

Each serving provides

kcal 358, **protein** 22 g, **fat** 16 g (of which saturated fat 7 g), **carbohydrate** 33 g (of which sugars 17 g), **fibre** 4 g

✓✓✓	B_6, B_{12}, C, E
✓✓	A, B_1, B_2, folate, niacin, calcium, potassium, selenium, zinc
✓	copper, iron

1 Put the salmon in a large saucepan with the bay leaf. Pour over the stock and add some of the milk, if needed, so the fish is covered with liquid. Slowly bring to the boil, then cover the pan and simmer over a low heat for 6–7 minutes or until the fish will flake easily. Remove the salmon with a draining spoon and break into large flakes, discarding any bones. Set aside. Pour the cooking liquid (with the bay leaf) into a jug or bowl and reserve.

2 Heat the butter and oil in the saucepan. Add the onion, leek and bacon, and cook over a low heat for 10 minutes or until soft, stirring frequently. Add the potatoes and cook the mixture for a further 2 minutes, stirring constantly.

3 Pour over the reserved cooking liquid and add the remaining milk. Bring to the boil, then half-cover the pan with a lid and simmer for 8 minutes, stirring occasionally. Add the diced tomatoes and cook for a further 3–4 minutes or until the potatoes have become tender, but have not started to disintegrate.

4 To thicken the soup, remove a ladleful or two and purée it in a bowl with a hand-held blender, or in a food processor, then return it to the soup in the pan and mix well.

5 Stir in the flaked salmon and 2 tbsp of the parsley. Simmer gently for 1–2 minutes or until the soup is piping hot. Discard the bay leaf. Season with salt and pepper to taste.

6 Ladle the soup into warmed serving bowls. Top each serving with 1 tbsp yogurt, swirling it round, and add a sprinkling of the remaining chopped parsley. Serve hot.

Plus points

• Salmon, like most fish, is an excellent source of protein as well as of vitamins B_6 and B_{12} and the minerals selenium and potassium. It also offers heart-healthy fats.

• Milk provides several important nutrients, most notably protein, calcium, phosphorus and many of the B vitamins. These nutrients are found in the non-fat part of milk, so lower fat varieties, such as semi-skimmed milk, actually contain more than full-fat milk.

Soups and starters

Some more ideas

• For a sweetcorn and blue cheese chowder, soften 1 chopped onion and 1 chopped celery stick in 15 g (½ oz) butter. Stir in 340 g (12 oz) peeled and diced potatoes, 450 ml (15 fl oz) semi-skimmed milk, 300 ml (10 fl oz) vegetable stock and 1 bay leaf. Half-cover and simmer for 12 minutes or until the potatoes are tender. Purée a third of the soup in a food processor or with a hand-held blender, then mix it with the rest of the soup. Stir in 1 can cream-style sweetcorn, about 420 g, 3 tbsp snipped fresh chives and salt and pepper to taste. Simmer for 2–3 minutes to heat through. Ladle into serving bowls and top each one with 1 tbsp fromage frais and 30 g (1 oz) crumbled blue cheese.

• Make a quick clam chowder. Soften 1 bunch sliced spring onions in 15 g (½ oz) butter. Add 340 g (12 oz) peeled and diced potatoes, 450 ml (15 fl oz) fish stock and 300 ml (10 fl oz) semi-skimmed milk. Half-cover and simmer for 12 minutes or until the potatoes are tender. Mash a few of the potatoes on the side of the pan to thicken the soup, then stir in 2 cans clams, about 175 g each, well drained, 1 can cream-style sweetcorn, about 420 g, 1 can chopped tomatoes, about 200 g, with the juice, 3 tbsp chopped parsley, 2 tbsp dry sherry and salt and pepper to taste. Simmer for about 5 minutes or until piping hot.

Borscht with crunchy mash

This healthy beetroot soup is a hearty version of the Russian favourite, which is often strained and served as a clear broth. Here the soup is puréed and accompanied by creamy mashed potatoes mixed with crunchy raw vegetables.

Serves 4

1 tbsp extra virgin olive oil

1 onion, chopped

1 large carrot

½ tsp lemon juice

1 bulb of fennel

500 g (1 lb 2 oz) raw beetroot

1 litre (1¾ pints) vegetable stock, preferably homemade light or rich

800 g (1¾ lb) floury potatoes, peeled and cut into small cubes

120 ml (4 fl oz) semi-skimmed milk

4 tbsp Greek-style yogurt

2 spring onions, finely chopped

salt and pepper

chopped leaves from the fennel bulb, herb fennel or parsley to garnish

Preparation time: about 35 minutes
Cooking time: about 50 minutes

Each serving provides Ⓥ

kcal 300, **protein** 11 g, **fat** 4 g (of which saturated fat 1 g), **carbohydrate** 56 g (of which sugars 21 g), **fibre** 7 g

✓✓✓	A, folate
✓✓	B₁, B₆, C
✓	iron

1 Place the oil in a large saucepan and add the onion. Set aside 55 g (2 oz) of the carrot for the mash, then chop the rest and add it to the pan. Mix well, cover and cook over a moderate heat for 5 minutes in order to soften the onion.

2 Place the lemon juice in a small bowl. Cut the bulb of fennel into quarters. Finely grate one quarter into the lemon juice and toss well. Finely grate the reserved carrot and add it to the grated fennel. Cover and set aside.

3 Chop the remaining fennel and add to the saucepan. Peel and dice the beetroot, and add it to the pan. Pour in the stock and bring to the boil. Reduce the heat, cover the pan and simmer for about 30 minutes or until all the vegetables are tender.

4 Meanwhile, bring another pan of water to the boil. Add the potatoes and boil for 10 minutes or until very tender. Drain the potatoes well and return them to the pan. Place over a low heat for about 1 minute to dry, shaking the pan occasionally to prevent the potatoes from sticking. Remove from the heat and set aside, covered to keep hot.

5 Purée the soup in a blender or food processor until smooth, or purée in the pan using a hand blender. Return the soup to the pan, if necessary, and reheat. Taste and adjust the seasoning.

6 While the soup is reheating, set the pan of potatoes over a moderate heat and mash until completely smooth, gradually working in the milk. Stir in the yogurt, grated fennel and carrot, spring onions and seasoning to taste.

7 Divide the mashed potato among 4 bowls, piling it up in the centre. Ladle the soup around the mash and sprinkle with chopped fennel or parsley. Serve at once.

Plus points

• Beetroot is a particularly rich source of the B vitamin folate, which may help to protect against heart disease and spina bifida. It also provides useful amounts of iron. The characteristic deep red colour comes from a compound called betacyanin, which has been shown to prevent the growth of tumours in animal studies.

• Adding grated raw vegetables to mashed potatoes is a good way of including them in a hot meal, especially for children.

• Fennel contains phytoestrogen, a naturally occurring plant hormone that encourages the body to excrete excess oestrogen. A high level of oestrogen is associated with increased risk of breast cancer. Fennel also contains useful amounts of folate.

Soups and starters

Some more ideas

● Other delicious raw vegetable additions to mashed potatoes are finely chopped celery, grated celeriac, finely shredded red or Savoy cabbage, shredded Brussels sprouts and coarsely chopped spring onions. They all contribute extra vitamins and minerals.

● Serve the borscht chunky instead of puréed, and add 2 tbsp hazelnut oil to the mashed potatoes instead of the yogurt.

● Instead of spooning the borscht around a pile of mash, garnish each bowl of soup simply with 1 tbsp Greek-style yogurt, soured cream or creamed horseradish, then sprinkle with chopped fresh fennel or parsley.

Vietnamese broth with noodles

Punchy flavours and aromatic ingredients transform this light broth into an exotic dish.
Unlike many oriental soups, the ingredients are not fried first so the fat content remains
low. Select prime-quality lean steak, which tastes excellent when poached.

Serves 2

25 g (scant 1 oz) dried shiitake mushrooms

75 g (2½ oz) fine rice noodles, such as
  vermicelli

170 g (6 oz) lean rump steak, diced

500 ml (17 fl oz) beef stock

2 tbsp fish sauce

1 heaped tsp grated fresh root ginger

30 g (1 oz) bean sprouts

½ small onion, thinly sliced

2 spring onions, thinly sliced

2 small fresh red bird's eye chillies or
  1 medium red chilli, seeded and finely
  chopped

1 tbsp shredded fresh mint

1 tbsp shredded fresh coriander

1 tbsp shredded fresh basil

To serve

lime wedges

soy sauce (optional)

Preparation time: 20 minutes, plus 20 minutes
  soaking

Cooking time: 10–15 minutes

Each serving provides

kcal 300, **protein** 23 g, **fat** 4 g (of which
saturated fat 1.5 g), **carbohydrate** 42 g (of
which sugars 2 g), **fibre** 0.8 g

✓✓✓ B₁, B₆, B₁₂, E, niacin

✓✓ iron, zinc

1 Rinse the shiitake mushrooms and
put them in a small bowl. Place the
rice noodles in a large bowl. Cover the
mushrooms with boiling water and
leave to soak for 20 minutes. Cover the
rice noodles with boiling water and soak
for 4 minutes, or according to the
packet instructions. Drain the noodles
and set aside until they are needed.

2 Drain the mushrooms and pour
the soaking liquid into a large
saucepan. Trim off and discard any
tough stalks from the mushrooms, then
slice them and add to the pan with the
diced steak, stock, fish sauce and
ginger. Bring to the boil, then simmer
for 10–15 minutes or until the steak is
cooked and tender. Skim off any scum
that rises to the surface of the soup
during cooking.

3 Divide the noodles, bean sprouts
and sliced onion between 2 large,
deep soup bowls. Use a draining spoon
to remove the steak and mushrooms
from the broth and divide them between
the bowls. Ladle the broth into the
bowls, then scatter the spring onions,
chillies, mint, coriander and basil over
the top.

4 Serve immediately, with the lime
wedges – the juice can be squeezed
into the broth to taste. Soy sauce can
also be added, if liked.

Plus points

● In common with other red meats, beef is a
good source of iron and zinc, and the iron in
meat is far more easily absorbed by the
body than iron from vegetable sources.

● Beef is now far leaner than it used to be,
and well-trimmed lean cuts can contain as
little as 4% fat.

Some more ideas

● For a vegetarian version of this soup, use tofu
and vegetable stock instead of beef and beef
stock, and soy sauce or dry sherry instead of
the fish sauce. Cook the tofu gently for only
2 minutes or until heated through.

● The bean sprouts can be replaced by shavings
of carrot and chopped celery. Vary the quantities
of spring onion, chilli and fresh herbs to taste.

● Any thin Oriental noodles can be used in
place of rice noodles, including the readily
available Chinese egg noodles. Cook or soak
the chosen noodles according to the packet
instructions.

● For a warm, spicy flavour, add a good pinch
of ground cinnamon with the ginger.

Soups and starters

Hearty mussel soup

This soup tastes fabulous and is packed full of healthy, fresh vegetables. The diced potatoes absorb the flavours and add body to the soup. Warm soda bread is an ideal partner, delicious for dunking and mopping up the last of the soup.

Serves 4

1 kg (2¼ lb) mussels in shells, scrubbed

2 tbsp extra virgin olive oil

1 onion, finely chopped

2 garlic cloves, finely chopped

2 leeks, thinly sliced

3 celery sticks, thinly sliced

2 carrots, diced

400 g (14 oz) potatoes, peeled and cut into small cubes

900 ml (1½ pints) vegetable stock, preferably homemade light

150 ml (5 fl oz) dry white wine

1 tbsp lemon juice

1 bay leaf

1 sprig of fresh thyme

4 tbsp chopped parsley

2 tbsp snipped fresh chives

salt and pepper

Preparation time: 30 minutes

Cooking time: 40–50 minutes

Each serving provides

kcal 260, **protein** 17 g, **fat** 8 g (of which saturated fat 1 g), **carbohydrate** 24 g (of which sugars 7 g), **fibre** 4.5 g

✓✓✓	A
✓✓	B₆, B₁₂, C, folate
✓	B₁, B₂, selenium

1 Discard any broken mussel shells or any that do not close when tapped. Put the wet mussels into a saucepan and cover tightly. Cook over a moderate heat for 4 minutes, occasionally shaking the pan. Check that the mussels are open – if not, cover and cook for a further 1–2 minutes. Drain the mussels, reserving the juices. Keep some mussels in their shells for garnish; remove the remainder from their shells and set aside. Discard the shells and any unopened mussels.

2 Heat the oil in the rinsed-out saucepan. Add the onion, garlic, leeks, celery and carrots, and cook gently for 5–10 minutes, stirring frequently, until the vegetables are softened but not browned. Add the potatoes, stock, wine, reserved mussel juices, lemon juice, bay leaf, thyme and salt and pepper. Bring to the boil, then reduce the heat to low. Cover the pan and simmer the soup for 20–30 minutes or until the vegetables are tender.

3 Remove the bay leaf and thyme, then add the shelled mussels, parsley and chives to the pan. Heat gently for about 1 minute. Do not let the soup boil or cook for longer than this or the mussels will become tough.

4 Ladle the soup into warm bowls and garnish with the reserved mussels. Serve while piping hot.

Another idea

● Cooked fresh mussels are available in most supermarkets, usually vacuum packed and displayed in chiller cabinets. Use 300 g (10½ oz) shelled weight of mussels. Alternatively, use 2 cans mussels in brine, each about 250 g, or 4 cans smoked mussels in vegetable oil, each about 85 g. Drain the canned mussels thoroughly and pat dry before adding them to the soup.

Plus points

● Like other shellfish, mussels are a good low-fat source of protein. They are an extremely good source of vitamin B₁₂ and provide useful amounts of copper, iodine, iron, phosphorus and zinc.

● Vitamin C from the potatoes, parsley and chives aids the absorption of iron from the mussels.

● Celery is said to have a calming effect on the nerves.

Soups and starters

Goat's cheese toasts

Indulge your taste buds with these morsels of toasted crusty baguette topped with slices
of plum tomato and tangy goat's cheese, sprinkled with pine nuts and fresh herbs. Choose
your favourite type of goat's cheese: delicate or strong in flavour, soft or firm in texture.

Makes 16 toasts

1 baguette, about 280 g (10 oz), cut into
   2.5 cm (1 in) slices

4 tbsp passata

2 tbsp sun-dried tomato paste

4 plum tomatoes, about 250 g (8½ oz) in total

140 g (5 oz) goat's cheese

1½ tbsp extra virgin olive oil

15 g (½ oz) pine nuts

few sprigs of fresh thyme or oregano, plus
   extra to garnish

Preparation time: 15 minutes

Cooking time: 4–5 minutes

1 Preheat the grill to moderate. Place
the baguette slices on a rack in the
grill pan and lightly toast on both sides.

2 Mix together the passata and
tomato paste and spread a little on
top of each toast, covering the surface
completely.

3 Slice the tomatoes lengthways,
discarding a slim slice from the
curved edges, to give 4 flat slices from
each tomato. Lay a slice of tomato on
top of each toast.

4 Place 1 small slice of firm goat's
cheese or about 1 tsp of soft goat's
cheese on top of each tomato slice, and
drizzle over a little olive oil. Scatter on
a few pine nuts and thyme or oregano
leaves.

5 Grill for 4–5 minutes or until the
cheese is beginning to melt and the
pine nuts are golden. Serve the toasts
hot, garnished with sprigs of thyme or
oregano.

Some more ideas

● Use a goat's cheese flavoured with garlic
and herbs.

● Serve the toasts on a bed of mixed soft salad
leaves as a starter or light lunch. Allow 4 toasts
per serving.

● Make fruity goat's cheese toasts. Instead of
the tomato topping, mix together 2 tbsp each of
cranberry sauce and mango, peach or another
fruit chutney. Spread this over the toasts, top

with the goat's cheese and scatter over a few
flaked almonds, then grill as in the main recipe.

● For tapenade goat's cheese toasts, put
100 g (3½ oz) stoned black olives, 1 can
anchovy fillets, about 50 g, drained, 3 tbsp
drained capers, 3 tbsp extra virgin olive oil, the
juice of ½ lemon and 2 crushed garlic cloves in
a blender or food processor and blend to a
paste (or pound to a paste with a pestle and
mortar). This makes 220 g (scant 8 oz)
tapenade; it can be kept, covered, in the fridge
for 2 weeks. Spread onto 4 large, thick slices of
toasted bread, then top with the goat's cheese
and grill for 3–4 minutes. Cut each slice into 8
fingers or triangles and serve warm, sprinkled
with chopped parsley. Makes 32 toasts.

Plus points

● Pine nuts are commonly found in Middle
Eastern rice dishes and stuffings. They are
also an important ingredient in the classic
Italian pesto sauce.

● Goat's cheese is a tasty source of protein
and calcium, as well as B vitamins (B_1, B_6,
B_{12} and niacin) and phosphorus. Medium-fat
goat's cheese contains about half the fat of
Cheddar cheese.

Each toast provides   Ⓥ

kcal 89, protein 3 g, fat 4 g (of which
saturated fat 1 g), carbohydrate 11 g (of
which sugars 1 g), fibre 0.5 g

✓   E

Soups and starters

Chicken and vegetable filo rolls

These filo pastry rolls make an excellent starter. The filling is a colourful mixture of low-fat minced chicken and plenty of vegetables, with a little smoked ham and fresh herbs to add to the flavour. The rolls are served with a piquant cranberry relish.

Serves 8 (makes 8)

1 large carrot, about 100 g (3½ oz), cut into
   very fine matchsticks

75 g (2½ oz) savoy cabbage, finely shredded

2 spring onions, cut into fine shreds

225 g (8 oz) minced chicken

55 g (2 oz) lean smoked ham, finely chopped

½ small onion, finely chopped

2 tbsp fresh white breadcrumbs

2 tsp chopped fresh sage

2 tsp chopped fresh thyme

4 large sheets filo pastry, each about
   46 x 28 cm (18 x 11 in)

2 tbsp extra virgin olive oil

15 g (½ oz) butter, melted

1 tsp sesame seeds

salt and pepper

Cranberry relish

3 tbsp cranberry sauce

1 tbsp extra virgin olive oil

1 tbsp red wine vinegar

1 tsp made English mustard

To serve

115 g (4 oz) mixed salad leaves

Preparation time: 40 minutes
Cooking time: 30 minutes

1 Blanch the carrot, cabbage and spring onions in boiling water for 1 minute. Drain, then plunge into a bowl of cold water to refresh. Drain again and pat dry with kitchen paper. Put the vegetables in a large mixing bowl with the chicken, ham, onion, breadcrumbs, herbs and seasoning. Mix together well, then set aside.

2 Preheat the oven to 190°C (375°F, gas mark 5). Halve each filo pastry sheet lengthways and then trim to a strip measuring 36 x 12 cm (15 x 5 in). Mix the oil and butter together.

3 Brush one pastry strip lightly with the butter mixture. Place an eighth of the filling at one end, shaping it into a sausage. Roll up the filling inside the pastry, folding in the long sides as you go, to make a spring roll-shaped parcel. Place on a baking sheet and brush with a little of the butter and oil mixture. Repeat to make another 7 parcels.

4 Score 3 diagonal slashes on top of each parcel. Sprinkle over the sesame seeds. Bake for 30 minutes or until the pastry is golden.

5 Meanwhile, put all the relish ingredients in a screw-top jar, season to taste and shake well.

6 Arrange the mixed salad leaves on serving plates, place a filo roll on each and drizzle around the relish.

Plus points

● Unlike most other types of pastry, filo contains very little fat – in 100 g (3½ oz) filo there are 2 g fat and 300 kcal. The same weight of shortcrust pastry contains 29 g fat and 449 kcal.

● Using a mixture of oil and butter to brush the sheets of filo reduces the amount of saturated fat, and brushing it on sparingly keeps the overall fat content down.

● By bulking out the poultry with plenty of vegetables you reduce the amount of fat in the dish as well as providing extra vitamins and dietary fibre.

Each roll provides
kcal 130, **protein** 8.5 g, **fat** 7.5 g (of which saturated fat 2 g), **carbohydrate** 7 g (of which sugars 4 g), **fibre** 1 g

✓   A, B₆

Soups and starters

Some more ideas

- Use minced turkey instead of chicken.
- For Greek-style chicken parcels, cook 30 g (1 oz) long-grain rice in boiling water for 12 minutes or until just tender; drain and rinse with cold water. Meanwhile, soften 1 finely chopped onion in 1 tsp extra virgin olive oil for 5 minutes, then set aside to cool. Put the rice and onion in a bowl with 225 g (8 oz) minced chicken or turkey, 2 tbsp toasted pine nuts, 2 tbsp raisins, 2 tbsp chopped fresh mint and 2 tbsp chopped fresh dill. Season to taste. Mix together well and divide into 8 equal portions. Cut the sheets of filo pastry into 8 strips as before. Brush each pastry strip lightly with the olive oil and butter mixture, and put one portion of the filling at one end. Fold the pastry over the filling into a triangle. Continue folding down the pastry strip to make a triangular-shaped parcel. Brush all the parcels with the butter and oil mixture, and scatter over 1 tsp poppy seeds. Bake for 30 minutes. Serve the filo triangles on a tomato and onion salad: thickly slice 3 beef tomatoes and scatter over 1 sliced red onion, 15 small black olives and 1 tbsp chopped fresh dill. Season with salt and pepper and drizzle over 1 tbsp extra virgin olive oil.

Tiger prawns with pepper salsa

A salsa is a Mexican-style vegetable or fruit sauce with a fresh zingy flavour. A tomato, pepper and chilli salsa makes a wonderful accompaniment for grilled prawn kebabs, here served with sweet melon and crusty bread.

Serves 4

32 large raw tiger prawns, peeled but tails left on

1 Charentais melon, seeded and cut into cubes

Marinade

2 tbsp lime juice

1 tsp bottled chopped garlic in oil, drained

1 tsp bottled chopped root ginger in oil, drained

Salsa

6 vine-ripened tomatoes, chopped

1 small red onion, finely chopped

1 red pepper, seeded and chopped

1 tsp bottled chopped garlic in oil, drained

1 fresh green chilli, seeded and finely chopped

2 tbsp lime juice

2 tbsp chopped fresh coriander

salt and pepper

shredded spring onions to garnish

Preparation and cooking time: 30 minutes

Each serving provides

kcal 150, **protein** 24 g, **fat** 1.5 g (of which saturated fat 0.5 g), **carbohydrate** 11 g (of which sugars 10 g), **fibre** 3 g

✓✓✓	A, B$_{12}$, C
✓✓	B$_6$, iron
✓	folate, niacin, potassium, selenium, zinc

1 Preheat the grill. Soak 8 bamboo skewers in cold water (this will prevent them from burning under the grill). Combine all of the ingredients for the marinade in a shallow dish. Add the prawns and stir to coat them with the marinade. Cover and chill while preparing the salsa.

2 Mix together all the salsa ingredients and season with salt and pepper to taste. Pile into a serving bowl. Thread the cubes of melon onto 8 unsoaked wooden skewers and place on a serving dish. Set aside.

3 Thread 4 prawns onto each of the soaked skewers, piercing them through both ends (this will help to keep them flat). Place under the grill and cook for 3–4 minutes or until they are pink, turning them once. Do not overcook or they will become tough.

4 Garnish the salsa with the shredded spring onions. Place the prawn kebabs on the serving dish with the melon and serve immediately, with the salsa alongside.

Some more ideas

● Make grilled chicken kebabs and serve with a fresh citrus salsa. Cut 550 g (1¼ lb) skinless boneless chicken breasts (fillets) into cubes and marinate as described in the main recipe. Grill the chicken on skewers for 10 minutes or until tender and cooked through. For the salsa, chop the flesh from 1 pink grapefruit and 1 orange and 1 crisp juicy apple (such as Jonagold), and mix with 2 chopped spring onions, 1 finely chopped fresh green chilli and 1 tbsp chopped fresh mint.

● Cubes of fresh pineapple can be speared onto skewers to accompany the prawn or chicken kebabs in place of melon.

Plus points

● The raw fruit and vegetables in the salsa are packed with vitamins. The tomatoes and red peppers are excellent sources of the antioxidants beta-carotene and vitamin C. Red peppers, in particular, are an excellent source of vitamin C. Weight for weight, they provide over twice as much vitamin C as oranges.

● Prawns are a high-protein, low-fat food.

Chicken liver mousse

A splash of brandy adds a special touch to this light mousse. Poaching the chicken livers with vegetables and herbs, instead of frying them, keeps the fat content low, and fromage frais adds the richness that would traditionally have come from butter.

Serves 4

250 g (9 oz) chicken livers, well trimmed

1 onion, finely chopped

1 garlic clove, crushed

600 ml (1 pint) vegetable stock or water

several sprigs of parsley

several sprigs of fresh thyme

1 bay leaf

1–1½ tbsp fromage frais

2 tsp garlic vinegar or white wine vinegar

2 tsp brandy or Calvados, or to taste

1 tbsp pink or green peppercorns in brine, drained and patted dry

2 tbsp finely chopped parsley

salt and pepper

Preparation time: 10 minutes, plus at least 4 hours chilling

Cooking time: about 15 minutes

Each serving provides

kcal 80, protein 12.5 g, fat 1.5 g (of which saturated fat 0.4 g), carbohydrate 3.5 g (of which sugars 2.5 g), fibre 1 g

✓✓✓	A, B₂, B₆, B₁₂, folate, iron
✓✓	C, copper, zinc
✓	B₁, niacin

1 Place the chicken livers, onion and garlic in a saucepan and add stock or water to cover. Tie the parsley, thyme and bay leaf into a bouquet garni and add to the pan. Slowly bring to the boil, skimming the surface as necessary, then reduce the heat and simmer gently for 5–8 minutes or until the livers are cooked through but still slightly pink in the centre when you cut into one.

2 Drain, and discard the bouquet garni. Tip the livers, onions and garlic into a food processor. Add 1 tbsp of the fromage frais, the vinegar and brandy, and process until smooth, adding the remaining ½ tbsp fromage frais if it is necessary for a lighter texture. Season to taste, then stir in the peppercorns. Alternatively, tip the livers, onions and garlic into a bowl and mash with a fork to a slightly coarse paste. Add the fromage frais, vinegar and brandy and mix well, then season and stir in the peppercorns.

3 Spoon the mousse into a serving bowl, or individual ramekins, and smooth the top. Sprinkle with a layer of finely chopped parsley. Cover with cling film and chill for at least 4 hours, but preferably overnight.

4 Before serving, allow the mousse to return to room temperature. Serve with slices of hot toast.

Some more ideas

● Replace the brandy with orange juice and add the finely grated zest of ½ orange.

● If you can't find pink or green peppercorns, substitute finely chopped drained capers.

● For a smooth mousse, made without a food processor, omit the onion, and sieve the cooked livers and garlic. Add 2 spring onions, finely chopped, with the peppercorns.

● For a less rich mousse to serve 6, omit the brandy and add 100 g (3½ oz) drained canned cannellini beans, rinsed and dried, to the food processor with ½ tbsp finely chopped fresh sage. This mousse is excellent on toasted slices of country-style bread, or spread on slices of baguette and then topped with sliced gherkins.

● Vary the herbs – chopped fresh chives, tarragon and mint all go well with chicken liver mousse.

Plus points

● Chicken livers are one of the richest sources of iron – each serving of this mousse provides more than half of the recommended daily intake.

● Many traditional recipes for chicken liver mousse and pâté seal the surface with a layer of melted or clarified butter for storage. In this version the fat is replaced by the chopped fresh herbs.

Soups and starters

Dolmades

Here's a healthy twist on these delicious Greek parcels. To boost the nutrient content, brown rice is used instead of white. The filling for the vine leaves is flavoured with garlic and herbs, with sweetness from the raisins and crunch from the walnuts.

Serves 8 (makes 24)

200 g (7 oz) long-grain brown rice

24 large vine leaves preserved in brine, about 115 g (4 oz) in total when drained

3 tbsp extra virgin olive oil

1 onion, finely chopped

1 large garlic clove, finely chopped

1 tbsp chopped parsley

1 tbsp chopped fresh mint

1 tbsp chopped fresh dill

grated zest and juice of 1 lemon

50 g (1¾ oz) raisins

50 g (1¾ oz) walnuts, chopped

salt and pepper

To garnish

lemon wedges

sprigs of fresh dill, parsley or mint

Preparation time: 1 hour

Cooking time: 10–15 minutes

Each serving provides Ⓥ

kcal 199, **protein** 4 g, **fat** 9 g (of which saturated fat 1 g), **carbohydrate** 27 g (of which sugars 6 g), **fibre** 1 g

✓✓✓ copper

✓ A, B₁, C, folate, calcium, iron, zinc

1 Put the rice in a saucepan and add 600 ml (1 pint) water. Bring to the boil. Stir, then cover with a tight-fitting lid and simmer very gently for 30–40 minutes or until the rice is tender and has absorbed all the water. Remove from the heat.

2 While the rice is cooking, drain the vine leaves, rinse with cold water and pat dry with kitchen paper. Put them to one side.

3 Heat 2 tbsp of the oil in a saucepan over a moderate heat. Add the onion and garlic, and cook, stirring occasionally, for 5–8 minutes or until soft but not browned. Remove from the heat and stir in the parsley, mint, dill, lemon zest and raisins.

4 Put the walnuts in a small frying pan and toast them over a moderate heat, stirring constantly, until lightly browned and aromatic.

5 Add the toasted walnuts to the onion mixture. Stir in the cooked rice and add the lemon juice (you may not need all of it), and salt and pepper to taste. Mix well.

6 Spread one of the vine leaves flat on a work surface and place about 2 teaspoons of the rice mixture in the centre. Fold over the stalk end, then fold in the sides. Roll up the leaf into a cylinder shape. Repeat with the remaining vine leaves and filling.

7 Place the rolls seam side down in a steamer and brush the tops with the remaining 1 tbsp olive oil. Cover and steam for 10–15 minutes or until piping hot. Serve hot or at room temperature, garnished with lemon wedges and sprigs of fresh herbs.

Plus points

• Brown rice has only the outer husk removed and therefore contains all the nutrients in the germ and outer layers of the grain. Raw brown rice contains 1.9 g fibre per 100 g (3½ oz) compared with 0.4 g fibre for the same weight of raw white rice. It also contains more B vitamins.

• Walnuts are high in unsaturated fats, especially linoleic acid. Recent studies have suggested that regular consumption of walnuts may help to protect against heart attacks.

• Raisins, currants and sultanas are all types of dried grapes. They are rich in sugars, mostly as glucose and fructose, and a useful source of iron, potassium and fibre.

Soups and starters

Another idea

● To make stuffed cabbage rolls, use 12 large Savoy cabbage leaves instead of the vine leaves. Blanch them for 1 minute in boiling water, then refresh under cold running water and pat dry. Cut out the tough cores. Cook the onion and garlic as in the main recipe, then add 1 tbsp chopped fresh thyme, the grated zest of 1 orange and 50 g (1¾ oz) each chopped dried apricots and chopped toasted almonds. Stir in the rice and the juice of ½ orange, and season with salt and pepper to taste. Roll up the filling in the cabbage leaves as instructed for the vine leaves. Make a simple tomato sauce by combining 2 tbsp extra virgin olive oil, 1 finely chopped onion and 1 can chopped tomatoes, about 400 g, with the juice, in a saucepan and simmering for 15–20 minutes or until the onion is soft and the sauce slightly thickened. Season to taste, then pour into a shallow baking dish. Place the cabbage rolls on top, seam side down, and cover the dish with foil. Bake in a preheated 180ºC (350ºF, gas mark 4) oven for 25 minutes or until piping hot.

Lemon mackerel pâté

Whether you are planning a family meal or a dinner party, this fresh-tasting smoked fish pâté makes a perfect starter, served with granary toast. For an elegant presentation, spoon it into scooped-out lemon shells, which will also enhance the tangy lemon flavour.

Serves 4

2 smoked mackerel fillets, about
    125 g (4½ oz) each, skinned

200 g (7 oz) fromage frais

finely grated zest and juice of 1 small lemon

2 tsp bottled soft green peppercorns, drained,
    rinsed and chopped, or 1 tsp dried green
    peppercorns, coarsely crushed

1 tbsp finely snipped fresh chives

1 tbsp finely chopped parsley

To serve

sprigs of parsley

lemon wedges

Preparation time: 10–15 minutes, plus
    30 minutes chilling

1 Using a fork, break up the mackerel fillets into large pieces and place in a bowl. Add the fromage frais, lemon zest, half of the lemon juice, the peppercorns, chives and parsley. Mash all the ingredients together with a fork. This will make a coarse-textured pâté. For a smooth version, combine the ingredients in a food processor and process. Taste the pâté and stir in more lemon juice if necessary.

2 Spoon the pâté into 4 ramekins, cover with cling film and chill for 30 minutes. Just before serving, top each with a sprig of parsley and serve with lemon wedges.

Some more ideas

• For a smoked trout pâté, substitute smoked trout fillets for the mackerel and add 1 tbsp creamed horseradish instead of the green peppercorns.

• Add a crushed garlic clove and use fresh dill instead of chives.

• Toast 50 g (1¾ oz) shelled walnuts or hazelnuts, chop coarsely and fold into the finished pâté. Season with freshly ground black pepper or a small pinch of cayenne pepper.

• Chill the pâté in a bowl, then scoop out using an ice-cream scoop or a spoon and serve in cup-shaped lettuce leaves. Offer crudités for dipping (such as celery, fennel and carrot sticks, strips of red pepper and whole radishes).

• To make lemon shells, cut a sliver off the stalk end of 4 lemons so they stand firmly upright. Cut off a lid from each lemon, about 1 cm (½ in) from the top. Using a grapefruit knife or pointed teaspoon, remove all the flesh from the lemons (keep it for another recipe). Fill the lemon shells with the mackerel pâté and top with the lids. Alternatively, cut the lemons in half horizontally, from the stalk end to the tip. Scoop out the flesh from the halves and fill with the pâté. Serve 2 halves per person.

Each serving provides

kcal 250, protein 16 g, fat 19 g (of which saturated fat 4 g), carbohydrate 3.5 g (of which sugars 3.5 g), fibre 0 g

✓✓✓	B₁, B₆, B₁₂, niacin
✓✓	selenium
✓	B₂, iron

Plus points

• Mackerel is an excellent source of vitamin D. Most people obtain all the vitamin D they need from the action of sunlight on skin, but those who remain indoors a lot would benefit from including this fish in their diet on a regular basis.

• Lemons, like other citrus fruits, contain excellent levels of vitamin C. Towards the end of the 18th century, lemon juice was used as a means of protecting sailors against scurvy, the disease caused by vitamin C deficiency.

Soups and starters

Pears grilled with pecorino

Many cuisines have traditions of combining fruit with cheese. This recipe stems from the Tuscan combination of juicy pears with salty pecorino. With some cheese melted over the pears and the rest combined with grapes and salad leaves, this is a very attractive dish.

Serves 4

55 g (2 oz) pecorino cheese

1 bunch of watercress, about 55 g (2 oz), leaves removed from stalks

115 g (4 oz) rocket leaves

55 g (2 oz) seedless green grapes, halved

2 dessert pears

Balsamic vinaigrette

2 tbsp extra virgin olive oil

1 tbsp best-quality balsamic vinegar

½ tsp Dijon mustard

pinch of caster sugar

salt and pepper

Preparation time: 15 minutes

Cooking time: about 2 minutes

Each serving provides Ⓥ

kcal 130, **protein** 4 g, **fat** 9 g (of which saturated fat 3 g), **carbohydrate** 9 g (of which sugars 9 g), **fibre** 2 g

✓✓	C
✓	A, B₁₂, folate, calcium

1 First make the dressing. Put the olive oil, balsamic vinegar, mustard, sugar, and salt and pepper to taste into a small screw-top jar. Screw on the lid and shake all the ingredients together until well blended. Keep the dressing in the fridge until required.

2 Preheat the grill to high. Place a strip of cooking foil on a baking tray and set aside.

3 Using a vegetable peeler, peel the pecorino cheese into fine shavings. Reserve half of these and finely chop the remainder. Put the watercress, rocket leaves and grapes into a salad bowl and toss together.

4 Peel, halve and core the pears. Arrange the pear halves, cut sides down, on the foil strip. Top the pears with the shavings of cheese, slightly overlapping them. Place under the grill, about 15 cm (6 in) from the heat, and grill for 2 minutes or until the cheese just starts to bubble and turn golden.

5 Meanwhile, shake the dressing, pour it over the salad and toss to coat the leaves. Add the chopped pecorino. Divide the salad equally among 4 plates.

6 Using a fish slice, carefully transfer one pear half to each plate, placing it on top of the bed of dressed salad. Serve at once.

Some more ideas

● Use diced kiwi fruit instead of grapes.

● Parmesan cheese, another Italian firm cheese, is suitable for this recipe and it has less fat.

● If you are in a hurry, just chop the pears and toss them in the salad with all the cheese.

● Substitute baby spinach leaves for the rocket.

● Grill the pear halves cut side up, then sprinkle a blue cheese, such as Shropshire blue, into the cavities and grill until it melts.

● A creamy goat's cheese could be used in a fruit and cheese salad instead of high-fat pecorino. Goat's cheese has a natural affinity with fresh raspberries, so for a delicious first course, omit the pears and pecorino cheese from the recipe above and replace the balsamic vinegar in the vinaigrette with raspberry vinegar. Toss 200 g (7 oz) raspberries with the salad. Toast 8 thin slices of baguette on one side under the grill, then turn over and top with slices of goat's cheese. Grill until the cheese is bubbling, then transfer 2 slices to each plate. Dress the salad and arrange next to the cheese-topped toasts.

Plus points

● This salad is a useful source of calcium, needed for healthy bones and teeth. The pecorino cheese, watercress and rocket all provide this vital mineral.

Parmesan-topped mussels

Make this stylish starter when you can buy large mussels, such as the green-lipped mussels from New Zealand, as small ones can toughen when grilled. Although you need only 24, buy at least 30 because some might have to be discarded. Serve with crusty French bread.

Serves 4

100 ml (3½ fl oz) white wine or fish stock, preferably homemade

1 large onion, very finely chopped

3 large garlic cloves, crushed

about 30 large mussels, scrubbed and beards removed

50 g (1¾ oz) fresh wholemeal bread

30 g (1 oz) parsley, chopped

30 g (1 oz) Parmesan cheese, freshly grated

½ tbsp finely grated lemon zest

pinch of cayenne pepper

1 tbsp extra virgin olive oil

lemon wedges to serve

Preparation and cooking time: 30 minutes

Each serving provides

kcal 167, **protein** 12 g, **fat** 7 g (of which saturated fat 2 g), **carbohydrate** 12 g (of which sugars 4 g), **fibre** 2 g

✓✓✓	B₁, B₆, B₁₂, niacin, iron
✓✓	selenium
✓	A, C, folate, calcium, copper, potassium, zinc

1 Pour the wine or stock into a large saucepan, add the onion and garlic, and bring to the boil over a high heat. Boil rapidly for 1 minute. Add the mussels, cover the pan tightly and cook for 2–3 minutes, shaking the pan occasionally. Uncover the pan and give the mussels a good stir. Using tongs, remove the mussels from the pan as soon as they open and set them aside. Discard any mussels that remain shut.

2 When the mussels are cool enough to handle, remove and discard the top shell. Place 24 mussels on the half shell in a single layer in a shallow flameproof dish, loosening the mussels from the shells but leaving them in place. Set the dish aside.

3 Preheat the grill to high. Put the bread in a food processor or blender and process to fine crumbs. Add the parsley, Parmesan, lemon zest, cayenne pepper and olive oil, and process again until well blended.

4 Using your fingers, put a mound of the cheese and crumb mixture on each mussel and pack it down firmly so the mussel is completely covered. Put the dish under the grill and cook for 2–3 minutes or until the crumb topping is crisp and lightly browned. Divide the mussels among individual plates and serve with lemon wedges.

Another idea

• Rather than grilling the mussels with the crumb and Parmesan topping, serve them French-style, cooked in cider. Put 1 litre (1¾ pints) dry cider in the pan with the onion and garlic and boil until reduced to 600 ml (1 pint). Stir in the parsley, lemon zest and cayenne pepper. Add the mussels and steam them open. Transfer the mussels to serving bowls. Season the cooking liquid to taste and ladle it over the mussels.

Plus points

• Mussels are a good source of iron, an essential component of haemoglobin in red blood cells responsible for transporting oxygen around the body.

• Parmesan cheese is a very hard cheese made from unpasteurised skimmed cow's milk. Although Parmesan has a high fat content, it also has a strong flavour and a little goes a long way in a recipe.

• Cayenne pepper, made from one of the smallest and hottest chillies, is often used in herbal medicine to stimulate the circulation.

Soups and starters

Main meals

Fish, poultry, vegetarian and meat dishes – here are main meals to suit all tastes and occasions. The selection includes delicate Thai-style crab cakes, Summer salmon and asparagus, Basil-stuffed chicken breasts, attractive Tomato and pecorino clafoutis, Herb and saffron risotto, Perfect pot roast, Fragrant lamb with spinach, and Sticky spare ribs. Packed with protein, many are also quick and simple to prepare.

Bulghur wheat and prawn salad

A coarsely ground wheat grain, Bulghur has already been parboiled, so it's quick to prepare and makes an ideal storecupboard standby to use in salads as well as in hot dishes. This nutty-textured, colourful salad is full of goodness, and is very attractive to the eye.

Serves 4

250 g (8½ oz) bulghur wheat

1 small red onion, very thinly sliced

1 carrot, coarsely grated

1 tomato, diced

6 baby corn, sliced into rounds

½ cucumber, diced

200 g (7 oz) peeled cooked prawns

Lime and chilli dressing

4 tbsp extra virgin olive oil

2 tbsp lime juice

1 garlic clove, crushed

¼ tsp crushed dried chillies

salt and pepper

Preparation and cooking time: 20–25 minutes

1 Put the bulghur wheat in a saucepan and pour over 650 ml (22 fl oz) water. Bring to the boil, then simmer for 10 minutes or until the bulghur is tender and all the water has been absorbed. Tip the bulghur into a flat dish, spread out and allow to cool slightly.

2 Combine the onion, carrot, tomato, corn, cucumber and prawns in a large salad bowl. Add the bulghur wheat and stir together.

3 For the dressing, put the oil, lime juice, garlic, chilli flakes, and salt and pepper to taste in a small bowl. Whisk with a fork until combined. Stir the dressing into the salad, tossing to coat all the ingredients evenly. If not serving the salad immediately, cover and keep in the fridge.

Some more ideas

● For a bulghur wheat and feta salad, replace the prawns with 200 g (7 oz) diced feta cheese. Another alternative to the prawns is diced tofu.

● To make a bulghur wheat and ham salad, combine the cooked bulghur wheat with 150 g (5½ oz) thinly sliced Parma or Serrano ham, trimmed of all fat and cut into strips, 3 chopped spring onions, 1 seeded and diced yellow pepper, 200 g (7 oz) halved cherry tomatoes and 3 tbsp capers. Make the dressing by whisking together 4 tbsp extra virgin olive oil, 2 tbsp red wine vinegar, 1 tsp clear honey and 6 finely crushed allspice berries. Season to taste and toss with the salad.

Plus points

● Bulghur wheat is a good source of starchy carbohydrate, dietary fibre and B vitamins, as it contains all the particularly nutritious outer layers of the grain except the bran itself.

● The inclusion of raw vegetables in this salad not only adds texture and colour but also vitamins, particularly those with antioxidant properties.

● Prawns, like all seafish, contain iodine, which is needed for the formation of the thyroid hormones and the functioning of the thyroid gland itself.

Each serving provides

kcal 399, **protein** 19 g, **fat** 13 g (of which saturated fat 2 g), **carbohydrate** 53 g (of which sugars 5 g), **fibre** 2 g

✓✓✓	B$_{12}$
✓✓	A, niacin, copper, iron
✓	B$_1$, C, E, calcium, potassium, selenium, zinc

Main meals

Provençal tuna and pepper salad

This bright, attractive salad is full of varied flavours and textures. Chunks of tuna, wedges of new potato, crisp beans and fleshy tomatoes re-create the original dish from the heart of Provence and are packed with healthy nutrients. Serve with crusty baguettes.

Serves 4

400 g (14 oz) new potatoes
55 g (2 oz) fine green beans
6 quail's eggs
225 g (8 oz) mixed salad leaves
1 tbsp chopped parsley
1 tbsp snipped fresh chives
1 small red onion, thinly sliced
1 tbsp tapenade (black olive paste)
2 garlic cloves, chopped
2 tbsp extra virgin olive oil
1 tbsp red wine vinegar
1 tsp balsamic vinegar
10–15 radishes, thinly sliced
1 can tuna in spring water, about 200 g,
    drained
100 g (3½ oz) cherry tomatoes
1 red pepper, seeded and thinly sliced
1 yellow pepper, seeded and thinly sliced
1 green pepper, seeded and thinly sliced
8 black olives
salt and pepper
fresh basil leaves to garnish

Preparation time: 45 minutes

Each serving provides

kcal 296, **protein** 20 g, **fat** 13 g (of which saturated fat 2 g), **carbohydrate** 26 g (of which sugars 10 g), **fibre** 5 g

✓✓✓	B$_1$, B$_6$, B$_{12}$, C, niacin, selenium
✓✓	A, folate, iron, potassium
✓	B$_2$, E, calcium, copper, zinc

1 Place the potatoes in a saucepan and cover with boiling water. Cook over a moderate heat for 10 minutes. Add the beans and cook for a further 5 minutes or until the potatoes are tender and the beans are just cooked. Drain well and set aside to cool.

2 Put the quail's eggs into a saucepan with cold water to cover and bring to the boil. Reduce the heat and cook at a low simmer for 3 minutes. Rinse well in cold water. Peel the eggs carefully and place in cold water.

3 Toss the salad leaves with the parsley, chives and red onion in a large shallow bowl.

4 To make the dressing, mix the tapenade with the garlic, olive oil, red wine vinegar and balsamic vinegar, and season with salt and pepper to taste. Pour two-thirds of the dressing over the salad leaves and toss well to mix.

5 Halve the potatoes and arrange them on top of the leaves with the green beans, radishes, chunks of tuna, tomatoes, peppers and olives. Halve the quail's eggs and add them to the salad. Pour over the remaining dressing, garnish with basil leaves and serve.

Some more ideas

• For a classic Italian cannellini bean and tuna salad, omit the potatoes and quail's eggs and add 1 can cannellini beans, about 400 g, well drained, to the salad leaves. Use the juice of ½ lemon in the dressing instead of balsamic vinegar.

• Try this salad using different varieties of tomatoes, such as yellow cherry tomatoes, baby plum tomatoes or quartered vine-ripened plum tomatoes.

Plus points

• Canned tuna retains a high vitamin content, particularly vitamins B$_{12}$ and D.

• In common with many other salad ingredients, radishes are a useful source of vitamin C and are very low in calories. The radish has a very hot flavour due to an enzyme in the skin that reacts with another substance to form a mustard type of oil.

• Green beans are a good source of dietary fibre and provide valuable amounts of folate.

Main meals

Thai-style crab cakes

Made from crab meat and white fish, together with classic Thai flavourings, these cakes are light but packed with protein, and come with a piquant dipping sauce and crunchy salad. Serve with fragrant Thai rice.

Serves 4

2 cans white meat crab, about 170 g each, drained and patted dry with kitchen paper
225 g (8 oz) skinless white fish fillets, such as cod or haddock, cut into chunks
1 tbsp Thai red curry paste
1 fresh lime leaf
2 tbsp chopped fresh coriander
½ tsp caster sugar
1 egg, beaten
2 carrots, finely chopped
½ cucumber, finely chopped
4 spring onions, finely chopped
2 tbsp groundnut or sunflower oil for frying
salt

Sweet and sour dipping sauce

3 tbsp white wine or cider vinegar
50 g (1¾ oz) caster sugar
1 tbsp fish sauce
1 fresh red chilli, seeded and finely chopped

To garnish

lime wedges
sprigs of fresh coriander

Preparation and cooking time: 30 minutes

Each serving provides

kcal 330, protein 30 g, fat 13 g (of which saturated fat 2 g), carbohydrate 23 g (of which sugars 22 g), fibre 2 g

✓✓✓	A, copper
✓✓	B_6, B_{12}, E, selenium, zinc
✓	B_1, folate, calcium, potassium

1 Place the crab and white fish in a food processor or blender and process until mixed. Add the red curry paste, lime leaf, chopped coriander, sugar, a pinch of salt and the egg. Process again to mix. Divide the mixture into 12 even-sized pieces. Roll each one into a ball, then flatten to make a small cake. Chill while making the dipping sauce.

2 Gently heat the vinegar, sugar, fish sauce and 2 tbsp water in a small pan until the sugar dissolves. Boil for 2–3 minutes or until syrupy, then remove from the heat and allow to cool before adding the chilli.

3 Mix together the carrots, cucumber and spring onions in a serving bowl or in 4 small individual dishes.

4 Heat the oil in a large non-stick frying pan. Fry the crab cakes for 2–3 minutes on each side or until golden and cooked through. Drain on kitchen paper. Serve garnished with lime wedges and sprigs of coriander, with the dipping sauce and the carrot and cucumber salad.

Some more ideas

● If you like a really hot dipping sauce, include the chilli seeds. Some chopped peanuts could also be added to the sauce.

● Halve the quantities of carrot, cucumber and spring onion, and add to the dipping sauce.

● For Thai-style prawn cakes, use 225 g (8 oz) peeled cooked prawns instead of the crab. Or make fish cakes using all white fish fillet – 450 g (1 lb) in total.

● Try Thai green curry paste instead of red – it is slightly milder and more aromatic.

● If you can't find lime leaves, use the grated zest of 1 lime instead.

Plus points

● Crab meat is an excellent low-fat source of protein and is a good source of phosphorus, which is important for healthy bones and strong teeth.

● Results from a study that compared the diets of over 5500 people in Holland, showed that those who ate fish regularly were less likely to develop dementia in later life.

● Some studies suggest that eating chillies can help to prevent gastric ulcers by causing the stomach lining to secrete a coating of mucus that protects it from damage by irritants such as aspirin or alcohol.

Main meals

102

Cod with spicy Puy lentils

Dark green Puy lentils, grown in the south of France, have a unique, peppery flavour that is enhanced by chilli. They do not disintegrate during cooking and their texture is a perfect complement for the flakiness of fresh cod. Serve this dish with warm crusty bread.

Serves 4

2 tbsp extra virgin olive oil

1 onion, chopped

2 celery sticks, chopped

2 medium-sized leeks, chopped

1–2 fresh red chillies, seeded and finely
 chopped

170 g (6 oz) Puy lentils, rinsed and drained

750 ml (1¼ pints) vegetable stock

1 sprig of fresh thyme

1 bay leaf

juice of 1 lemon

pinch of cayenne pepper

4 pieces of skinless cod fillet or cod steaks,
 about 140 g (5 oz) each

salt and pepper

lemon wedges to serve

Preparation and cooking time: about 35 minutes

1 Preheat the grill to moderately high. Heat 1 tbsp of the olive oil in a saucepan, add the onion, celery, leeks and chillies, and cook gently for 2 minutes. Stir in the lentils. Add the vegetable stock, thyme and bay leaf and bring to the boil. Lower the heat and simmer for about 20 minutes or until the lentils are tender. If at the end of this time the lentils have not absorbed all the stock, drain them (you can use the excess stock to make a soup).

2 While the lentils are cooking, mix together the remaining 1 tbsp oil, the lemon juice and cayenne pepper. Lay the cod in the grill pan, skinned side up, season with salt and pepper, and brush with the oil mixture. Grill for 6–7 minutes or until the fish will flake easily. There is no need to turn the fish over.

3 Spread the lentils in a warmed serving dish and arrange the pieces of cod on top. Serve immediately, with lemon wedges.

Some more ideas

● For cod with mustard lentils, cook the lentils as in the main recipe, omitting the chillies. Mix 125 g (4½ oz) fromage frais or crème fraîche with 1–2 tbsp Dijon mustard and stir into the cooked lentils. Spread a thin layer of Dijon mustard over the seasoned cod, drizzle with olive oil and grill. Serve the cod on top of the lentils, garnished with grilled cherry tomatoes.

● Hake, halibut, salmon or hoki can be used instead of cod.

Plus points

● White fish such as cod is low in calories. Frying it in batter more than doubles the calorie content, whereas brushing it with a little oil and grilling it keeps the fat and therefore calories at healthy levels.

● Lentils, which are small seeds from a variety of leguminous plants, are classified as pulses, but unlike other pulses they do not need to be soaked before cooking. Lentils are a good source of protein, starch, dietary fibre and B vitamins. Iron absorption from lentils is poor, but vitamin C-rich foods, such as the lemon juice in this recipe, can improve this process considerably.

● Thyme has been used as an antiseptic since Greek and Roman times.

Each serving provides

kcal 324, **protein** 38 g, **fat** 7.5 g (of which saturated fat 1 g), **carbohydrate** 26 g (of which sugars 6 g), **fibre** 7.5 g

✓✓✓	B_1, B_6, niacin, selenium
✓✓	B_{12}, C
✓	A, E, folate, iron, potassium

Main meals

Griddled halibut steaks with tomato and red pepper salsa

Firm-fleshed halibut is well suited to quick cooking on a ridged cast-iron grill pan, which produces attractive markings. A hot salsa adds colour and a spicy touch. Serve with a mixed salad and crusty bread for a balanced meal.

Serves 4

4 halibut steaks, about 140 g (5 oz) each

3 tbsp extra virgin olive oil

juice of 1 small orange

1 garlic clove, crushed

1 orange, cut into wedges, to garnish

Tomato and red pepper salsa

200 g (7 oz) ripe plum tomatoes, diced

½ red pepper, seeded and diced

½ red onion, finely chopped

juice of 1 small orange

15 g (½ oz) fresh basil, chopped

1 tbsp balsamic vinegar

1 tsp caster sugar

salt and pepper

Preparation time: 15 minutes

Cooking time: 4–6 minutes

1 Place the halibut steaks in a shallow non-metallic dish. Mix together the oil, orange juice, garlic and salt and pepper to taste, and spoon over the fish steaks.

2 Combine all the salsa ingredients and season with salt and pepper to taste. Spoon into a serving bowl.

3 Heat a lightly oiled ridged cast-iron grill pan or heavy-based frying pan over a high heat. Place the fish steaks on the grill pan or in the frying pan and cook for 2–3 minutes on each side, basting from time to time with the oil mixture, until the fish will just flake easily.

4 Place the fish steaks on warm serving plates and grind over some black pepper. Garnish with wedges of orange and serve with the salsa.

Some more ideas

• Other white fish steaks such as cod, haddock, hoki or swordfish, or monkfish fillets, can be cooked in the same way.

• For a tomato and olive salsa, combine the diced tomatoes with ½ diced cucumber, 4 chopped spring onions, 45 g (1½ oz) chopped stoned green or black olives and 15 g (½ oz) chopped fresh basil. Or use 1 tbsp drained and rinsed capers instead of olives.

• In summer, the fish can be cooked outdoors on a barbecue. Lay the steaks on a sheet of foil to prevent the delicate flesh slipping through the barbecue grid.

Plus points

• Red peppers are an excellent source of vitamin C – half a raw pepper provides over twice the recommended daily intake of this vitamin. They also supply beta-carotene and a small amount of vitamin E.

• Halibut is a good source of niacin, which has an important role to play in the release of energy within cells. Niacin is one of the most stable vitamins, and there are little or no losses during preparation or cooking.

Each serving provides

kcal 254, **protein** 31 g, **fat** 11 g (of which saturated fat 2 g), **carbohydrate** 7.5 g (of which sugars 6.5 g), **fibre** 1 g

✓✓✓	B₁, B₆, C, niacin
✓✓	A, B₁₂, E
✓	iron, potassium

Main meals

Herbed fish crumble

This tasty fish crumble is comfort food at its healthiest: smoked haddock and whiting in a smooth sauce, covered with a crisp herby topping. Baked jacket potatoes, baby carrots and peas go well with this dish.

Serves 4

200 g (7 oz) whiting fillet

200 g (7 oz) smoked haddock fillet

1 medium-sized leek, thinly sliced

300 ml (10 fl oz) semi-skimmed milk

2 bay leaves

45 g (1½ oz) butter

75 g (2½ oz) wholemeal flour

3 tbsp freshly grated Parmesan cheese

2 tbsp chopped fresh marjoram or 2 tsp dried marjoram

4 tsp cornflour

100 g (3½ oz) button mushrooms, thinly sliced

2 tbsp chopped fresh flat-leaf parsley

salt and pepper

sprigs of fresh marjoram to garnish

Preparation time: 25 minutes

Cooking time: 35–40 minutes

Each serving provides

kcal 319, **protein** 28 g, **fat** 14 g (of which saturated fat 9 g), **carbohydrate** 22 g (of which sugars 5 g), **fibre** 3 g

✓✓✓	B₁, B₆, niacin, selenium
✓✓	A, B₁₂, calcium, copper
✓	B₂, C, folate, iron, potassium, zinc

1 Preheat the oven to 190ºC (375ºF, gas mark 5). Put the fish in a single layer in a large saucepan or frying pan and add the leek, milk and bay leaves. Season with salt and pepper to taste. Bring just to the boil, then simmer gently for 5 minutes. Take the pan off the heat and leave to stand for about 5 minutes.

2 Meanwhile, in a bowl rub the butter into the flour with your fingertips to make fine crumbs. Stir in the cheese, marjoram and seasoning to taste.

3 Lift the fish out of the milk with a fish slice and put it onto a plate. Remove the skin and flake the flesh, discarding any bones.

4 Mix the cornflour to a smooth paste with a little water, add to the milk in the pan and bring to the boil, stirring until the sauce has thickened. Discard the bay leaves. Stir in the sliced mushrooms and cook for 1 minute. Gently stir in the flaked fish and chopped parsley and season with salt and pepper to taste.

5 Pour the fish mixture into a 1.2 litre (2 pint) shallow ovenproof dish. Spoon the crumble mixture evenly over the top. Bake for 35–40 minutes or until the top is golden. Serve at once, garnished with marjoram.

Plus points

● Milk is an excellent source of calcium, which is essential for healthy, strong bones and forms part of the structure of the teeth. An adult requires a daily intake of 700mg, although this varies with age and sex. A lack of calcium in childhood and adolescence can lead to osteoporosis in later life.

● Mushrooms contain useful amounts of the B vitamins B₂ and niacin. They are also a good source of copper, which is needed for bone growth.

Some more ideas

● Some children do not like the taste of wholemeal flour, so it's a good trick to mix it with an equal quantity of white flour.

● Make up a large batch of crumble topping and store it in a plastic box in the freezer. Then simply take out as much as you need and cook from frozen.

● For a Welsh-inspired cod crumble, poach 340 g (12 oz) cod or other firm white fish fillet in the milk with the leeks and bay leaves. Skin and flake the fish. Make the sauce, and stir in a jar of pickled cockles, about 160 g, drained and well rinsed, and 2 tbsp snipped fresh chives with the mushrooms. Top with a crumble made without the herbs and cheese, and flavoured instead with 1 tsp wholegrain mustard rubbed into the mixture with the butter.

Main meals

Summer salmon and asparagus

Fresh young vegetables and succulent salmon make this casserole highly nutritious and it is also quick to prepare. Choose tiny leeks, tender asparagus, sugarsnap peas, which all look superb, and boiled new potatoes to complete the meal.

Serves 4

4 pieces skinless salmon fillet, about 140 g
   (5 oz) each
200 g (7 oz) baby leeks
250 g (8½ oz) tender asparagus spears
150 g (5½ oz) sugarsnap peas
4 tbsp dry white wine
200 ml (7 fl oz) fish or vegetable stock,
   preferably bought chilled stock
30 g (1 oz) butter, cut into small pieces
salt and pepper
1 tbsp snipped fresh chives to garnish

Preparation time: 10 minutes
Cooking time: about 20 minutes

1 Run your fingertips over each salmon fillet to check for stray bones, pulling out any that remain between the flakes of fish. Arrange the leeks in a single layer in the bottom of a large shallow flameproof casserole. Lay the pieces of salmon on top. Surround the fish with the asparagus and sugarsnap peas. Pour in the wine and stock, and dot the butter over the fish. Season with salt and pepper.

2 Bring to the boil, then cover the casserole with a tight-fitting lid and reduce the heat so the liquid simmers gently. Cook the fish and vegetables for 12–14 minutes or until the salmon is pale pink all the way through and the vegetables are tender. Sprinkle the chives over the salmon and serve.

Some more ideas

● Mackerel fillets can be casseroled in the same way. Season the mackerel fillets and fold them loosely in half, with the skin outside. Use baby carrots, or large carrots cut into short, thick sticks, instead of the asparagus, and medium-dry cider instead of the wine. Add 2 sprigs of fresh rosemary to the vegetables before arranging the mackerel on top and pouring in the cider and stock.

● For a quick Oriental fish casserole, use cod or halibut fillet instead of salmon, 4 spring onions instead of the leeks, and 300 g (10½ oz) whole button mushrooms instead of the asparagus.

Arrange the vegetables and fish as in the main recipe, adding 4 tbsp Chinese rice wine or dry sherry with the stock instead of the white wine. Omit the butter and sprinkle 1 tbsp soy sauce, 1 tbsp grated fresh root ginger and 1 tbsp toasted sesame oil over the fish. Garnish with chopped fresh coriander instead of chives and serve with plain boiled rice.

Each serving provides

kcal 360, **protein** 33 g, **fat** 22 g (of which saturated fat 7 g), **carbohydrate** 4 g (of which sugars 4 g), **fibre** 3 g

✓✓✓	B₁₂
✓✓	B₆, C, folate
✓	B₁, niacin, iron, selenium

Plus points

● Asparagus contains asparagine, a phytochemical that acts as a diuretic. The ancient Greeks used the plant to treat kidney problems. Today modern-day naturopaths recommend eating asparagus to help relieve bloating associated with pre-menstrual syndrome (PMS).

● Salmon is a rich source of omega-3 fatty acids, a type of polyunsaturated fat thought to help protect against coronary heart disease and strokes by making blood less 'sticky' and therefore less likely to clot. A diet rich in omega-3 fatty acids may also be helpful in preventing and treating arthritis.

Main meals

Prawn gumbo

A bowl of steaming gumbo – a thick and spicy cross between a soup and a stew, full of peppers, tomatoes, okra, herbs and prawns – brings you all the good tastes of the Louisiana bayou. Serve with steamed rice or crusty bread so you can enjoy all the sauce.

Serves 4

1 tbsp extra virgin olive oil

2 onions, chopped

1 red pepper, seeded and chopped

2 celery sticks, chopped

3 garlic cloves, chopped

75 g (2½ oz) lean smoked back bacon
  rashers, rinded and diced

1 tbsp plain flour

1 tbsp paprika

1 litre (1¾ pints) fish stock, preferably
  homemade

1 tsp chopped fresh thyme

1 can chopped tomatoes, about 225 g

2 tbsp chopped parsley

2 bay leaves

2 tsp Worcestershire sauce

Tabasco sauce to taste

100 g (3½ oz) okra, sliced crossways

340 g (12 oz) peeled raw prawns

55 g (2 oz) fine green beans, cut into
  bite-sized lengths

salt and pepper

3 spring onions, thinly sliced, to garnish

Preparation time: 25 minutes

Cooking time: 40 minutes

1 Heat the oil in a large saucepan, add the onions, pepper and celery, and cook for 5–6 minutes or until lightly browned. Stir in the garlic and bacon and cook for a further 3–4 minutes. Stir in the flour, increase the heat slightly and cook for 2 minutes, stirring. Stir in the paprika and cook for 2 more minutes. Gradually add the stock, stirring well to dissolve the flour mixture.

2 Add the thyme, tomatoes with their juice, parsley, bay leaves and Worcestershire sauce. Bring to the boil, then reduce the heat to a simmer and add Tabasco sauce to taste. Add the okra and simmer for 15 minutes or until the okra is tender and the gumbo mixture has thickened.

3 Add the prawns and green beans and cook for 3 minutes or until the prawns turn pink and the beans are tender. Remove the bay leaves and season the gumbo with salt and pepper to taste. Serve in bowls, sprinkled with spring onions.

Some more ideas

● Try a gumbo with the flavours of Trinidad. Instead of lean bacon, use 75 g (2½ oz) lean smoked sausage such as kabanos. In step 2, add 1 tsp chopped fresh root ginger, ½ tsp Angostura bitters, 1 small can red kidney beans, about 200 g, drained, and 1 tbsp dark rum with the tomatoes and other ingredients. Replace half the parsley with fresh coriander.

● Use a mixture of 170 g (6 oz) prawns and 170 g (6 oz) canned crab meat, adding the crab at the very end, with the final seasoning.

Plus points

● Okra contains a mucilaginous substance that is useful to thicken the liquid in dishes such as this (the name gumbo comes from the African word for okra). The nutrient content of okra is very similar to other green vegetables in that it provides useful amounts of dietary fibre, potassium, calcium, folate and vitamin C.

● Bacon is a good source of vitamin B_1, which is essential for maintaining a healthy nervous system.

Each serving provides

kcal 206, **protein** 23 g, **fat** 6 g (of which saturated fat 1 g), **carbohydrate** 17 g (of which sugars 10 g), **fibre** 4 g

✓✓✓	B_1, B_6, B_{12}, C, niacin
✓✓	A, E, iron, potassium
✓	folate, calcium, copper, selenium, zinc

Main meals

Turbot with sauce maltaise

To enhance its excellent flavour, the turbot is simply poached and served with a lower-fat version of a classic hollandaise-style sauce flavoured with oranges. Steamed new potatoes, mangetout and baby corn add taste, colour and healthy vitamins.

Serves 4

300 ml (10 fl oz) fish stock, preferably homemade

1 shallot, sliced

1 lemon slice

1 bay leaf

6 black peppercorns, crushed

4 turbot fillets, about 140 g (5 oz) each

Sauce maltaise

85 g (3 oz) unsalted butter

1 tbsp blood orange juice

1 tbsp white wine vinegar

3 black peppercorns, lightly crushed

2 egg yolks

1 tsp lemon juice

1 tsp finely grated orange zest

125 g (4½ oz) tomatoes, skinned, seeded and finely diced

salt and pepper

fresh tarragon sprigs to garnish

Preparation and cooking time: 30 minutes

Each serving provides

kcal 331, **protein** 27 g, **fat** 24 g (of which saturated fat 13 g), **carbohydrate** 2 g (of which sugars 2 g), **fibre** 0.5 g

✓✓✓	B₁, B₁₂, niacin
✓✓	A
✓	B₆, C, E, calcium, iron, potassium

1 Place the stock, shallot, lemon slice, bay leaf and peppercorns in a pan wide enough to hold the fillets in a single layer. Bring to the boil, then remove from the heat and set aside to infuse while you make the sauce.

2 Melt the butter in a small saucepan. Pour off the clear golden liquid into a small bowl, discarding the milky sediment, and set aside to cool slightly.

3 Put the orange juice, vinegar, peppercorns and 1 tbsp water in a small saucepan and boil for 2 minutes or until reduced by half. Transfer to the top of a double boiler or a heatproof bowl set over a saucepan of simmering water. The base of the pan or bowl should not touch the water.

4 Whisk in the egg yolks and continue whisking for 4–5 minutes or until the mixture thickens and becomes pale. Gradually whisk in the melted butter, drop by drop. Continue whisking after all the butter has been incorporated, until the sauce is thick enough to hold a ribbon trail on the surface when the whisk is lifted – this will take 4–5 minutes.

5 If at any point the sauce begins to curdle, immediately remove it from the heat, add an ice cube and whisk briskly until it comes together again. Remove the ice cube, return to the heat and continue whisking in the butter.

6 Stir in the lemon juice and orange zest and season with salt and pepper to taste. Remove the saucepan or double boiler from the heat. Stir in the tomatoes, then cover and set aside while you poach the fish.

7 Strain the cooled fish stock and return it to the pan. Add the fish fillets – the liquid should just cover the fillets; if there is too much, spoon it off and reserve to use in fish soups. Slowly increase the heat so the stock just simmers but doesn't boil, and poach the fish fillets for about 5 minutes, depending on the thickness, until they will flake easily.

8 Remove the fillets with a fish slice, gently shaking off any excess liquid, and set on warmed plates. Spoon over the sauce, garnish with tarragon sprigs and serve.

Plus points

• Turbot is an excellent source of niacin, which is needed to release energy from carbohydrate foods.

• Black pepper has been viewed traditionally as a digestion stimulant, in addition to improving the circulation of the body.

Some more ideas

● Turbot is an expensive fish. For a more economical version, you can use 8 skinned sole fillets, about 70 g (2¼ oz) each, poaching them as in the main recipe.

● Instead of the sauce maltaise, serve the fish with a fresh orange and tomato salsa. Halve and finely chop 200 g (7 oz) mixed red and yellow cherry tomatoes. Peel and segment 2 oranges, and chop the segments. Toss the oranges and tomatoes together. Season with salt and pepper to taste, and sprinkle over 2 tbsp finely chopped fresh herbs, such as tarragon, parsley and chives. Stir gently, then cover and chill until required.

● The poaching liquid can be cooled and stored in the fridge for up to a day to use as the base of a fish soup.

Tuna and tomato pizzas

Add canned fish to a tomato sauce, spread it on a ready-made pizza base and you have a delicious, healthy pizza without a heavy cheese quotient. If you don't want to use a bought pizza base, virtually any type of crusty bread can be used instead.

Serves 4

3 tsp extra virgin olive oil

1 onion, finely chopped

1 can chopped tomatoes, about 400 g

½ tsp dried oregano

good pinch of sugar

2 ready-made thick pizza bases, 230 g
   (8¼ oz) each

2 tbsp tomato purée

1 can tuna in spring water, about 150 g,
   drained and flaked into chunks

4 tsp capers

8 stoned black olives, sliced

salt and pepper

fresh basil leaves to garnish

Preparation time: 15 minutes

Cooking time: 10 minutes

1 Preheat the oven to 220°C (425°F, gas mark 7). Heat 1 tsp of the oil in a small pan, add the onion and cook over a moderate heat for 4 minutes or until softened. Add the tomatoes and their juice, the oregano and sugar. Season with salt and pepper to taste. Leave the sauce to bubble for 10 minutes, stirring occasionally.

2 Put the pizza bases on 2 baking sheets. Spread 1 tbsp of tomato purée over each base. Spoon the tomato sauce over the pizzas, then add the tuna. Sprinkle with the capers and sliced olives, and drizzle the remaining 2 tsp of olive oil over the top.

3 Bake the pizzas for 10 minutes or until the bases are crisp and golden. Sprinkle with torn basil leaves and serve at once.

Some more ideas

• Use part-baked ciabatta bread, halved lengthways, as the base for the pizza. Add the topping, then bake according to the packet instructions. Alternatively, use a French stick or 4 wholemeal muffins, split in half. The muffins will provide more fibre.

• Any canned fish will work well on these pizzas. Oil-rich fish such as sardines, pilchards, anchovies, salmon and mackerel are particularly good as they are excellent sources of omega-3 essential fatty acids.

• For clam and tomato pizzas, use 1 can baby clams, about 280 g, rinsed and drained. Make the sauce by heating 1 tsp extra virgin olive oil in a pan, adding 85 g (3 oz) sliced chestnut mushrooms and frying for 3 minutes. Add 4 chopped spring onions, 1 can chopped tomatoes, about 400 g, with the juice, and 1 tsp chilli sauce. Simmer for 10 minutes to reduce the sauce, then stir in the clams, 2 tbsp chopped parsley and seasoning to taste. Spread the tomato purée over the pizza bases and spoon the clam filling on top, spreading it almost to the edges. Add 8 sliced green olives, then bake as in the main recipe.

• For a meaty pizza, cut 125 g (4½ oz) wafer-thin slices of cooked ham or turkey into fine shreds and arrange them on the tomato sauce, pushing them under the sauce a little. Sprinkle 50 g (1¾ oz) diced mozzarella cheese over the top, then bake.

Each serving provides

kcal 300, **protein** 28 g, **fat** 9 g (of which saturated fat 3 g), **carbohydrate** 37 g (of which sugars 9 g), **fibre** 3 g

✓✓ B$_6$, B$_{12}$, C, selenium

✓ E, niacin, copper

Plus point

• Canned tomatoes and tomato purée are healthy storecupboard ingredients – they are both rich sources of the phytochemical lycopene (other good sources include pink grapefruit, watermelon and guava), which can help to protect against several types of cancer and heart disease.

Main meals

Basil-stuffed chicken breasts

This stylish main course is, surprisingly, not laden with fat. The chicken breasts can be prepared in advance and kept, covered, in the fridge. Tagliatelle tossed with a little grated lemon zest makes a good accompaniment, plus ciabatta with olives or sun-dried tomatoes.

Serves 4

4 skinless boneless chicken breasts (fillets), about 140 g (5 oz) each

100 g (3½ oz) mozzarella cheese, thinly sliced

1 tomato, thinly sliced

1 garlic clove, crushed

1 bunch of fresh basil, about 20 g (¾ oz)

4 slices Parma ham, about 55 g (2 oz) in total

1 tbsp extra virgin olive oil

salt and pepper

Green salad

2 tbsp extra virgin olive oil

juice of ½ lemon

125 g (4½ oz) pack gourmet lettuce selection or mixed salad leaves

1 bunch of watercress, large stalks discarded

Preparation time: 25–30 minutes
Cooking time: about 15 minutes

Each serving provides

kcal 339, protein 40 g, fat 19 g (of which saturated fat 6 g), carbohydrate 1.5 g (of which sugars 1 g), fibre 1 g

✓✓✓	B$_6$
✓✓	A, B$_{12}$, C, niacin, calcium, iron
✓	B$_1$, B$_2$, E, folate, copper, potassium, zinc

1 Preheat the oven to 220°C (425°F, gas mark 7). Make a slit along the length of each chicken breast and enlarge to form a pocket.

2 Divide the mozzarella among the chicken breasts, sliding the slices into the pockets. Top the cheese with the tomato slices and crushed garlic. Roughly chop a little of the basil and add a sprinkling to each pocket.

3 Season each chicken breast. Place a large sprig of basil on each, then wrap in a slice of Parma ham, making sure the ham covers the slit in the chicken. Tie the ham securely in place with three or four pieces of string on each breast.

4 Heat the oil in a heavy-based frying pan (preferably one with an ovenproof handle). Add the chicken breasts and fry over a high heat for 3–4 minutes, turning to brown both sides. Transfer the pan to the oven (or transfer the chicken to an oven dish) and bake for 10–12 minutes or until the chicken is cooked through; the juices should run clear when the thickest part of the chicken is pierced with a knife.

5 Meanwhile, make the salad. Put the oil and lemon juice in a bowl, season and mix well together. Add the lettuce and watercress. Toss together, then divide among 4 serving plates.

6 Remove the string from the chicken breasts. Cut each breast across into slices, holding it together so it keeps its shape. Place on the salad and garnish with the remaining basil.

Another idea

• As an alternative to the mozzarella filling, use a mixture of feta cheese and watercress. Soften ½ finely chopped red onion in 15 g (½ oz) butter for 3–5 minutes, then add 75 g (2½ oz) watercress sprigs and cook for a further 1 minute or until the watercress has just wilted. Crumble in 100 g (3½ oz) feta cheese, and season with nutmeg and black pepper.

Plus points

• The Greeks and Romans believed that eating watercress could cure madness. We, too, attribute healing powers to this green leaf, as it contains powerful phytochemicals that help to protect against cancer. It is also a good source of many B vitamins plus vitamins C, E and beta-carotene, which the body converts into vitamin A.

• Mozzarella contains less fat than many other cheeses. For example, 100 g (3½ oz) mozzarella has 21 g fat and 289 kcal, while the same weight of Cheddar has 34 g fat and 412 kcal.

Chicken with apricots and cumin

Tender, flavourful chicken thighs are excellent in a casserole. Fresh apricots and a bulb of fennel make good partners, especially when spiced up with cumin. Plain boiled or saffron rice, boiled new potatoes or baked potatoes go well with this dish.

Serves 4

2 tbsp sunflower oil

8 chicken thighs, about 450 g (1 lb) in total

1 onion, sliced

2 garlic cloves, chopped

2 tsp ground cumin

2 tsp ground coriander

300 ml (10 fl oz) chicken stock

3 carrots, halved crossways, then each half cut into 6–8 thick fingers

1 bulb of fennel, halved lengthways, then cut crossways into slices

300 g (10½ oz) ripe but firm apricots, stoned and quartered

salt and pepper

chopped fennel leaves from the bulb, or herb fennel, to garnish

Preparation time: 15 minutes

Cooking time: 50 minutes

1 Heat the oil in a large flameproof casserole and fry the chicken thighs for 5–10 minutes, turning occasionally, until golden brown all over. Remove from the pan. Add the onion and garlic to the casserole and fry for 5 minutes or until soft and golden.

2 Stir in all the spices and fry for 1 minute, then add the stock. Return the chicken to the casserole together with the carrots and fennel. Bring to the boil. Stir well, then cover and simmer gently for 30 minutes or until the chicken is tender. Remove the lid. If there is too much liquid, boil to reduce it slightly.

3 Add the apricots to the casserole and stir gently to mix. Simmer over a low heat for a further 5 minutes.

4 Season to taste with salt and pepper. Sprinkle with the fennel leaves and serve with rice or potatoes.

Plus points

● Chicken is a good source of protein.

● Both apricots and carrots provide some vitamin A in the form of beta-carotene, which gives them their distinctive colour, but carrots are by far the better source, providing about 20 times more of this nutrient per 100 g (3½ oz) than apricots. Vitamin A is essential for proper vision and increasingly valued for its role as an antioxidant, helping to prevent cancer and coronary heart disease.

Some more ideas

● Most of the fat in chicken is contained in the skin, so removing the skin before cooking will reduce the calories per serving to 310 kcal and the fat content per serving to 16 g, of which 3 g is saturated fat.

● For a different flavour, omit the ground cumin and coriander and add 8 tbsp black bean sauce at the end of step 3 and heat through.

● Replace the apricots with 1 fresh mango, cut into slices or chunks. Sprinkle with fresh coriander instead of fennel leaves.

● Use 1 can of apricot halves in natural juice, about 400 g, drained and cut in half, instead of fresh apricots.

Each serving provides

kcal 370, **protein** 26 g, **fat** 24 g (of which saturated fat 6 g), **carbohydrate** 12 g (of which sugars 11 g), **fibre** 4 g

✓✓✓	A
✓✓	B₆, C
✓	B₁, B₂, folate, copper, iron, potassium, selenium, zinc

Main meals

121

Indian-style grilled chicken breasts

Tandoori dishes are often the healthiest option in Indian restaurants as they are cooked without fat. At home, a hot grill gives a similar result. These lean chicken breasts come with creamy low-fat raita. All that is needed to complete the meal is rice or naan bread.

Serves 4

4 skinless boneless chicken breasts (fillets), about 140 g (5 oz) each

sunflower oil for brushing

lemon or lime wedges to serve

sprigs of fresh coriander to garnish

Yogurt marinade

1 garlic clove, crushed

1 tbsp finely chopped fresh root ginger

1½ tsp tomato purée

1½ tsp garam masala

1½ tsp ground coriander

1½ tsp ground cumin

¼ tsp turmeric

pinch of cayenne pepper, or to taste

100 g (3½ oz) plain low-fat yogurt

Raita

340 g (12 oz) plain low-fat yogurt

1 cucumber, about 300 g (10½ oz), cut into quarters lengthways and seeded

100 g (3½ oz) tomato, very finely chopped

½ tsp ground coriander

½ tsp ground cumin

pinch of cayenne pepper

pinch of salt

Preparation time: about 15 minutes

Cooking time: 15 minutes

1 Preheat the grill to high. To make the marinade, put all the marinade ingredients into a large bowl and whisk together well. If you prefer, put the ingredients into a blender or food processor and process until well blended. Transfer to a bowl large enough to hold all the chicken breasts.

2 Score 2 slits on each side of the chicken breasts. Place them in the marinade, turning to coat and rubbing the marinade into the slits. (If you have time, leave the chicken to marinate in the fridge overnight.)

3 Brush the grill rack with oil, then place the chicken breasts on top. Grill for 12–15 minutes, turning and basting with the remaining marinade, until the juices run clear when the chicken is pierced with a knife, and the marinade looks slightly charred.

4 Meanwhile, make the raita. Place the yogurt in a bowl. Coarsely grate the cucumber, then squeeze to remove as much moisture as possible. Add the cucumber to the yogurt together with the tomato, ground coriander, cumin, cayenne and salt. Stir well to mix. Spoon the raita into a serving bowl.

5 Transfer the chicken breasts to a serving plate. Add lemon or lime wedges and garnish with coriander sprigs. Serve with the raita on the side.

Plus points

● Chicken is a low-fat source of protein and this marinade adds very little extra fat.

● Yogurt is an excellent source of protein and calcium, needed for healthy bones and teeth, and it provides useful amounts of phosphorus and vitamins B_2 and B_{12}, as well as beneficial bacteria.

Each serving provides

kcal 250, **protein** 40 g, **fat** 5 g (of which saturated fat 1.5 g), **carbohydrate** 11 g (of which sugars 11 g), **fibre** 1 g

✓✓✓	B_6, niacin
✓✓	B_2, calcium, potassium, selenium
✓	B_1, B_{12}, C, E, folate, copper, iron, zinc

Main meals

Some more ideas

- For a crisper texture on the grilled breasts, omit the yogurt from the marinade, double all the other ingredients and stir in 1 tbsp white distilled vinegar.

- Try this onion and herb raita with either version of the grilled chicken breasts: very finely chop 200 g (7 oz) sweet onion, such as Vidalia, or the same weight of spring onions, and place in a bowl. Stir in 4–6 tbsp finely chopped fresh mint, 2 tbsp finely chopped fresh coriander, 1 fresh green chilli or to taste, finely chopped, and 340 g (12 oz) plain low-fat yogurt. Heat a dry frying pan over a high heat, add 2 tsp cumin seeds and fry, stirring constantly, until they give off their aroma and start to jump. Immediately tip them on top of the raita.

- For Indian-style kebabs, cut the breasts into cubes before you put them in the marinade. While preheating the grill, soak 8 bamboo skewers in water. Thread the chicken cubes onto the skewers, alternating with chunks of courgette and red and yellow pepper cubes. Grill, basting with the marinade and turning the skewers over several times, for 12–15 minutes or until the chicken juices run clear.

- A quick alternative to raita is to serve the chicken breasts with a simple salad of chopped tomatoes and onions on lettuce leaves with finely chopped coriander sprinkled over the top.

Main meals

French-style chicken in wine

This up-dated and low-fat version of a classic bistro dish contains shallots, mushrooms and carrots, all you need to add is potatoes – and, of course, lots of fresh French bread – for a truly satisfying meal.

Serves 4

12 shallots or button onions

1½ tbsp garlic-flavoured olive oil

55 g (2 oz) back bacon, cut across into thin strips

12 chestnut or button mushrooms

4 chicken joints such as breasts, about 170 g (6 oz) each

several sprigs of parsley, stalks bruised

several sprigs of fresh thyme

1 bay leaf

150 ml (5 fl oz) chicken stock, preferably homemade

360 ml (12 fl oz) full-bodied red wine, such as Burgundy

300 g (10½ oz) carrots, cut into chunks

pinch of caster sugar

1 tbsp cornflour

salt and pepper

chopped parsley to garnish

Preparation time: 15 minutes

Cooking time: about 1¼ hours

Each serving provides

kcal 372, **protein** 37 g, **fat** 9 g (of which saturated fat 2 g), **carbohydrate** 22 g (of which sugars 7 g), **fibre** 3 g

✓✓✓	A, B$_6$, niacin, copper
✓✓	B$_1$, B$_2$, iron, potassium, selenium, zinc
✓	E, folate

1 Put the shallots or onions in a heatproof bowl and pour over enough boiling water to cover. Leave for 30 seconds, then drain. When cool enough to handle, peel and set aside.

2 Heat 1 tbsp of the oil in a flameproof casserole. Add the bacon and fry for about 3 minutes, stirring often, until crispy. Remove with a draining spoon and set aside.

3 Add the shallots to the casserole and fry, stirring often, over a moderately high heat for 5 minutes or until browned all over. Remove with a draining spoon and set aside.

4 Add the mushrooms to the casserole, with the remaining ½ tbsp oil if needed, and fry for 3–4 minutes, stirring often, until golden.

5 Return half of the bacon and shallots to the casserole. Place the chicken joints on top and sprinkle with the remaining bacon and shallots. Tie the herbs into a bouquet garni and add to the casserole with the stock and wine. Season generously with pepper.

6 Bring to the boil, then reduce the heat to very low and simmer for 15 minutes. Add the carrots and continue simmering over a low heat for a further 30 minutes or until the chicken is cooked through and the carrots are tender but still crisp.

7 Lift out the chicken and arrange on a warmed serving platter. Strain the liquid into a saucepan. Add the bacon, mushrooms, shallots and carrots to the chicken and keep warm.

8 Put the bouquet garni back in the strained liquid, add the sugar and bring to the boil. Boil until the sauce is reduced to about 360 ml (12 fl oz). Mix the cornflour with a little water to make a smooth paste. Add to the sauce, stirring, and simmer until thickened. Adjust the seasoning to taste and discard the bouquet garni. Spoon the sauce over the chicken and vegetables, sprinkle with the parsley and serve.

Plus points

• Unlike most vegetables, which are most nutritious when eaten raw, cooking carrots increases their nutritional value. Because raw carrots have tough cell walls, the body can convert only about 25% of the beta-carotene present into vitamin A. Cooking breaks down the cell membrane, making it easier for the body to absorb and convert the beta-carotene.

• Red wine contains flavonoid compounds, which may help to protect against heart disease.

Main meals

Some more ideas

• If you cannot find garlic-flavoured olive oil, use extra virgin olive oil and fry 1 garlic clove, crushed, with the mushrooms.

• For chicken with Riesling, typical of the Alsace region of north-eastern France, take 550 g (1¼ lb) skinless boneless chicken breasts or thighs and cut into large chunks. Use Riesling instead of red wine. Add the carrots with the chicken and simmer for 30 minutes, then add 200 g (7 oz) frozen peas, straight from the freezer, and continue simmering for about 5 minutes.

Strain and reduce the cooking liquid as above, then thicken and enrich with 4 tbsp whipping cream or soured cream. Serve the chicken with egg noodles, boiled and tossed with finely chopped parsley or poppy seeds.

Marsala chicken with fennel

Cooking with a little wine gives depth to a sauce: nearly all the alcohol and calories burn away, leaving only great flavour behind. This sauce is thickened with a mixture of egg and lemon juice, which is typically Mediterranean and less rich than beurre manié or cream.

Serves 4

1 chicken, about 1.35 kg (3 lb), jointed
2 tbsp plain flour
2 tbsp extra virgin olive oil
1 large leek, coarsely chopped
1 tbsp chopped parsley
1 tsp fennel seeds
90 ml (3 fl oz) Marsala
500 ml (17 fl oz) chicken stock, preferably
   homemade
2 medium-sized bulbs of fennel, trimmed and
   cut into chunks
280 g (10 oz) shelled fresh or frozen peas
juice of 1 lemon
1 egg, lightly beaten
salt and pepper
To garnish
chopped parsley
shreds of lemon zest

Preparation time: 15 minutes
Cooking time: 45 minutes

Each serving provides
kcal 380, **protein** 46 g, **fat** 12 g (of which
saturated fat 2.5 g), **carbohydrate** 18 g (of
which sugars 5 g), **fibre** 5.5 g

✓✓✓	B$_6$, niacin
✓✓	B$_1$, B$_2$, C, folate, iron, potassium, selenium, zinc
✓	A, B$_{12}$, E, calcium, copper

1 Remove the skin from the chicken joints, except for any small pieces such as the wings which would be too difficult to skin. Season the flour and dust over the joints.

2 Heat 1 tbsp of the oil in a sauté pan and add the leek, parsley and fennel seeds. Cook over a moderate heat until the leek is softened, stirring frequently. Remove from the pan with a draining spoon and set aside.

3 Add the remaining 1 tbsp of oil to the pan and sauté the chicken for 6–7 minutes or until just golden all over. Remove the chicken from the pan and set aside. Pour in the Marsala and bubble until it is reduced to about 2 tbsp of glaze. Pour in the stock, and return the leek mixture and dark meat chicken joints and wings to the pan (wait to add the breasts as they can overcook). Add the chunks of fennel. Cover and simmer over a low heat for 10–15 minutes, then add the breasts and continue to cook, covered, for 15 minutes or until all the chicken joints are tender. Add the peas for the last 5 minutes of cooking.

4 Using a draining spoon, remove the chicken pieces and vegetables to a platter. Keep warm.

5 In a small bowl, mix the lemon juice into the egg. Slowly add about 4 tbsp of the hot cooking liquid to the lemon and egg mixture, stirring well, then slowly stir this mixture back into the liquid in the pan. Return the chicken and vegetables to the pan and gently warm it all through, taking care to ensure that the heat is very low so the sauce does not curdle into scrambled egg. Season to taste. Serve hot, garnished with parsley and shreds of lemon zest.

Plus points

● Bulb fennel contains more phytoestrogen than most vegetables. This naturally occurring plant hormone encourages the body to excrete excess oestrogen (a high level of oestrogen is linked with greater risk of breast cancer).

● Peas provide good amounts of the B vitamins B$_1$, B$_6$ and niacin. They also offer dietary fibre, particularly the soluble variety, plus some folate and vitamin C.

● The dark meat of chicken contains twice as much iron and zinc as the light meat.

Main meals

Some more ideas
• Use 8 skinless boneless chicken thighs, about 500 g (1 lb 2 oz) in total, instead of a jointed chicken.
• Replace the leek with 2 chopped onions.

• For chicken with asparagus and fennel seeds, omit the peas and bulb fennel. Cut 1 bunch of asparagus (about 225 g/8 oz) into bite-sized pieces and add to the simmering chicken at the end of step 3, just before you remove the

chicken joints and leeks. Thicken with the egg and lemon mixture, as above. Do not overcook the asparagus: 1–2 minutes should be enough. Asparagus is an excellent source of folate, and a good source of beta-carotene.

Pan-fried turkey escalopes with citrus honey sauce

Here, tangy orange and lemon, with honey and shallots, create a tasty, low-calorie sauce to complement the mild flavour of turkey escalopes. Serve on a stack of green beans and for a simple accompaniment, steam some new potatoes.

Serves 4

4 small skinless turkey breast steaks, about 115 g (4 oz) each
30 g (1 oz) butter
4 large shallots, thinly sliced
1 garlic clove, crushed
400 g (14 oz) fine French beans, trimmed
2 tbsp clear honey
grated zest and juice of 1 orange
grated zest and juice of 1 lemon
salt and pepper

Preparation time: 15 minutes
Cooking time: about 15 minutes

Each serving provides

kcal 245, **protein** 27 g, **fat** 9 g (of which saturated fat 5 g), **carbohydrate** 14 g (of which sugars 13 g), **fibre** 2.5 g

✓✓✓	B₁₂
✓✓	B₆, C, folate, niacin, iron, zinc
✓	A, copper, potassium

1 Put the turkey steaks between sheets of cling film and pound them to flatten to about 5 mm (¼ in) thickness. Set these escalopes aside.

2 Melt the butter in a large frying pan, add the shallots and garlic, and cook, stirring, for 2–3 minutes or until softened but not brown. Remove the shallots from the pan with a draining spoon and set aside.

3 Put the turkey escalopes in the pan, in one layer, and fry them for 2–3 minutes on each side.

4 Meanwhile, cook the beans in a saucepan of boiling salted water for 3–4 minutes or until just tender. Drain and rinse briefly in cold water to stop the cooking. Keep the beans warm.

5 Mix the honey with the zest and juice of the orange and lemon. Remove the turkey escalopes from the pan and keep hot. Pour the honey mixture into the pan, return the shallots and garlic, and add seasoning to taste. Bring to the boil and bubble for about 2 minutes, stirring constantly.

6 Make a pile of beans on 4 plates and place a turkey escalope on top of each pile. Spoon over the sliced shallots and pan juices, and serve.

Some more ideas

● Use 4 skinless boneless turkey breast fillets, about 125 g (4½ oz) each. Being a bit thicker than escalopes, they will need to be cooked for 5 minutes on each side.

● Replace the turkey steaks with 4 small boneless duck breasts, about 550 g (1¼ lb) in total. Remove the skin and all fat from the breasts. Pan-fry for 3 minutes on each side, if you like duck a little pink, or a little longer for well-done duck. For the sauce, use the zest and juice from a pink grapefruit instead of the orange and lemon. Also add a piece of stem ginger, cut into fine slivers, and 1 tbsp of the stem ginger syrup.

● Replace the beans with 3 finely shredded leeks, stir-fried in 1 tbsp sunflower oil.

Plus points

● Turkey contains even less fat than chicken, making it one of the lowest fat meats available.

● All citrus fruits are an excellent source of vitamin C. Studies have shown a correlation between a regular intake of vitamin C and the maintenance of intellectual function in elderly people.

Main meals

Turkey kebabs with fennel and red pepper relish

Lean bites of turkey are marinated with wine and herbs, and then threaded onto skewers to be grilled or barbecued. A colourful raw-vegetable relish provides vitamin C as well as a delightful taste contrast. A complex carbohydrate such as couscous goes nicely.

Serves 4

450 g (1 lb) skinless turkey breast steak

3 garlic cloves, chopped

1½ tbsp lemon juice

2 tbsp dry white wine

1 tbsp chopped fresh sage or 2 tsp dried sage, crumbled

1 tbsp chopped fresh rosemary

1½ tsp fresh thyme leaves or ½ tsp dried thyme

1 tsp fennel seeds, lightly crushed

2½ tbsp extra virgin olive oil

1 red pepper, seeded and finely diced

1 bulb of fennel, finely diced

1 tbsp black olive paste (tapenade) or 10 black Kalamata olives, finely diced

8 stalks of fresh rosemary (optional)

8 shallots or button onions

salt and pepper

Preparation time: 20 minutes, plus at least 10 minutes marinating

Cooking time: 15 minutes

1 Cut the turkey into 24 pieces, each about 5 x 2 cm (2 x ¾ in). Combine the turkey pieces with 2 of the chopped garlic cloves, 1 tbsp lemon juice, the wine, sage, rosemary, thyme, fennel seeds, 2 tbsp of the olive oil and seasoning. Toss so that all the turkey pieces are covered with the herb mixture. Leave to marinate for at least 10 minutes, or up to an hour if you have the time.

2 Meanwhile, make the relish. Put the red pepper, diced fennel and olive paste or diced olives in a bowl together with the remaining garlic, ½ tbsp lemon juice and ½ tbsp olive oil. Season to taste. Mix well, then set aside.

3 Preheat the grill to high, or prepare a charcoal fire in the barbecue. Thread the marinated turkey pieces onto the rosemary stalks if using, or onto skewers, and top each one with a shallot or button onion.

4 Grill or barbecue the kebabs for about 15 minutes or until cooked through and the turkey pieces are lightly browned in spots. Turn the kebabs and baste with the remaining marinade frequently. Serve the kebabs hot, with the red pepper relish.

Plus points

• Red peppers are an excellent source of vitamin C and they are rich in beta-carotene. Both of these nutrients are powerful antioxidants that can help to counteract the damaging effects of free radicals and protect against many diseases including cancer and heart disease.

• Fennel provides useful amounts of both potassium and the B vitamin folate. It is also low in calories – 100 g (3½ oz) contains 12 kcal.

Each serving provides

kcal 224, protein 28 g, fat 9.5 g (of which saturated fat 1.5 g), carbohydrate 7 g (of which sugars 6 g), fibre 2.5 g

✓✓✓	B_6, B_12, C
✓✓	A, niacin
✓	E, folate, copper, iron, potassium, zinc

Main meals

Some more ideas

● Instead of making a vegetable relish, add the red pepper and fennel to the kebabs. Cut the pepper and fennel into 2.5 cm (1 in) chunks. Alternate the vegetable chunks with pieces of turkey on the skewers, and brush all over with the turkey marinade. Grill or barbecue as above,

then serve the turkey and vegetable kebabs drizzled with the remaining extra virgin olive oil and lemon juice.

● Another delicious relish, containing no oil, can be made with roasted red pepper and tomatoes. Cut a large red pepper in half and grill the skin side until it is blistered and

charred. Put into a polythene bag and leave until cool enough to handle, then peel off the skin. Finely dice the flesh and mix with 1 diced tomato, 1 finely chopped shallot, 2 chopped garlic cloves, 2 tbsp chopped fresh basil or parsley, a splash of balsamic vinegar, and salt and pepper to taste.

Spiced stir-fried duck

In this dish, strips of duck are stir-fried with onions, water chestnuts, pak choy and – for sweetness – fresh pear. Little oil is needed to stir-fry, and adding lots of vegetables keeps the quantity of meat down. Serve with rice noodles or with plain boiled or steamed rice.

Serves 4

400 g (14 oz) boneless duck breasts

2 tsp five-spice powder

2 tbsp sunflower oil

100 g (3½ oz) button onions, thinly sliced

4 small celery sticks, thinly sliced, plus a few leaves to garnish

1 large firm pear, peeled, cored and diced

1 can water chestnuts, about 225 g, drained and sliced

1 tbsp clear honey

3 tbsp rice vinegar or sherry vinegar

1 tbsp light soy sauce

200 g (7 oz) pak choy, shredded

150 g (5½ oz) bean sprouts

Preparation time: about 15 minutes

Cooking time: about 10 minutes

1 Remove the skin and all fat from the duck breasts, then cut them across into thin strips. Sprinkle with the five-spice powder and toss to coat. Set aside for a few minutes while the vegetables are prepared.

2 Heat a wok or heavy-based frying pan until really hot, then add the oil and swirl to coat the wok. Add the duck pieces and stir-fry for 2 minutes. Add the onions and celery and continue to stir-fry for 3 minutes or until softened. Add the pear and water chestnuts and stir to mix.

3 Add the honey, rice vinegar and soy sauce. When the liquid is bubbling, reduce the heat to low and simmer for 2 minutes.

4 Turn the heat up to high again. Add the pak choy and bean sprouts, and stir-fry for 1 minute or until the pak choy is just wilted and the bean sprouts are heated through.

5 Transfer to a warmed serving dish and serve immediately, garnished with celery leaves.

Plus points

• Removing the skin and fat from duck lowers the fat content substantially. Skinless duck breast contains only a fraction more fat than skinless chicken breast.

• Dark green, leafy vegetables such as pak choy provide good amounts of vitamin C, as well as vitamin B$_6$, folate and niacin.

• Bean sprouts are a good source of vitamin C and also offer B vitamins.

• Water chestnuts provide small amounts of potassium, iron and fibre, and contain no fat and very few calories.

Some more ideas

• For a less piquant sauce, replace the rice vinegar or sherry vinegar with red wine or apple or orange juice.

• If in season, use an Asian pear instead of an ordinary pear. Or substitute 3–4 ripe but firm plums, sliced, for the pear.

• For a duck stir-fry with a citrus flavour, use ground star anise instead of five-spice powder, and 170 g (6 oz) sliced and seeded kumquats instead of the pear. Replace the pak choy with ½ head Chinese leaves, shredded. Instead of rice vinegar, use orange juice or red wine.

• Use skinless boneless chicken or turkey breasts, cut into strips, instead of the duck.

Each serving provides

kcal 200, **protein** 13 g, **fat** 9 g (of which saturated fat 2 g), **carbohydrate** 17 g (of which sugars 13 g), **fibre** 2.5 g

✓✓✓	B$_{12}$
✓✓	B$_6$, C, E, folate, copper, iron
✓	B$_1$, B$_2$, niacin, calcium, potassium, zinc

Main meals

Pheasant casseroled with ginger

Casseroling is an excellent way to cook pheasant, as it produces succulent pieces of both breast and dark meat and the goodness from both creates a rich sauce. Herby mashed potatoes, baby carrots and broccoli are good accompaniments for this aromatic dish.

Serves 4

1 large bulb of fennel, about 300 g
  (10½ oz)

1 tbsp sunflower oil

1 pheasant, about 1 kg (2¼ lb), jointed into
  4 or 8 pieces

100 g (3½ oz) shallots or button onions,
  halved

4 pieces stem ginger, about 115 g (4 oz) in
  total, cut into thin strips

4 tbsp ginger wine

300 ml (10 fl oz) chicken stock, preferably
  homemade

salt and pepper

Preparation time: 15 minutes
Cooking time: about 1¼ hours

1 Preheat the oven to 190°C (375°F, gas mark 5). Trim the fennel, retaining any feathery leaves for the garnish, then cut the bulb lengthways into 8 wedges. Set aside.

2 Heat the oil in a large flameproof casserole over a moderately high heat. Add the pheasant joints and shallots or button onions and fry to brown on all sides.

3 Add the fennel wedges. Turn the pheasant joints skin side up and sprinkle over the strips of ginger. Add the ginger wine and enough stock to come halfway up the pheasant joints but not cover them. Season to taste.

4 Bring to the boil, then cover the casserole and transfer to the oven. Cook for 1–1¼ hours or until the pheasant is tender. Serve garnished with the reserved fennel leaves.

Plus points

• There is evidence to suggest that onions help to prevent circulatory diseases such as thrombosis and many conditions associated with strokes, because they appear to contain a substance that stops blood clotting.

• Pheasant is an excellent source of protein as well as iron and B vitamins. Although it is higher in fat than other game birds, most of this fat is monounsaturated.

Some more ideas

• Try a pheasant casserole with chestnuts and cabbage. Brown the pheasant joints and shallots, then add 200 g (7 oz) vacuum-packed chestnuts and 200 g (7 oz) red cabbage, cut into 4 wedges, instead of the fennel wedges. Replace the stem ginger with 2 tbsp marmalade and use red wine instead of ginger wine.

• Other game birds can be jointed and cooked in the same way.

• When game is out of season, use duck or chicken joints.

Each serving provides

kcal 235, **protein** 30 g, **fat** 11 g (of which saturated fat 3 g), **carbohydrate** 3.5 g (of which sugars 3 g), **fibre** 2 g

✓✓✓	B₆, B₁₂, niacin, iron
✓✓	B₂, potassium, zinc
✓	E, folate, calcium, copper

Main meals

Pot-roasted partridge with sage

Naturally low in calories, partridge is perfect for pot-roasting. Cooking in cider and stock keeps the meat moist, and sage, pickled walnuts and apple add wonderful flavours. Carrot and celeriac purée is an ideal extra, or try potato mash with spring onions.

Serves 4

4 partridges

15 g (½ oz) fresh sage

1 tbsp extra virgin olive oil

15 g (½ oz) butter

1 onion, finely chopped

1 tbsp plain flour

300 ml (10 fl oz) dry cider

150 ml (5 fl oz) chicken stock, preferably homemade

2 tsp German mustard

3 pickled walnuts, about 45 g (1½ oz) in total, thinly sliced

1 red-skinned dessert apple, cored and cut into thick slices

salt and pepper

Preparation time: 10 minutes

Cooking time: about 1¼ hours

Each serving provides

kcal 350, **protein** 43 g, **fat** 14 g (of which saturated fat 4.5 g), **carbohydrate** 9 g (of which sugars 5 g), **fibre** 1 g

✓✓✓ iron

✓ potassium

1 Preheat the oven to 160°C (325°F, gas mark 3). Tuck some sage sprigs into the body cavity of each partridge, reserving a few sprigs for garnish.

2 Heat the oil and butter in a flameproof casserole just large enough to hold the birds. Add the partridges and fry over a moderately high heat for 3–4 minutes, turning until evenly browned. Lift the birds out of the casserole and set aside.

3 Add the onion to the casserole and cook for 3 minutes, stirring, until lightly browned. Sprinkle in the flour and stir well to mix with the onion, then add the cider, stock, mustard and seasoning to taste. Bring to the boil, stirring constantly. Add the walnuts.

4 Return the partridges to the casserole, breast side down. Cover the casserole and transfer to the oven. Cook for 1 hour or until tender.

5 Lift the partridges out of the casserole and place on a warmed serving plate. Cover and keep hot.

6 Set the casserole on top of the cooker and boil the cooking liquid for 5 minutes or until reduced by a third. Add the apple slices for the last 2 minutes of cooking.

7 Spoon the apple slices around the birds and garnish with the reserved sage sprigs. Serve with the sauce.

Some more ideas

● To make a carrot and celeriac purée, cook 340 g (12 oz) each peeled and diced celeriac and carrots in boiling water for 20 minutes or until very tender. Drain and mash, or purée in a food processor, with 3 tbsp semi-skimmed milk and seasoning to taste. Spoon into a serving dish and sprinkle with a little freshly grated nutmeg.

● For partridge pot-roasted with mushrooms, soak 15 g (½ oz) dried porcini mushrooms in 300 ml (10 fl oz) boiling water for 30 minutes. Drain, reserving the soaking liquid. Make the liquid up to 300 ml (10 fl oz) with the juice of 1 orange and chicken stock. Add 2 tsp tomato purée and 300 ml (10 fl oz) red wine. Use this as the cooking liquid. Replace the sage with fresh thyme, and add the soaked mushrooms instead of the pickled walnuts. Omit the apple, and garnish the dish with orange slices and a sprinkling of fresh thyme leaves.

Plus points

● Walnuts, like most nuts, are quite fatty, however, this is not a bad thing as it is mostly the healthy form of unsaturated fatty acids. Recent tests have shown that a daily consumption of 85 g (3 oz) of walnuts – when used in place of saturated fats as part of a low-fat diet – lowers blood cholesterol.

Main meals

Tagliatelle with green sauce

This simple vegetable and yogurt sauce is bursting with fresh flavours and irresistibly creamy, though it is much lighter than the classic cream sauce for pasta. A salad of crisp radicchio and Lollo Rosso lettuce completes the meal.

Serves 4

225 g (8 oz) baby spinach, thick stalks
    discarded
100 g (3½ oz) watercress, thick stalks
    discarded
125 g (4½ oz) frozen peas
500 g (1 lb 2 oz) fresh tagliatelle
2 tsp cornflour
200 ml (7 fl oz) Greek-style yogurt
4 tbsp chopped parsley
6 sprigs of fresh basil, torn into pieces
salt and pepper

Preparation time: 5 minutes
Cooking time: 7–8 minutes

1 Rinse the spinach and watercress and place in a large saucepan with just the water clinging to the leaves. Cover and cook over a moderate heat for 2 minutes, stirring and turning the vegetables occasionally, until they have wilted.

2 Add the peas and heat through, uncovered, for 2 minutes – there should be enough liquid in the pan to cook the peas. Tip the greens and their liquid into a bowl. Set aside.

3 Cook the pasta in a large saucepan of boiling water for 3 minutes, or according to the packet instructions, until al dente.

4 Meanwhile, blend the cornflour to a smooth paste with the yogurt, and put into the pan used for cooking the vegetables. Stir over a moderate heat until just bubbling. Add the vegetables, parsley, basil and seasoning to taste and stir well. Heat the sauce through, then remove the pan from the heat.

5 Drain the pasta and add to the sauce. Toss to mix with the sauce, then serve.

Some more ideas

● When fresh peas are in season, use them instead of frozen. Add to the spinach and watercress in step 1 and cook for 4 minutes.
● For a creamy broccoli and pea sauce, replace the spinach and watercress with 200 g (7 oz) broccoli. Cook the broccoli in a little boiling water for 5–8 minutes, then drain, refresh in cold running water, drain well again and return to the pan. Mash the broccoli with a potato masher, then add the yogurt mixed with the cornflour and 5 tbsp semi-skimmed milk. Stir in 125 g (4½ oz) frozen peas and 2 spring onions, finely chopped. Bring to the boil, stirring, and cook for 1–2 minutes to thicken. Season to taste and add a dash of lemon juice if you like. Toss with the freshly cooked pasta, then sprinkle with plenty of chopped parsley.

Plus points

● Spinach and watercress are high on the list of foods that assist in the fight against cancer. They are also full of calcium and carotenoids and contain good amounts of vitamins C and E, and some B vitamins.
● Heat can destroy vitamin C. The best way to cook leafy green vegetables, such as spinach and watercress, and still retain the maximum vitamin C, is to wilt them briefly.
● Peas provide protein. They are also rich in fibre, some of it soluble, and this helps to keep blood sugar levels and cholesterol under control.

Each serving provides　Ⓥ
kcal 215, **protein** 11 g, **fat** 6 g (of which saturated fat 3 g), **carbohydrate** 30 g (of which sugars 3 g), **fibre** 4 g

✓✓✓	A
✓✓	C, E, folate, calcium
✓	B₂, niacin, copper, iron, zinc

Main meals

Pea curry with Indian paneer

Paneer is a low-fat Indian cheese, similar to ricotta but drier. It's often combined with peas in a curry. This delicious version uses homemade paneer, which is simple to make. Serve with basmati rice for a well-balanced meal.

Serves 4

Paneer

2.3 litres (4 pints) full-fat milk

6 tbsp lemon juice

Pea and tomato curry

3 tbsp sunflower oil

1 large onion, chopped

2 garlic cloves, finely chopped

5 cm (2 in) piece fresh root ginger, finely chopped

1 fresh green chilli, seeded and thinly sliced

1 tbsp coriander seeds, crushed

1 tbsp cumin seeds, crushed

1 tsp turmeric

1 tbsp garam masala

450 g (1 lb) firm tomatoes, quartered

340 g (12 oz) frozen peas

85 g (3 oz) spinach leaves

15 g (½ oz) fresh coriander, roughly chopped

salt

Preparation time: 15 minutes, plus about
   45 minutes draining and 3 hours pressing
Cooking time: about 20 minutes

Each serving provides   Ⓥ

kcal 298, **protein** 20 g, **fat** 15 g (of which saturated fat 5 g), **carbohydrate** 22 g (of which sugars 14 g), **fibre** 7 g

✓✓✓	A, C, E
✓✓	B$_1$, B$_{12}$, folate, niacin, calcium, zinc
✓	B$_2$, B$_6$, copper, iron, potassium

---

1 First make the paneer. Pour the milk into a large saucepan and bring to the boil. Immediately reduce the heat to low and add the lemon juice. Stir for 1–2 minutes or until the milk separates into curds and whey. Remove the pan from the heat.

2 Line a large sieve or colander with muslin, or a clean, tight-knit dishcloth, and set over a large bowl. Pour in the milk mixture. Leave to drain for about 15 minutes or until cool.

3 Bring together the corners of the muslin or cloth to make a bundle containing the drained curds. Squeeze them, then leave to drain for a further 30 minutes or until all the whey has dripped though the sieve into the bowl. Reserve 240 ml (8 fl oz) of the whey.

4 Keeping the curds wrapped in the muslin or cloth, place on a board. Set another board on top and press down to flatten the ball shape into an oblong block. Place cans or weights on top and leave in a cool place for about 3 hours or until firm.

5 Carefully peel off the muslin and cut the cheese into squares about 2 cm (¾ in). Heat 1 tbsp of the oil in a large non-stick frying pan and cook the paneer for 1–2 minutes on each side or until golden. As the pieces are browned, remove from the pan with a draining spoon and set aside.

6 For the curry, heat the remaining 2 tbsp oil in the pan. Add the onion and cook gently for 5 minutes or until softened. Stir in the garlic and ginger, and cook gently for 1 minute, then stir in the chilli, coriander and cumin seeds, turmeric and garam masala. Cook for 1 more minute, stirring constantly.

7 Add the tomatoes, the reserved whey and a pinch of salt, and stir well to mix. Cover and cook gently for 5 minutes.

8 Add the peas and bring back to the boil, then reduce the heat, cover again and simmer for 5 minutes. Add the spinach, stirring it in gently so as not to break up the tomatoes too much. Simmer for 3–4 minutes or until the spinach has just wilted and the peas are hot and tender.

9 Stir in most of the chopped fresh coriander, then transfer the curry to a serving dish and scatter the paneer on top. Spoon the curry gently over the paneer to warm it, then sprinkle with the rest of the coriander and serve.

Plus point

• Paneer is low in fat and very nutritious, providing protein, calcium and vitamins, including vitamins A and D.

Some more ideas

- Use frozen minted peas.
- For a cottage cheese and vegetable curry, which is similar but much quicker to make, cook 600 g (1 lb 5 oz) peeled potatoes, cut into large chunks, in a large pan of boiling water for 5 minutes. Add 400 g (14 oz) cauliflower florets to the pan and cook for 5 more minutes. Finally, add 200 g (7 oz) halved fine green beans and cook for a further 3–4 minutes or until all the vegetables are tender. While the vegetables are cooking, place 350 g (12½ oz) cottage cheese in a sieve and leave to drain off any excess liquid. Cook the onion and spices as in step 6 of the main recipe, then add 300 ml (10 fl oz) vegetable stock and cook gently for a further 5 minutes. Add the drained potatoes, cauliflower and beans to the spiced sauce and stir to coat. Season with salt to taste. Fold in the cottage cheese and heat through gently. Serve hot, with wholewheat parathas or naan bread.

Tomato and pecorino clafoutis

For this savoury version of a classic French batter pudding, sweet cherry tomatoes are baked in a light, fluffy batter flavoured with pecorino cheese. Crusty bread or boiled new potatoes and green beans go well with this dish.

Serves 4

2 tsp extra virgin olive oil

450 g (1 lb) cherry tomatoes

4 tbsp snipped fresh chives

85 g (3 oz) mature pecorino cheese, coarsely grated

6 large eggs

45 g (1½ oz) plain flour

3 tbsp soured cream

300 ml (10 fl oz) semi-skimmed milk

Preparation time: 20 minutes
Cooking time: 30–35 minutes

1 Preheat the oven to 190°C (375°F, gas mark 5). Lightly oil 4 shallow ovenproof dishes, each 12–15 cm (5–6 in) in diameter. Divide the cherry tomatoes among the dishes, spreading them out, and sprinkle over the chives and 75 g (2½ oz) of the cheese.

2 Break the eggs into a bowl and whisk them together, then gradually whisk in the flour until smooth. Add the soured cream, then gradually whisk in the milk to make a thin, smooth batter. Season with salt and pepper to taste.

3 Pour the batter over the tomatoes, dividing it evenly among the dishes. Sprinkle over the remaining cheese and an extra grinding of pepper. Bake for 30–35 minutes or until set, puffed and lightly golden.

4 Remove the clafoutis from the oven and leave to cool for a few minutes before serving, as the tomatoes are very hot inside.

Some more ideas

• Bake one large clafoutis, using a lightly oiled 23 cm (9 in) round ovenproof dish that is about 5 cm (2 in) deep. Increase the baking time to 35–40 minutes.

• Use torn fresh basil leaves or chopped fresh oregano instead of chives.

• For a Red Leicester and onion clafoutis, cut 250 g (8½ oz) red onions into thin wedges and fry in 1 tbsp extra virgin olive oil for about 5 minutes or until golden. Stir in 1 tbsp fresh thyme leaves towards the end of the cooking. Scatter the onions over the bottom of a lightly oiled 23 cm (9 in) round ovenproof dish that is about 5 cm (2 in) deep. Coarsely grate 85 g (3 oz) Red Leicester cheese and sprinkle all but a small handful of it over the onions. Make the batter as in the main recipe and pour over the onions. Give the mixture a stir, then sprinkle over the remaining cheese and a few sprigs of fresh thyme. Bake for 35–40 minutes or until puffed and golden.

Plus points

• Pecorino is a hard Italian cheese made from sheep's milk. Like Parmesan, it is quite high in fat, but need only be used in small quantities as it has a rich, strong flavour.

• Both soured cream and single cream – the fresh version of soured cream – contain considerably more calcium than other creams.

• Tomatoes contain lycopene, a valuable antioxidant that may help to protect against prostate, bladder and pancreatic cancers if tomatoes are included in the diet regularly.

Each serving provides

kcal 392, protein 26 g, fat 26 g (of which saturated fat 11 g), carbohydrate 17 g (of which sugars 8 g), fibre 1.5 g

✓✓✓	B_{12}, calcium
✓✓	A, B_2, C, E, niacin, zinc
✓	B_1, B_6, folate, copper, iron, potassium, selenium

Main meals

Leek and spring green filo pie

Spring vegetables, lively herbs and zesty lemon make a refreshing filling for a crisp filo crust that is easy to prepare and healthy too. Add baby carrots and new potatoes boiled in their skins to create a well-balanced meal.

Serves 4

finely grated zest of 1 lemon
2 tbsp extra virgin olive oil
225 g (8 oz) leeks, thinly sliced
115 g (4 oz) spring greens, thinly sliced
170 g (6 oz) frozen petits pois
2 tbsp chopped fresh tarragon
1 tbsp chopped fresh mint
2 large eggs
4 tbsp plain low-fat yogurt
85 g (3 oz) Gruyère cheese, diced
115 g (4 oz) filo pastry
salt and pepper

Preparation time: 20 minutes
Cooking time: 20–25 minutes

1 Mix the lemon zest with the oil and set aside to infuse for about 5 minutes. Heat half the lemon-infused oil in a large saucepan. Add the leeks, spring greens, petits pois, tarragon and mint. Mix well to coat the vegetables with the oil, then cover and cook over a low heat for about 5 minutes, stirring occasionally, until the greens are lightly cooked and have wilted.

2 Season the vegetables to taste, then transfer them to a 20 cm (8 in) pie dish or flan dish. Preheat the oven to 220°C (425°F, gas mark 7).

3 Beat the eggs with the yogurt. Add a little seasoning and the Gruyère cheese, then pour the mixture evenly over the vegetables and mix lightly.

4 Brush a sheet of filo pastry very sparingly with a little of the remaining lemon-infused oil and lay it over the vegetables, tucking the edges neatly inside the rim of the dish. Brush the remaining sheets of filo with oil and place them on top of the pie, oiled side up, pinching and pleating them into folds to cover the top fairly evenly.

5 Lay a piece of foil loosely over the top of the pie, and bake for about 10 minutes. Remove the foil and bake for a further 10–15 minutes or until the pastry is crisp and golden brown. Serve immediately.

Some more ideas

• Replace the spring greens and petit pois with mushrooms and spinach. Slice 125 g (4½ oz) button mushrooms and cook with the leeks and herbs, adding 2 garlic cloves, crushed, and 1 bunch of spring onions, sliced. Place in the bottom of the pie dish. Wash 225 g (8 oz) spinach and place in a saucepan, then cover and cook for about 2 minutes or until the leaves are wilted and tender (the water remaining on the leaves will provide sufficient moisture). Drain well, pressing out excess liquid, then coarsely chop the spinach and place on top of the mushrooms. Sprinkle evenly with 100 g (3½ oz) crumbled feta cheese and pour over the egg and yogurt mixture (omit the Gruyère). Top with the filo and bake.

• Curly kale and chickpeas are another good combination. Use 115 g (4 oz) kale, shredded, and 1 can chickpeas, about 400 g, drained, instead of the spring greens and petit pois.

Plus points

• Filo pastry can be cooked with just a little fat to give light and crisp results. It is an ideal alternative to rich pastries.

• Like other dark green, leafy vegetables, spring greens are an excellent source of antioxidant carotenoids which help to prevent degenerative diseases.

Each serving provides Ⓥ
kcal 300, **protein** 18 g, **fat** 18 g (of which saturated fat 6 g), **carbohydrate** 15 g (of which sugars 6 g), **fibre** 5 g

✓✓✓	B$_{12}$, C, folate, calcium
✓✓	A, B$_1$, B$_2$, B$_6$, E, niacin, iron
✓	zinc

Main meals

Baked aubergines with yogurt

In this delicious low-calorie dish, grilled slices of aubergine and courgette are layered with a rich tomato sauce and cumin-flavoured yogurt, then baked. Thick slices of Greek daktyla bread and a crisp green salad are perfect accompaniments.

Serves 4

3 tbsp extra virgin olive oil
1 red onion, finely chopped
2 garlic cloves, finely chopped
1 can chopped tomatoes, about 400 g
2 tsp sun-dried tomato paste
6 tbsp dry red wine
1 bay leaf
2 tbsp chopped parsley
3 aubergines, about 675 g (1½ lb) in total, cut into 1 cm (½ in) slices
3 courgettes, about 450 g (1 lb) in total, thinly sliced
½ tsp ground cumin
400 g (14 oz) plain low-fat yogurt
2 eggs, beaten
30 g (1 oz) Parmesan cheese, freshly grated
salt and pepper

Preparation time: about 50 minutes
Cooking time: 40–45 minutes

Each serving provides (V)

kcal 304, **protein** 17 g, **fat** 16 g (of which saturated fat 4 g), **carbohydrate** 20 g (of which sugars 18.5 g), **fibre** 6 g

✓✓✓ C, calcium

✓✓ A, B$_6$, B$_{12}$, folate, copper, potassium, zinc

✓ B$_1$, B$_2$, E, niacin, iron, selenium

Main meals

1 Heat 1 tbsp of the oil in a saucepan, add the onion and cook for about 8 minutes or until softened. Add the garlic and cook for a further minute, stirring. Stir in the chopped tomatoes with their juice, the tomato paste, wine and bay leaf. Cover and simmer gently for 10 minutes.

2 Take the lid off the pan and let the sauce bubble for a further 10 minutes or until thickened, stirring occasionally. Remove the bay leaf from the sauce. Stir in the parsley and season with salt and pepper to taste.

3 While the sauce is simmering, preheat the grill to moderate. Lightly brush the aubergine and courgette slices with the remaining 2 tbsp oil. Cook under the grill, in batches, for 3–4 minutes on each side or until browned and very tender.

4 Preheat the oven to 180°C (350°F, gas mark 4). Stir the cumin into half of the yogurt.

5 Arrange a third of the aubergine slices, in one layer, in a large ovenproof dish that is about 2.5 litres (4 pints) capacity. Spoon over half of the tomato sauce. Arrange half of the courgette slices on top, in one layer, then drizzle with half of the cumin-flavoured yogurt. Repeat the layers, then finish with a layer of the remaining aubergine slices.

6 Mix the remaining 200 g (7 oz) yogurt with the beaten eggs and half of the Parmesan. Spoon the yogurt mixture over the aubergines, spreading with the back of the spoon to cover evenly. Sprinkle with the remaining Parmesan.

7 Bake for 40–45 minutes or until the top is lightly browned and set, and the sauce is bubbling. Serve hot, in the baking dish.

Plus points

• The normal gut flora can be upset by antibiotics, stress and poor diet. Including yogurt in the diet helps to maintain the 'good' bacteria in the gut and prevent the growth of less desirable bacteria.

• Aubergines are a useful vegetable to include in dishes, because they add bulk and dietary fibre without adding calories – 100 g (3½ oz) contains just 15 kcal.

• Flavonoids are compounds found in onions, which can help to protect against heart disease. Although they occur in both red and white onions, red onions have been shown to have higher levels of flavonoids.

Another idea

● For a chicken, spinach and yogurt layered bake, cook 2 large sliced leeks in lightly boiling water for 4–5 minutes or until just tender. Drain and spread half over the bottom of a large ovenproof dish that is 1.7 litres (3 pints) capacity. Cut 300 g (10½ oz) cooked skinless boneless chicken breasts (fillets) into thick slices and arrange on top of the leeks. Set aside. Pack 450 g (1 lb) rinsed spinach into a large saucepan, cover and cook gently for 2–3 minutes, shaking the pan occasionally, until the spinach is wilted. Drain in a colander, but do not squeeze dry. Soften 2 finely chopped shallots in 15 g (½ oz) butter in the wiped-out saucepan. Add 1 crushed garlic clove and cook for a further minute. Stir in 170 g (6 oz) curd cheese, 3 tbsp semi-skimmed milk, 1 tsp wholegrain mustard, a pinch of freshly grated nutmeg, and salt and pepper to taste. Heat gently, stirring, until smoothly blended, then stir in the spinach. Spoon the mixture over the chicken and spread the remaining leeks on top. Mix 150 g (5½ oz) plain low-fat yogurt with 15 g (½ oz) grated Gruyère cheese, 1 beaten egg, and seasoning to taste. Spoon over the leeks and sprinkle with a further 15 g (½ oz) grated Gruyère. Bake in a preheated 180ºC (350ºF, gas mark 4) oven for 35 minutes. Leave to stand for 5 minutes, then serve with baked jacket potatoes.

Herb and saffron risotto

This fragrant, fresh-tasting risotto should be eaten as soon as it is cooked – if it is left to stand, the starch will begin to set, resulting in a heavy texture. Lemon zest and juice and fresh herbs stirred in at the end add a wonderful burst of flavour.

Serves 6

15 g (½ oz) butter

2 tbsp extra virgin olive oil

1 small onion, chopped

340 g (12 oz) risotto rice

150 ml (5 fl oz) dry white wine

small pinch of saffron strands

1.5 litres (2¾ pints) hot vegetable stock

grated zest of 1 lemon

2 tbsp lemon juice

2 tbsp chopped fresh chives

2 tbsp chopped parsley

salt and pepper

To serve

15 g (½ oz) Parmesan cheese

snipped fresh chives

Preparation time: 10 minutes

Cooking time: about 25 minutes

1 Heat the butter and oil in a large saucepan, add the onion and cook gently for 4–5 minutes or until softened, stirring from time to time.

2 Add the rice and cook for 1 minute, stirring to coat all the grains with the butter and oil. Stir in the wine and boil until it has almost all evaporated.

3 Stir the saffron into the hot stock. Add a ladleful of the stock to the pan and bubble gently until it has almost all been absorbed, stirring frequently. Continue adding the stock a ladleful at a time, letting each be almost all absorbed before adding the next, and stirring frequently. Total cooking time will be 15–20 minutes. The risotto is ready when the rice is tender but the grains are still whole and firm, and the overall texture is moist and creamy.

4 Remove the pan from the heat and stir in the lemon zest and juice, chives and parsley. Season with salt and pepper to taste.

5 Using a vegetable peeler, take thin shavings from the Parmesan and scatter them over the risotto together with the chives. Serve immediately.

Some more ideas

● Stir 100 g (3½ oz) lightly cooked asparagus tips or thawed frozen peas into the risotto towards the end of cooking.

● To make an artichoke risotto, omit the onion and cook the rice as in the main recipe, adding 2 tbsp lemon juice with the wine. A few minutes before the end of cooking, stir in 1 jar or can of artichoke hearts in water, about 340 g, drained. Add mint instead of parsley, and sprinkle with 30 g (1 oz) chopped walnuts instead of the Parmesan shavings.

Plus points

● Vitamin loss from rice is reduced when it is cooked by the absorption method, as in making a risotto – the vitamins remain in the liquid, which is then absorbed into the dish.

● Parsley is one of the most nutritious of herb garnishes and it also contains useful amounts of vitamin C and iron. Fresh parsley is also a great breath freshener, and if chewed after a meal can neutralise the after-taste of ingredients such as garlic.

Each serving provides Ⓥ

kcal 287, **protein** 6 g, **fat** 7 g (of which saturated fat 2 g), **carbohydrate** 44 g (of which sugars 1 g), **fibre** 0.2 g

✓ niacin, copper, zinc

Main meals

Broccoli and red pepper quiche

This vegetable-packed quiche is cooked in a deep tin and the pastry is rolled out thinly to give a generous amount of filling and small proportion of pastry in each slice. Serve warm, rather than piping hot or chilled, with a lightly dressed, crisp salad.

Serves 8

15 g (½ oz) butter

1 tbsp extra virgin olive oil

225 g (8 oz) onions, thinly sliced

1 red pepper, seeded and finely chopped

85 g (3 oz) broccoli, cut into small florets

3 large eggs, beaten

225 ml (7½ fl oz) semi-skimmed milk

3 tbsp finely chopped parsley or fresh chives

125 g (4½ oz) shiitake mushrooms or small closed-cup mushrooms, sliced

115 g (4 oz) frozen sweetcorn, thawed and drained

salt and pepper

Pastry

125 g (4½ oz) plain flour

125 g (4½ oz) plain wholemeal flour

pinch of cayenne pepper (optional)

125 g (4½ oz) butter, chilled and diced

Preparation time: 1¼ hours, plus at least 30 minutes chilling

Cooking time: 40–45 minutes

Each serving provides ⓥ

kcal 330, **protein** 9 g, **fat** 20 g (of which saturated fat 11 g), **carbohydrate** 32 g (of which sugars 5 g), **fibre** 3 g

✓✓✓	C
✓✓	A, B₁₂, E, folate
✓	B₁, niacin, calcium, iron, selenium

1 First make the pastry. Sift both types of flour and the cayenne pepper, if using, into a large bowl, adding the bran left in the sieve. Rub in the butter until the mixture resembles fine crumbs. Sprinkle with 2 tbsp of ice-cold water and mix to form a dough, adding an extra 1 tbsp water, if necessary.

2 Gather the dough into a ball, then roll it out on a lightly floured surface into a 28 cm (11 in) circle, about 3 mm (⅛ in) thick. Use the pastry to line a loose-bottomed 23 cm (9 in) fluted flan tin, about 3 cm (1¼ in) deep. Prick the pastry case all over with a fork, then cover and chill for at least 30 minutes.

3 Place a baking sheet in the oven and preheat it to 200°C (400°F, gas mark 6). Melt the butter with the olive oil in a frying pan or large saucepan. Add the onions and stir well, then cover and cook over a very low heat for 30 minutes or until very tender.

4 Meanwhile, blanch the red pepper in a saucepan of boiling water for 1 minute. Remove with a slotted spoon, place the pepper in a colander and refresh under cold water, then drain well. Add the broccoli to the same water and blanch for 30 seconds, then remove, refresh and drain well.

5 Line the chilled pastry case with a piece of greaseproof paper and cover with baking beans or rice. Place on the hot baking sheet and bake for 20 minutes. Remove the paper and beans, and continue baking the pastry case for 5 minutes. Brush the bottom of the pastry case with a little of the beaten egg and bake for a further 2 minutes. Remove from the oven, leaving the baking sheet inside. Reduce the oven to 190°C (375°F, gas mark 5).

6 Beat the milk with the eggs. Add the herbs and seasoning to taste. Spread the onions in the pastry case, then add the red pepper, broccoli, mushrooms and sweetcorn. Pour the egg mixture over the vegetables.

7 Place the quiche in the oven, on the hot baking sheet, and bake for 40–45 minutes or until the filling is set. Leave to cool for at least 10 minutes before serving.

Plus points

● Eggs have received a 'bad press' in recent years because of their cholesterol content, but they are an excellent source of many nutrients, including protein, iron and vitamins A, B group and E. They are also low in fat.

Some more ideas

• For a crisp Mediterranean-style pastry, low in saturated fat, replace the butter with 125 ml (4½ fl oz) olive oil. Use 2–4 tbsp lukewarm water rather than ice cold. Gather the pastry together into a soft ball, then press it over the bottom and up the side of the flan tin, trimming off any excess pastry. This delicate pastry must be handled with care. Cover and chill for at least 30 minutes. Do not blind bake: add the filling to the uncooked pastry case and bake at 180ºC (350ºF, gas mark 4) for 55–60 minutes. Leave the quiche to set and cool before serving. Cut it with a serrated knife.

• Other suitable vegetables to include are finely chopped seeded tomatoes, shelled peas and sliced courgettes. For an aniseed-like flavour, soften a thinly sliced bulb of fennel with the onions. Chopped, well-drained cooked spinach can also be added, spread out in a thin layer over the onions.

Feta and couscous salad

In this salad, couscous makes a great background for raw and lightly steamed vegetables, together with toasted almonds, fresh mint and creamy feta cheese. A touch of chilli gives extra bite to the dressing.

Serves 4

225 g (8 oz) couscous

300 ml (10 fl oz) hot vegetable stock

170 g (6 oz) slim asparagus spears, halved

2 courgettes, cut into thin sticks

1 red pepper, seeded and cut into thin strips

30 g (1 oz) toasted flaked almonds

handful of fresh mint leaves, finely chopped

170 g (6 oz) feta cheese

Chilli dressing

3 tbsp extra virgin olive oil

grated zest of 1 lemon

1 tbsp lemon juice

1 garlic clove, finely chopped

½ tsp crushed dried chillies

salt and pepper

Preparation and cooking time: 30–35 minutes

Each serving provides Ⓥ

kcal 388, **protein** 14 g, **fat** 22 g (of which saturated fat 7.5 g), **carbohydrate** 35 g (of which sugars 5 g), **fibre** 2 g

✓✓✓	A, C
✓✓	E, folate, calcium, iron
✓	B₁, B₆, B₁₂, niacin, copper, potassium, zinc

1 Put the couscous into a large bowl and pour over the hot stock. Set aside to soak for 15–20 minutes or until all the liquid has been absorbed.

2 Meanwhile, steam the asparagus for 3 minutes. Add the courgettes and continue steaming for 2 minutes or until the vegetables are just tender but still retain some crunch. Tip the vegetables into a colander and refresh under cold running water. Drain well.

3 To make the dressing, combine the oil, lemon zest and juice, garlic, chillies, and salt and pepper to taste in a screw-top jar. Shake well to blend.

4 Fluff up the couscous with a fork, then fold in the pepper strips, almonds, mint, and steamed asparagus and courgettes. Pour over the dressing and stir gently together. Crumble the feta over the top, and serve.

Some more ideas

● If you can get yellow courgettes, use 1 yellow and 1 green for even more colour.

● Instead of, or as well as, mint, use other herbs such as chopped fresh coriander.

● For a halloumi and lentil salad, cook 85 g (3 oz) Puy lentils in plenty of boiling water for 15–20 minutes or until just tender. At the same time, cook 115 g (4 oz) long-grain rice in boiling water for 10–15 minutes, or according to the packet instructions, until tender. Add 170 g (6 oz) broad beans or peas (fresh or frozen) to

the lentils for the last 4 minutes of the cooking time. Drain the rice and lentils well, then mix them together. Stir in 3 finely chopped spring onions, 1 red pepper, seeded and diced, and 30 g (1 oz) toasted flaked almonds. Make the chilli dressing as in the main recipe, and toss with the rice and lentil salad. Cut 170 g (6 oz) halloumi cheese into 8 slices. Brush each slice with a little extra virgin olive oil, using about 1 tbsp oil in all, then grill or griddle for a few minutes or until golden on both sides. Serve the salad topped with the cheese and an extra grinding of black pepper.

Plus points

● Feta cheese is quite salty. If you are concerned about your sodium intake you can reduce the salt content of the cheese by soaking it in milk for 30 minutes before use (discard the milk).

● Couscous, made from semolina, is low in fat and high in starchy carbohydrate.

● Courgettes belong to the same family as melons, cucumbers and pumpkins. Their skin is a rich source of beta-carotene, which the body can convert into vitamin A. This vitamin helps to maintain healthy eyesight and skin, and a properly functioning immune system.

Main meals

Cheese and watercress soufflé

Soufflés have a undeserved reputation for being difficult to make. This tasty soufflé is, in fact, quick and easy to prepare and makes a satisfying lunch with crusty bread and a side salad. Semi-skimmed milk and cornflour keep it lower in calories than other soufflés.

Serves 4

1 tsp butter
15 g (½ oz) Parmesan cheese, freshly grated
15 g (½ oz) fine dry breadcrumbs
85 g (3 oz) watercress
3 tbsp cornflour
300 ml (10 fl oz) semi-skimmed milk
4 eggs, separated
1 tbsp wholegrain mustard
85 g (3 oz) Gruyère cheese, grated
salt and pepper

Preparation time: 20 minutes
Cooking time: 30–35 minutes

Each serving provides ⓥ
kcal 293, **protein** 19 g, **fat** 18 g (of which saturated fat 8 g), **carbohydrate** 16 g (of which sugars 4 g), **fibre** 1 g

✓✓✓	A, B₁₂, niacin, calcium
✓✓	E, niacin, zinc
✓	B₂, C, folate, copper, iron, selenium

1 Preheat the oven to 200°C (400°F, gas mark 6). Lightly butter the inside of a 1.5 litre (2¾ pint) soufflé dish. Mix together the Parmesan and breadcrumbs, and sprinkle half of this mixture over the bottom and sides of the dish, turning and tilting the dish to coat evenly. Set aside.

2 Remove the thicker stalks from the watercress and discard. Finely chop the rest of the watercress and set aside.

3 Mix the cornflour with a little of the milk to make a smooth paste. Heat the rest of the milk until almost boiling, then pour onto the cornflour mixture, stirring constantly. Return to the pan and stir over a moderate heat until the sauce thickens and is smooth.

4 Remove from the heat and add the egg yolks, beating them thoroughly into the sauce. Stir in the chopped watercress, mustard, Gruyère cheese, and salt and pepper to taste.

5 In a clean, dry bowl, whisk the egg whites until they will hold soft peaks. Fold a quarter of the whites into the sauce mixture to lighten it, then gently fold in the rest of the whites.

6 Spoon the mixture into the soufflé dish and sprinkle the top with the remaining Parmesan and breadcrumb mixture. Bake the soufflé for 30–35 minutes or until well risen and golden brown. Serve immediately.

Some more ideas

● Instead of Gruyère, use a blue cheese such as Gorgonzola, Stilton or Danish blue.

● Try a Greek-style feta and watercress soufflé, replacing the Gruyère cheese with 75 g (2½ oz) crumbled feta. Sprinkle the soufflé with a pinch of freshly grated nutmeg before serving.

● For a smoked haddock and spinach soufflé, use 85 g (3 oz) smoked haddock fillet and 85 g (3 oz) fresh spinach leaves. Cook the haddock gently in the milk for 5–6 minutes, then drain, reserving the milk for the sauce. Flake the haddock, discarding any skin and bones. Wash the spinach, then cook for 2–3 minutes, with just the water clinging to the leaves, until wilted. Drain well, squeezing out excess moisture, then chop the spinach. Add the haddock and spinach to the sauce in step 4, in place of the Gruyère and watercress.

Plus points

● Gruyère cheese has a distinctive flavour and creamy, melting texture. It contributes to the protein and calcium content of this soufflé, as well as providing zinc, a mineral that has an important role to play in wound healing.

● Most soufflés are based on a mixture of butter and flour called a roux. This version uses cornflour instead, which works just as well and keeps the total fat content low.

Main meals

Moroccan-style pumpkin and butter beans

Middle Eastern spices flavour this low-fat vegetarian casserole, which is full of fibre-rich ingredients. It is a great recipe for a cook-ahead meal as the flavours improve when the casserole is chilled overnight, then reheated for serving. Try it with couscous.

Serves 4

600 ml (1 pint) boiling water

1 vegetable stock cube, crumbled, or
   2 tsp vegetable bouillon powder or paste

½ tsp turmeric

½ tsp ground coriander

pinch of ground cumin

200 g (7 oz) leeks, halved lengthways and
   sliced

225g (8 oz) parsnips, cut into 1 cm (½ in)
   cubes

600 g (1 lb 5 oz) piece of pumpkin, peeled,
   seeded and cut into 1cm (½ in) cubes

400 g (14 oz) yellow or green courgettes,
   sliced

1 red pepper, seeded and chopped

100 g (3½ oz) ready-to-eat dried apricots,
   chopped

1 can butter beans, about 400 g, drained

pinch of crushed dried chillies, or to taste
   (optional)

salt and pepper

To garnish

30 g (1 oz) pine nuts

chopped parsley or fresh coriander

Preparation time: about 10 minutes
Cooking time: about 20 minutes

1 Pour the boiling water into a flame proof casserole. Stir in the stock cube, powder or paste, the turmeric, ground coriander and cumin. Add the leeks and parsnips and bring to the boil. Reduce the heat to moderate, cover the pan and simmer the vegetables for 5 minutes.

2 Add the pumpkin, courgettes and red pepper to the pan, then bring the stock back to the boil. Stir in the apricots, butter beans and chilli flakes, if using, adding more to taste for a spicier result. Season with salt and pepper. Reduce the heat, cover the pan and simmer for 10 minutes or until all the vegetables are tender.

3 Meanwhile, toast the pine nuts in a non-stick frying pan over a moderate heat, stirring constantly, until just beginning to brown and giving off their nutty aroma. Tip the pine nuts onto a board and chop them coarsely.

4 Taste the casserole and adjust the seasoning, if necessary, then ladle it into deep bowls. Sprinkle with the chopped pine nuts and parsley or fresh coriander and serve.

Plus points

● Pumpkin is a rich source of beta-carotene and other carotenoid compounds. Save the seeds, and roast or toast them to enjoy as a snack, as they provide good amounts of protein and zinc.

● Dried apricots are an excellent source of beta-carotene and a useful source of the mineral calcium.

● Parsnips provide useful amounts of potassium, folate and vitamin B_1.

Each serving provides
kcal 250, **protein** 12 g, **fat** 7 g (of which saturated fat 1 g), **carbohydrate** 35 g (of which sugars 21 g), **fibre** 11 g

✓✓✓	A, C, iron
✓✓	B_1, B_6, folate
✓	calcium

Main meals

Some more ideas

• This casserole is delicious ladled over couscous. Place 340 g (12 oz) couscous in a heatproof bowl. Add salt to taste and pour in 600 ml (1 pint) boiling water to cover. Cover the bowl and leave to stand for about 5 minutes or until all the water has been absorbed and the couscous is plumped up and tender. Add 15 g (½ oz) butter and fluff up the couscous with a fork, to separate the grains.

• Try other vegetables with the pumpkin – for example, broccoli florets can be added with the pumpkin instead of the courgettes. The distinctive flavour of turnips is also good with the other vegetables.

• For a fresh, peppery flavour, garnish the casserole with 55 g (2 oz) grated red radishes or large white radish (mooli).

Beef and mushroom Stroganoff

This version of the classic East European dish of quick-fried steak with mushrooms shows how vegetables can be used to enhance and 'stretch' a modest portion of meat. The result is every bit as special and delicious as true Stroganoff, but much lower in fat.

Serves 4

2 tbsp extra virgin olive oil

200 g (7 oz) chestnut mushrooms, halved

1 red pepper, seeded and cut into fine strips

200 g (7 oz) broccoli, cut into small florets

150 ml (5 fl oz) beef stock

1 onion, sliced

300 g (10½ oz) fillet steak, cut into thin strips

2 tbsp brandy

3 tbsp creamed horseradish (optional)

150 ml (5 fl oz) soured cream

salt and pepper

Preparation time: 10 minutes

Cooking time: about 12 minutes

1 Heat half of the oil in a large saucepan. Add the mushrooms and fry for 2 minutes or until beginning to soften. Stir in the red pepper and broccoli florets and continue to fry, stirring, for 3–4 minutes.

2 Pour in the stock and bring to the boil. Cover the pan, reduce the heat and simmer for about 5 minutes or until the broccoli is just tender.

3 Meanwhile, heat the remaining 1 tbsp of oil in a large frying pan and stir-fry the onion for about 5 minutes or until softened and beginning to brown.

4 Add the strips of beef to the onions and stir-fry for 1 minute or until the beef begins to change colour. Stand back from the pan, pour in the brandy and set light to it.

5 As soon as the flames subside, stir in the creamed horseradish, if using, and the soured cream. Add the vegetables with their cooking liquid. Stir well, season to taste and serve immediately. A rice pilaff is the traditional Russian accompaniment for Stroganoff; tagliatelle is very popular today. Boiled new potatoes are also delicious with this vegetable-rich version.

Plus points

● Although not eaten in large quantities, horseradish contributes some fibre, B-group vitamins and vitamin C.

● Broccoli is a good source of vitamin C, which helps to increase the absorption of iron from the beef in this recipe.

● Mushrooms are low in fat and calories and they provide useful amounts of copper as well as many B vitamins.

Some more ideas

● Try lean gammon steak, cut into fine strips, instead of the fillet steak and replace the mushrooms and broccoli with 200 g (7 oz) white or green cabbage, shredded, and 150 g (5½ oz) frozen peas. Use vegetable stock instead of beef stock and cider instead of brandy (cider will not flame). Stir in 2 tbsp Dijon mustard (or your favourite mustard) instead of the creamed horseradish.

● Lean pork fillet or chicken or turkey breast fillets are good alternatives to the beef.

● For a vegetarian Stroganoff, omit the steak and use vegetable stock. Increase the quantity of mushrooms to 450 g (1 lb), including a variety such as open cap, shiitake and chestnut, and use 2 peppers.

Each serving provides

kcal 370, **protein** 20 g, **fat** 29 g (of which saturated fat 14 g), **carbohydrate** 6 g (of which sugars 5 g), **fibre** 3 g

✓✓✓	A, B₁₂, C
✓✓	B₂, B₆, E, folate, copper, iron, zinc
✓	B₁, niacin, potassium, selenium

Main meals

Perfect pot roast

This long-simmered, one-pot meal is wonderfully satisfying, with its mixture of beef and chunky vegetables. The dish can be prepared ahead of time, so it's perfect for family dinners as well as for informal entertaining. Serve with a crunchy mixed salad and bread.

Serves 6

1 tsp extra virgin olive oil

1 kg (2¼ lb) piece boneless beef chuck, about 7.5 cm (3 in) thick, trimmed of fat and tied

2 large onions, finely chopped

1 celery stick, finely chopped

3 garlic cloves, crushed

250 ml (8½ fl oz) dry red or white wine

1 can chopped tomatoes, about 225 g

1 large carrot, grated

1 tsp chopped fresh thyme

450 ml (15 fl oz) beef stock, preferably home-made

600 g (1 lb 5 oz) new potatoes, scrubbed and quartered

340 g (12 oz) celeriac, cut into 2.5 cm (1 in) cubes

340 g (12 oz) swede, cut into 2.5 cm (1 in) cubes

4 carrots, about 280 g (10 oz) in total, sliced

salt and pepper

3 tbsp chopped parsley to garnish

Preparation and cooking time: 4 hours

Each serving provides

kcal 399, **protein** 43 g, **fat** 12 g (of which saturated fat 4 g), **carbohydrate** 33 g (of which sugars 15 g), **fibre** 8 g

✓✓✓	A, B₁, B₆, B₁₂, C, folate, niacin, zinc
✓✓	B₂, iron
✓	selenium

1 Preheat the oven to 160°C (325°F, gas mark 3). Heat the oil in a large flameproof casserole. Add the beef and brown it over a moderately high heat for 6–8 minutes or until it is well coloured on all sides. Remove the meat to a plate.

2 Reduce the heat to moderate. Add the onions, celery and garlic and cook, stirring frequently, for about 3 minutes or until the onions begin to soften. Add the wine and let it bubble for about 1 minute, then add the tomatoes with their juice and the grated carrot. Cook for a further 2 minutes.

3 Return the beef to the casserole together with any juices that have collected on the plate and the chopped thyme. Tuck a piece of greaseproof paper or foil around the top of the meat, turning back the corners so that it doesn't touch the liquid, then cover with a tight-fitting lid. Transfer the casserole to the oven and cook for 2½ hours.

4 About 20 minutes before the end of the cooking time, bring the stock to the boil in a deep saucepan with a lid. Add the potatoes, celeriac, swede and sliced carrots. Cover and simmer gently for 12–15 minutes or until they are starting to become tender.

5 Meanwhile, remove the beef from the casserole and set aside. Remove any fat from the cooking liquid, either by spooning it off or by using a bulb baster, then purée the casseroled vegetables and liquid in a blender or food processor until smooth. Season to taste.

6 Drain the potatoes and other root vegetables, reserving the liquid. Make a layer of the vegetables in the casserole, put the beef on top and add the remaining root vegetables and their cooking liquid. Pour over the puréed sauce. Cover the casserole and return to the oven to cook for 20 minutes or until the root vegetables are tender.

7 Remove the beef to a carving board, cover and leave to rest for 10 minutes. Keep the vegetables and sauce in the oven turned down to low.

8 Carve the beef and arrange on warmed plates with the vegetables and sauce. Sprinkle with the parsley and serve immediately.

Plus points

• Swede is a member of the cruciferous family of vegetables. It is a useful source of vitamin C and beta-carotene and rich in phytochemicals that are believed to help protect against cancer.

• A freshly dug potato may contain as much as ten times more vitamin C than one that has been stored.

Some more ideas

- Brisket can be used instead of chuck, as can topside of beef.
- Any leftover beef can be chopped or shredded and mixed with the sauce and/or a freshly made tomato sauce, then served over spaghetti or other pasta.
- Substitute a boneless gammon joint, soaked if necessary, for the beef. Soften 1 chopped onion in 1 tsp extra virgin olive oil with 2 chopped garlic cloves (omit the celery). Add the wine (use white) and gammon (there is no need to brown it first). Omit the tomatoes, grated carrot and thyme and add 750 ml (1¼ pints) unsalted vegetable stock, 3 cloves, 1½ tsp mustard powder and 1 strip of orange zest. Cover and simmer for 1¼ hours, adding the root vegetables after 25 minutes. When the meat is cooked, transfer it to a carving board as in step 7. Strain the cooking liquid and remove the fat, then boil rapidly until reduced to 600 ml (1 pint). Stir in 2 tbsp cornflour mixed with 1½ tbsp cold water and boil until the liquid has thickened. Finish as in the main recipe.

Keema curry

With just a hint of chilli, this mellow curry is ideal for those who like to experiment with new tastes, but are unused to spicy food. Team with steamed basmati rice and warm naan bread, for a meal that is packed full of protein and vitamins.

Serves 4

500 g (1 lb 2 oz) lean minced beef

1 onion, finely chopped

450 g (1 lb) potatoes, peeled and diced

3 garlic cloves, chopped

2.5 cm (1 in) piece fresh root ginger, peeled and finely chopped

1 cinnamon stick, halved

1 tsp turmeric

1 tsp cumin seeds, roughly crushed

1 tsp coriander seeds, roughly crushed

½ tsp crushed dried chillies

1 can chopped tomatoes, about 400 g

300 ml (10 fl oz) beef or lamb stock, preferably home-made

150 g (5½ oz) baby leaf spinach

salt and pepper

fresh mint leaves to garnish

Raita

150 g (5½ oz) plain low-fat yogurt

¼ cucumber, finely diced

4 tsp chopped fresh mint

Preparation time: 10–15 minutes

Cooking time: 35 minutes

Each serving provides

kcal 369, **protein** 35 g, **fat** 14 g (of which saturated fat 6 g), **carbohydrate** 30 g (of which sugars 10 g), **fibre** 4 g

✓✓✓ B₁, B₆, B₁₂, C, E, folate, iron, zinc

✓✓ A, B₂

---

1 Fry the beef and onion in a large saucepan for 5 minutes or until evenly browned, stirring to break up the meat. Add the potatoes, garlic, ginger and spices and fry for 2 minutes, stirring. Add the tomatoes with their juice and the stock and season with salt and pepper to taste. Bring to the boil, then cover and simmer for 20 minutes, stirring occasionally.

2 Meanwhile, make the raita. Mix the yogurt, cucumber and mint together with a little seasoning. Spoon into a small bowl and chill until required.

3 Stir the spinach into the curry and heat through for 1 minute, then taste for seasoning. Spoon the curry onto warmed plates and sprinkle with fresh mint leaves. Serve immediately, with the chilled raita.

Some more ideas

● If you prefer, you can cook the curry in the oven. Brown the beef and onion in a flameproof casserole, then add the other ingredients and bring to the boil. Cover and cook in a preheated 180°C (350°F, gas mark 4) oven for 1 hour. Add the spinach, toss with the meat, then cover and return to the oven to cook for 10 minutes.

● If you don't have the individual dried spices, you can use 2 tbsp mild curry paste instead.

● Use Swiss chard or spring greens in place of the spinach. Tear into bite-sized pieces before adding to the meat.

● For a fruity curry, add 55 g (2 oz) sultanas and 1 sliced dessert apple with the potatoes. Omit the spinach. Garnish the curry with 1 diced banana tossed with the juice of ½ lemon, 2 tbsp chopped fresh coriander and 2 tbsp toasted desiccated coconut.

● Any leftover curry is delicious reheated and served in folded chapattis or warmed pitta bread pockets.

● To vary the raita, add ½ grated carrot, 2 chopped spring onions or a sprinkling of toasted cumin seeds to the basic mixture.

● If you don't have any fresh mint, use 1½ tsp ready-made mint sauce instead.

Plus points

● A raita or sauce of yogurt, cucumber and mint is often served with curries to act as a cooling agent against the heat of the chillies and spices. Banana can also be used.

● Yogurt contains vitamin B₂ which is needed to release energy from food. Bio-yogurts contain cultures which are claimed to be particularly beneficial to the digestion.

Main meals

163

Slow-braised beef and barley

Here, beef is simmered until meltingly tender while nourishing pot barley thickens the gravy to make a hearty casserole and juniper berries add a distinctive flavour. Serve with mashed potatoes and a green vegetable such as French beans or spring greens.

Serves 4

500 g (1 lb 2 oz) beef chuck or lean braising steak, trimmed and cut into 5 cm (2 in) cubes

2 garlic cloves, halved

3 bay leaves

6 juniper berries, lightly crushed

1 sprig of fresh thyme

250 ml (8½ fl oz) full-bodied red wine

12 button onions, about 400 g (14 oz) in total

1 tbsp extra virgin olive oil

55 g (2 oz) pot barley

400 ml (14 fl oz) beef stock

3 large carrots, cut into large chunks, about 425 g (15 oz) in total

2 celery sticks, sliced

300 g (10½ oz) swede, cut into 4 cm (1½ in) chunks

salt and pepper

Preparation time: 20 minutes, plus 8 hours marinating

Cooking time: 2–2¼ hours

Each serving provides

kcal 367, **protein** 31 g, **fat** 10 g (of which saturated fat 3 g), **carbohydrate** 29 g (of which sugars 18 g), **fibre** 8 g

✓✓✓	A
✓✓	C
✓	B₁, B₆, E, folate, niacin, calcium, copper, iron, potassium, zinc

1 Put the beef in a bowl with the garlic, bay leaves, juniper berries and thyme. Pour over the wine, then cover and leave to marinate in the fridge for 8 hours or overnight.

2 The next day, preheat the oven to 160°C (325°F, gas mark 3). Put the button onions in a bowl and pour over enough boiling water to cover. Leave for 2 minutes, then drain. When cool enough to handle, peel off the skins. Set the onions aside.

3 Remove the beef from the marinade and pat dry on kitchen paper. Heat the oil in a large flameproof casserole over a moderately high heat. Add the beef and brown on all sides. Do this in batches, if necessary, so the pan is not overcrowded. Remove the beef from the casserole and set aside on a plate.

4 Add the onions to the casserole and cook gently for 3–4 minutes or until lightly coloured all over. Add the barley and cook for 1 minute, stirring, then return the beef and any beefy juices to the casserole. Pour in the stock and bring to a simmer.

5 Strain the marinade into the casserole, and add the bay leaves and sprig of thyme. Season with salt and pepper to taste. Cover with a tight-fitting lid, transfer to the oven and braise for 45 minutes.

6 Add the carrots, celery and swede, and stir to mix. Cover again and braise for a further 1–1¼ hours or until the beef, barley and vegetables are tender. Remove the bay leaves and thyme stalk before serving.

Plus points

• Pot barley retains the outer layers of the grain (these are removed in the milling of pearl barley), and it therefore contains all the nutrients of the whole grain.

• The barley grain contains gummy fibres called beta-glucans, which appear to have significant cholesterol-lowering properties.

• Beef is an excellent source of iron in a form that can be efficiently absorbed and used by the body.

Some more ideas

- The gravy will be quite thick. If you prefer it slightly thinner, stir in an extra 120 ml (4 fl oz) beef stock 20 minutes before the end of the cooking time.

- For slow-braised lamb and barley, use lean boneless stewing lamb instead of beef, and marinate overnight in 250 ml (8½ fl oz) dry cider mixed with 2 tsp Dijon mustard, 1 tsp molasses and 1 tsp Demerara sugar. Dry and fry the lamb as for the beef in the main recipe. Add 1 sliced onion to the casserole and cook for 4–5 minutes or until beginning to colour, then add the barley and stir for 1 minute. Pour in 250 ml (8½ fl oz) lamb or vegetable stock, 150 ml (5 fl oz) tomato juice and the marinade, and add a sprig of fresh rosemary. Cover and braise for 45 minutes. Stir in 250 g (8½ oz) baby carrots and 250 g (8½ oz) halved or quartered small turnips. Braise for a further 1–1¼ hours or until everything is tender.

Thai-style stir-fried beef with mango

This colourful dish is bursting with fresh flavours and contrasting textures. The dressing is oil-free, so although a little oil is used to stir fry the beef, the dish is still very light in fat. No extra salt is needed because of the spicy dressing and the saltiness of soy sauce.

Serves 4

400 g (14 oz) lean steak, such as sirloin

3 garlic cloves, finely chopped

1 tsp caster sugar

2 tsp soy sauce

1½ tbsp sunflower oil

Ginger and honey dressing

2 tsp paprika

2 tsp mild Mexican-style chilli powder

1½ tbsp clear honey

2.5 cm (1 in) piece fresh root ginger, grated

4 tbsp rice vinegar or cider vinegar

juice of 1 lime or lemon

Salad

1 ripe but firm mango, peeled and cut into strips

2 ripe but firm plums, sliced

¼ medium-sized red cabbage, shredded

55 g (2 oz) watercress leaves

½ cucumber, cut into matchsticks

½ red pepper, cut into thin strips

3–4 spring onions, cut into diagonal pieces

45 g (1½ oz) mixed fresh mint and coriander

2 tbsp coarsely chopped roasted unsalted peanuts

Preparation time: 30 minutes

Cooking time: about 10 minutes

1 To make the dressing, put the paprika, chilli powder, honey, ginger and vinegar in a saucepan and slowly add 250 ml (8½ fl oz) of water, stirring. Bring to the boil, then reduce the heat and simmer for 5 minutes. Remove from the heat and stir in the lime or lemon juice. Set aside.

2 Combine all the salad ingredients, except the peanuts, in a large shallow serving dish and toss gently together until evenly mixed. Set aside.

3 Cut the steak into thin strips for stir-frying. Put the steak in a bowl with the garlic, sugar and soy sauce and mix together so the strips of steak are seasoned. Heat a wok or non-stick pan on a high heat, then add the oil. Add the beef and stir-fry until the strips are evenly browned and cooked to taste.

4 Spoon the stir-fried beef over the top of the salad. Drizzle the dressing over the top and sprinkle with the peanuts. Serve immediately.

Some more ideas

• Add cubes of fresh or canned pineapple (canned in juice rather than syrup) or kiwi fruit to the salad, to increase the fruit content.

• Spice up the salad with very thin strips of fresh red chilli – particularly if you have a cold, as scientists have suggested that eating chillies can help to alleviate nasal congestion.

• Replace the mango with 2 nectarines, unpeeled and sliced.

• For a vegetarian version, omit the stir-fried beef and increase the quantity of peanuts to 150 g (5½ oz). Peanuts are an excellent source of protein and contain much less saturated fat than meat.

Plus points

• All orange and red fruit and vegetables, such as mango, red cabbage and red peppers, are excellent sources of beta-carotene and vitamin C – both antioxidants that help to protect against heart disease and cancer. The vitamin C aids the absorption of iron from the steak.

• Apart from adding delicious spiciness to the dressing, ginger also aids digestion.

Each serving provides

kcal 265, **protein** 27 g, **fat** 8 g (of which saturated fat 3 g), **carbohydrate** 20 g (of which sugars 18 g), **fibre** 3 g

✓✓✓	B_{12}, C
✓✓	A, B_6, iron, zinc
✓	B_1, B_2, E, folate, niacin, copper

Fragrant lamb with spinach

Warmly spiced rather than fiery hot, thanks to the cooling effect of the yogurt, this curry has a wonderful flavour. The lamb is infused with spices, and Basmati rice, chapattis and a tomato and cucumber chutney make this an irresistible meal that is also low in calories.

Serves 4

2 tbsp sunflower oil

2 onions, finely chopped

4 garlic cloves, crushed

5 cm (2 in) piece fresh root ginger, peeled and chopped

1 red chilli, seeded and sliced

2 tsp paprika

2 tsp ground cumin

2 tsp ground coriander

1 tsp ground white pepper

½ tsp ground cinnamon

seeds from 8 green cardamom pods, crushed

2 bay leaves

½ tsp salt

200 g (7 oz) Greek-style yogurt

500 g (1 lb 2 oz) lean boneless lamb, cubed

2 large tomatoes, chopped

225 g (8 oz) fresh baby spinach

4 tbsp chopped fresh coriander

sprigs of fresh coriander to garnish

Preparation time: 20–25 minutes

Cooking time: 1 hour 20 minutes

Each serving provides

kcal 350, **protein** 32 g, **fat** 22 g (of which saturated fat 8 g), **carbohydrate** 7 g (of which sugars 6 g), **fibre** 2 g

✓✓✓ B₁₂

✓✓ A, B₆, C, folate, phosphorus, iron, zinc

✓   B₁, B₂, E, niacin, calcium, copper, potassium, selenium

1 Heat the oil in a large saucepan or flameproof casserole. Add the onions, garlic and ginger, and fry for about 15 minutes, stirring frequently, until the onions are golden.

2 Stir in the chilli, paprika, cumin, coriander, white pepper, cinnamon, crushed cardamom seeds, bay leaves and salt. Stir briefly over a moderate heat, then stir in the yogurt and 150 ml (5 fl oz) water. Add the lamb, mix well and cover the pan. Simmer gently for 1¼ hours or until the lamb is tender.

3 Add the tomatoes, spinach and chopped coriander. Cook for 2–3 minutes, stirring, until the tomatoes have softened slightly and the spinach has wilted. Taste for seasoning and remove the bay leaf. Serve garnished with fresh coriander.

Some more ideas

● The basic curry sauce in this recipe can be used to cook other meats or vegetables. Cubes of skinless boneless chicken or turkey breast (fillet) are delicious, as are lean boneless pork chops. All of these need only 40 minutes simmering in the sauce to cook. A mixture of vegetables – halved new potatoes, cauliflower florets, sliced carrots and chunks of parsnip – is good too. Use 500 g (1 lb 2 oz) total weight and cook for 30 minutes.

● To make a refreshing fresh chutney to serve with the curry, finely chop and mix together 4 plum tomatoes, ½ cucumber, 1 small onion, 1 seeded fresh green chilli and 4 tbsp chopped fresh coriander.

Plus points

● Onions contain a type of dietary fibre called fructoligosaccarides (FOS), which is also found in chicory, leeks, garlic, Jerusalem artichokes, asparagus, barley and bananas. It is thought to stimulate the growth of friendly bacteria in the gut while inhibiting bad bacteria.

● Cardamom is believed to help relieve digestive problems such as indigestion, flatulence and stomach cramps, and it can help prevent acid regurgitation and belching.

Main meals

Lamb burgers with fruity relish

The advantage of making your own burgers is that you know exactly what's in them – and with good lean meat they can make a healthy meal. A fruity relish, full of vitamin C, adds a fresh flavour to these juicy burgers. Serve with a green or mixed salad.

Serves 4

400 g (14 oz) lean minced lamb

1 carrot, about 125 g (4½ oz), grated

1 small onion, finely chopped

50 g (1¾ oz) fresh wholemeal breadcrumbs

pinch of freshly grated nutmeg

2 tsp fresh thyme leaves or 1 tsp dried thyme

1 large egg, beaten

2 tsp extra virgin olive oil

4 wholemeal baps, weighing about
    55 g (2 oz) each

salt and pepper

shredded lettuce to garnish

Orange and raspberry relish

1 orange

100 g (3½ oz) fresh or thawed frozen
    raspberries

2 tsp demerara sugar

Preparation and cooking time: 30 minutes

Each serving provides

kcal 390, **protein** 29 g, **fat** 13 g (of which saturated fat 5 g), **carbohydrate** 40 g (of which sugars 12 g), **fibre** 6 g

✓✓✓	A, B₁₂
✓✓	B₁, B₆, C, niacin, copper, iron, selenium, zinc
✓	B₂, folate, calcium, potassium

1 Preheat the grill. Put the lamb into a large bowl. Add the carrot, onion, breadcrumbs, nutmeg and thyme, and season with salt and pepper to taste. Mix roughly with a spoon. Add the egg and use your hands to mix the ingredients together thoroughly.

2 Divide the mixture into 4 and shape each portion into a burger about 10–12 cm (4–5 in) in diameter, or about 2.5 cm (1 in) bigger than the diameter of the baps. Brush both sides of the burgers with oil, then put them in the grill pan. Cook for 4–5 minutes on each side, depending on thickness.

3 Meanwhile, make the relish. Cut the peel and pith from the orange with a sharp knife and, holding it over a bowl to catch the juice, cut between the membrane to release the segments. Roughly chop the segments and add them to the juice. Add the raspberries and sugar, lightly crushing the fruit with a fork to mix it together.

4 Split the baps and toast briefly under the grill. Put a lamb burger in each bap and add some lettuce to garnish and a good spoonful of relish. Serve with the remaining relish.

Another idea

● Make turkey burgers with an orange and summer fruit relish. Use minced turkey instead of lamb, and flavour with the zest of ½ lemon and 4 tbsp chopped parsley in place of the nutmeg and thyme; omit the breadcrumbs. Serve in toasted sesame buns, with rocket leaves and a relish made by simmering 100 g (3½ oz) frozen summer fruits for about 3 minutes or until thawed, and mixing with 1 tbsp caster sugar and the chopped orange.

Plus points

● Although lamb still tends to contain more fat than other meats, changes in breeding, feeding and butchery techniques mean that lean cuts only contain about one-third of the fat that similar cuts contained 20 years ago. More of the fat is monounsaturated, which is good news for healthy hearts.

● Using wholemeal baps instead of white ones doubles the amount of fibre intake. The bread also provides B-complex vitamins, iron and calcium.

● A fruity relish gives a huge bonus of protective antioxidants. It also provides useful amounts of potassium and fibre, especially from the raspberries.

Main meals

Hotpot with golden parsnips

The influence of the Middle-East brings beans, aubergines, apricots, garlic and warm spices to this lamb hotpot. The topping is in traditional British style – a golden layer of parsnip slices - which is low in calories and supplies more vitamins.

Serves 6

115 g (4 oz) dried black-eyed beans, soaked overnight

2 tbsp extra virgin olive oil

2 onions, sliced

1 garlic clove, chopped

500 g (1 lb 2 oz) boneless leg of lamb, cut into 2.5 cm (1 in) cubes

1 large aubergine, cubed

115 g (4 oz) ready-to-eat dried apricots, quartered

2 carrots, diced

225 g (8 oz) turnips, diced

½ tsp ground cinnamon

1 tsp ground cumin

1 tsp ground coriander

675 g (1½ lb) parsnips, thinly sliced

about 900 ml (1½ pints) vegetable stock, preferably home-made

salt and pepper

sprigs of fresh flat-leaf parsley to garnish

Preparation time: 30 minutes, plus overnight soaking

Cooking time: 1½ hours

Each serving provides

kcal 375, **protein** 25 g, **fat** 15 g (of which saturated fat 5 g), **carbohydrate** 38 g (of which sugars 19 g), **fibre** 10 g

✓✓✓	B_{12}
✓✓	A, B_1, C, E, folate, copper, iron, zinc
✓	B_6, niacin, calcium, potassium

1 Preheat the oven to 160°C (325°F, gas mark 3). Drain the soaked black-eyed beans and place them in a saucepan. Add cold water to cover, bring to the boil and boil rapidly for 10 minutes, then drain well. Set aside.

2 Reserve 1 tsp of the oil and heat the remainder in a large flameproof casserole. Add the onions and garlic, and cook for 2–3 minutes or until softened. Add the lamb and cook for about 5 minutes, stirring frequently, until browned. (If you do not have a suitable flameproof casserole, cook the onions and lamb in a frying pan, then transfer to an ovenproof dish. Bring the stock to the boil in the pan before pouring it into the dish.)

3 Stir in the aubergine, apricots, carrots, turnips, cinnamon, cumin and coriander, with seasoning to taste. Add the black-eyed beans and stir well.

4 Arrange the parsnip slices in a thick layer on top of the hotpot, slightly overlapping them, then pour in sufficient stock to come just below the surface of the parsnips. Bring to the boil, then cover the casserole and transfer to the oven. Cook for 1½ hours.

5 Preheat the grill. Brush the reserved 1 tsp of oil over the parsnips and place under the grill to crisp the top. Serve hot, garnished with parsley sprigs.

Plus points

● A high proportion of vegetables, pulses and additional flavouring ingredients can extend a modest portion of lean meat into a heart-healthy dish.

● Dried apricots are a valuable source of many minerals – phosphorus, potassium and iron – as well as fibre.

● Eaten in moderation, red meat, such as lamb or beef, makes a valuable contribution in a well-balanced diet. As well as being high in protein, meat provides zinc and iron in a form that is readily absorbed by the body. Red meat also provides most of the B vitamins.

Some more ideas

● Use other varieties of beans, such as red kidney beans, borlotti beans or pinto beans, instead of the black-eyed beans.

● Add the grated zest and juice of 1 large orange with the spices.

● Replace the aubergine with 450 g (1 lb) pumpkin, butternut squash or kabocha squash flesh, cut into large cubes.

Main meals

Mediterranean stuffed vegetables

An array of colourful stuffed vegetables can make an appetising and satisfying main dish. The mixture of lean lamb, fresh vegetables and rice makes this a very balanced and healthy main course. Lots of French bread and a mixed leaf salad complete the meal.

Serves 4

100 g (3½ oz) long-grain rice

250 g (8½ oz) lean minced lamb

1 onion, chopped

4 peppers

4 beefsteak tomatoes, ripe but firm

2 large courgettes, about 225 g (8 oz) each

1 tbsp extra virgin olive oil

3 garlic cloves, coarsely chopped

170 g (6 oz) baby spinach leaves

2 tbsp shredded fresh basil

1 egg, lightly beaten

salt and pepper

To serve

2–3 tbsp shredded fresh basil

Preparation time: 45 minutes

Cooking time: 45–50 minutes

Each serving provides

kcal 324, **protein** 21 g, **fat** 15 g (of which saturated fat 5 g), **carbohydrate** 27 g (of which sugars 18 g), **fibre** 7 g

✓✓✓	A, B₁, B₆, B₁₂, C, E, folate, niacin, zinc
✓✓	B₂, iron, potassium
✓	calcium

1 Cook the rice in a saucepan of boiling water for 10–12 minutes, or according to the packet instructions, until tender. Drain.

2 While the rice is cooking, put the lamb and onion in a non-stick frying pan and fry until the lamb is lightly browned and cooked through and the onion has softened. Turn and break up the meat as it cooks so it browns evenly. Place a sieve over a bowl and tip the meat into it. The fat will drip through and can be discarded.

3 Cut each pepper in half lengthways through the stalk and remove the core and seed. Cut the tops (stalk end) off the tomatoes and hollow out the insides. Chop the tops and hollowed-out flesh and place in a bowl with any tomato juices. Cut the courgettes in half lengthways and hollow out the centres to leave shells 5 mm (¼ in) thick. Chop the hollowed-out courgette flesh and add it to the chopped tomatoes.

4 Preheat the oven to 180ºC (350ºF, gas mark 4). Heat the olive oil in a non-stick frying pan, add the garlic and chopped vegetables, and cook, stirring, until they soften slightly. Add the spinach and cook over a moderate heat for a minute or so until wilted. Remove from the heat and add the basil, rice and lamb. Add the egg, season with salt and pepper to taste and mix well.

5 Spoon the stuffing into the pepper, tomato and courgette shells. Arrange the peppers and courgettes in a single layer in 1 or 2 roasting tins. The vegetables should not be too crowded together. Cover with foil or a lid and roast for 15 minutes. Add the tomatoes and continue roasting for 15 minutes or until the vegetables are almost tender.

6 Uncover the vegetables and roast for a further 15–20 minutes or until they are tender and the tops are lightly browned. Serve either warm or cool, sprinkled with the shredded fresh basil.

Plus points

• Peppers, tomatoes, courgettes and spinach are high in phytochemicals and antioxidant vitamins. They all contain beta-carotene whose antioxidant properties help to protect cells from damage by free radicals produced in the body in response to stress.

• Courgettes belong to the same family as melons, pumpkins and cucumber. Their skin is particularly rich in beta-carotene, and they also provide niacin and vitamin B₆.

Main meals

Another idea

• Make Middle Eastern-style stuffed vegetables. Use brown rice instead of white rice and combine it with the fried lamb and onion. Add 3 thinly sliced spring onions, 3 chopped garlic cloves, 2 tbsp each chopped fresh dill and mint, ½ tsp ground cumin, a good pinch of ground cinnamon, 3 tbsp plain low-fat yogurt, 2 tbsp raisins, the juice of ½ lemon, and salt and pepper to taste. Cut 2 aubergines in half lengthways and steam for 5 minutes or until just tender. Leave until cool enough to handle, then hollow them out, leaving shells about 5 mm (¼ in) thick. Dice the flesh and add it to the rice and lamb mixture. Blanch 4 large Savoy cabbage leaves for 30–60 seconds or until pliable. Arrange the aubergine shells in a roasting tin and spoon in some of the filling. Roll the rest of the filling in the cabbage leaves and place in the tin. Mix 1 can chopped tomatoes, about 225 g, and their juices with 120 ml (4 fl oz) lamb or vegetable stock and spoon around the vegetables. Cover the tin with foil. Roast for 30 minutes. Uncover and continue roasting for 15–20 minutes or until the tops of the vegetables are tinged a light brown. Serve hot or cool, garnished with chopped fresh mint.

Gingered roast pork

Roast pork with apple sauce, an all-time favourite, is given a new twist in this dish inspired by German cuisine, and is kept healthy by using stock instead of fat. It is absolutely delicious served with roast or jacket baked potatoes and seasonal green vegetables.

Serves 6

900 g (2 lb) boned loin of pork without skin, trimmed of fat

3 dessert apples

1 small onion, finely chopped

75 g (2½ oz) ready-to-eat prunes, chopped

75 g (2½ oz) gingersnap biscuits, crushed

1 egg yolk

300 ml (10 fl oz) chicken stock

200 ml (7 fl oz) dry white wine

4 tbsp extra virgin olive oil

900 g (2 lb) parsnips, quartered

1 tbsp clear honey

500 g (1 lb 2 oz) shallots

salt and pepper

Apple sauce

500 g (1 lb 2 oz) cooking apples, peeled, cored and chopped

2.5 cm (1 in) piece fresh root ginger, finely chopped

2 tbsp caster sugar

Preparation time: 1¼ hours

Cooking time: 2 hours

Each serving provides

kcal 391, **protein** 8 g, **fat** 12 g (of which saturated fat 3 g), **carbohydrate** 60 g (of which sugars 43 g), **fibre** 12 g

✓✓✓	B₁, B₂, B₆, C, E, folate, niacin
✓✓	potassium
✓	B₂, calcium, iron, zinc

1 Preheat the oven to 180°C (350°F, gas mark 4). Place the pork, skinned side down, on a chopping board. Slit the joint lengthways, cutting two-thirds of the way through the meat, then open it out like a book.

2 Peel, core and finely chop 1 of the dessert apples, then mix with the onion, prunes, biscuits, egg yolk and seasoning to taste. Spoon onto the pork, spreading evenly, then press the joint back together. Tie into a neat shape with fine string.

3 Put the joint, skinned side up, into a roasting tin and pour in the stock and wine. Cover the tin with foil, twisting the ends tightly over the edges. Put into the oven and roast for 2 hours.

4 After 45 minutes, heat the oil in a second roasting tin on the shelf above the pork for 5 minutes. Add the parsnips and put to roast, turning them once or twice.

5 Meanwhile, make the apple sauce. Put the apples, ginger, sugar and 2 tbsp water into a small saucepan. Cover and simmer, stirring occasionally, for 10 minutes or until pulpy. Remove from the heat and set aside.

6 When the pork has been cooking for 1¼ hours, remove the foil and drizzle the meat with the honey. Add the shallots to the parsnips, toss together and continue roasting.

7 About 20 minutes before the end of the cooking time, peel, core and thickly slice the remaining 2 dessert apples, then add them to the vegetables.

8 Transfer the pork to a carving board, cover with foil and keep warm. Strain the cooking liquid into a saucepan, then skim off any fat. Boil the cooking liquid, stirring constantly, for 2 minutes. Pour into a sauceboat. Carve the pork and serve immediately, with the roasted vegetables, apple sauce and gravy.

Plus points

• Prunes supply useful amounts of iron, potassium and vitamin B₆, and they also contain fibre, which helps to prevent constipation. Prune juice contains an ingredient that has an additional laxative effect, which is why some people drink the juice rather than eat the fruit itself.

• Apples are relatively low in calories and contain a high proportion of fructose, a simple sugar that is sweeter than sucrose (table sugar) and metabolised more slowly, so helping to control blood sugar levels.

Some more ideas

• Instead of fresh pork use smoked pork loin, which is slightly milder and sweeter than smoked gammon. Look for it in the cooked meats section of large supermarkets, or ask your butcher if he can get it for you.

• Spice the pork and sauce with cardamom rather than ginger. In the stuffing, substitute fresh breadcrumbs for the gingersnap biscuits and 85 g (3 oz) chopped ready-to-eat dried apricots for the diced apple and add the seeds of 4 crushed cardamom pods. In the apple sauce replace the ginger with the seeds of 6–8 crushed cardamom pods. Serve the cardamom pork with spiced roast vegetables: add 500 g (1 lb 2 oz) potatoes, peeled and cut in chunks, to the parsnips. Toss in the hot oil, then sprinkle with 1 tsp each crushed coriander and cumin seeds and turmeric.

• For an alternative accompaniment, stir-fry 500 g (1 lb 2 oz) finely shredded red cabbage in 1 tbsp sunflower oil for 5 minutes. Add 2 diced dessert apples, 3 tbsp wine vinegar, 3 tbsp water, 2 tbsp honey and salt and pepper to taste. Mix together, cover and simmer for 4–5 minutes.

• As a change from roast vegetables, serve with puréed celeriac. Cook 900 g (2 lb) diced celeriac in boiling water for 15 minutes, then mash or purée with 4 tbsp milk and seasoning.

Goulash in a hurry

This rich, short-cut version of classic Hungarian goulash keeps the calories low. Lean pork, red cabbage and green pepper taste excellent with the traditional flavourings of paprika and caraway seeds. Serve rice or noodles and a simple green salad alongside.

Serves 4

2 tbsp extra virgin olive oil

1 large onion, finely chopped

2 garlic cloves, crushed

3 thick lean pork loin steaks, about 300 g
   (10½ oz) total weight, cut into thin strips

1 tbsp plain flour

1 can tomatoes, about 800 g

120 ml (4 fl oz) extra dry white vermouth

2 tbsp paprika

1 tsp caraway seeds

1 tsp caster sugar

1 pork or chicken stock cube, crumbled

1 large green pepper, seeded and chopped

200 g (7 oz) red cabbage, finely shredded

salt and pepper

To serve

4 tbsp Greek-style yogurt

paprika

fresh chives

Preparation time: 10 minutes
Cooking time: about 20 minutes

Each serving provides

kcal 280, **protein** 21 g, **fat** 13 g (of which saturated fat 3.5 g), **carbohydrate** 16 g (of which sugars 12 g), **fibre** 4 g

✓✓✓	B₁₂, C
✓✓	B₁, B₆
✓	folate, niacin, iron, selenium, zinc

1 Heat the oil in a large frying pan or saucepan. Add the onion, garlic and pork, and cook over a high heat for about 3 minutes or until the meat has changed colour and become firm and the onion is slightly softened. Meanwhile, blend the flour with 4 tbsp juice from the canned tomatoes to make a smooth paste; set aside.

2 Add the vermouth, paprika, caraway seeds and sugar to the pan and stir, then add the tomatoes with the rest of their juice, breaking them up as you mix them in. Stir in the stock cube, and the flour and tomato juice mixture. Bring to the boil, stirring, and cook until the juices thicken.

3 Stir in the green pepper and red cabbage until both are thoroughly coated in the cooking juices. Reduce the heat, cover the pan and simmer the goulash for about 15 minutes or until the meat is cooked and the vegetables are just tender, but still slightly crisp.

4 Taste the goulash and season with salt and pepper, if necessary. Ladle the goulash into bowls and top each portion with a spoonful of Greek-style yogurt and a sprinkle of paprika. Garnish with chives and serve.

Some more ideas

● To make a vegetarian goulash, omit the pork and red cabbage. Cut 1 aubergine into large chunks and add to the softened onion and garlic in step 1 with 6 halved sun-dried tomatoes, 2 thickly sliced celery sticks and 2 thickly sliced courgettes. Follow the main recipe, using a vegetable stock cube or 2 tsp bouillon powder or paste. Simmer for 25 minutes or until the vegetables are tender, then stir in 1 can chickpeas, about 400 g, and 1 can red kidney beans, about 200 g, both well drained. Cook for a further 5 minutes. Serve the goulash topped with Greek-style yogurt or soured cream.

● Halved small new potatoes are good in the vegetarian version, above. Add them with the other vegetables and leave out the canned red kidney beans.

Plus points

● Several studies have shown that eating garlic can reduce the risk of heart attack and stroke by making the blood less sticky and likely to clot. Garlic can also help to reduce high blood pressure.

● As the red cabbage is cooked in the dish, the vitamin C from this vegetable is retained in the juice. Cabbage is thought to offer some protection from cancer.

Spiced pork with sweet potatoes

Try this modern casserole for a healthy example of fusion cooking, marrying ingredients and flavours from diverse cuisines. Here, oriental spices, sweet potatoes and fruit go very well with the pork. A simple green salad makes a refreshing accompaniment.

Serves 4

1 tbsp sunflower oil

4 pork loin steaks or boneless pork chops, about 140 g (5 oz) each, trimmed of fat

1 red onion, coarsely chopped

2 celery sticks, chopped

1 large orange-fleshed sweet potato, about 400 g (14 oz), peeled and cut into sticks

150 ml (5 fl oz) sweetened cranberry juice

150 ml (5 fl oz) chicken stock, preferably home-made

1 piece of preserved stem ginger, drained and cut into fine sticks

1 tbsp thick-cut orange marmalade

1 tbsp dry sherry

1 tsp Chinese five-spice powder

2 star anise

4 plum tomatoes, quartered lengthways

salt and pepper

3 spring onions, shredded, to garnish

Preparation time: 30 minutes

Cooking time: about 30 minutes

1 Heat the oil in a large flameproof casserole or deep sauté pan. Add the pork steaks and brown them for 3–4 minutes on each side. Transfer the pork to a plate and set aside.

2 Add the onion and celery to the oil remaining in the casserole and cook, stirring, over a moderate heat for 2–3 minutes. Add the sweet potato, cover the pan and sweat the vegetables for 3–4 minutes or until softened.

3 Stir in the cranberry juice drink, stock, ginger, marmalade, sherry, five-spice powder, star anise and a little salt and pepper. Bring to the boil, then reduce the heat and return the pork to the casserole. Cover and cook gently for 15 minutes.

4 Add the tomatoes to the casserole, cover and cook gently for a further 5 minutes or until the tomatoes are lightly cooked, but still hold their shape. Taste for seasoning, adding more salt and pepper if necessary, and serve, garnished with spring onions.

Some more ideas

● Add 400 g (14 oz) cubed pumpkin or butternut squash instead of the sweet potato, and 1 small bulb of fennel, chopped, instead of the celery sticks.

● Tomato rice goes well with this casserole. Bring 200 ml (7 fl oz) water to the boil and add 225 g (8 oz) rinsed Basmati rice, 1 can chopped tomatoes, about 400 g, with the juice and 4 chopped sun-dried tomatoes. Cover and cook gently for 10 minutes or until the rice is tender and has absorbed all the water.

● For a rich fruit casserole, add 200 g (7 oz) pitted, ready-to-eat prunes and 2 cored and thickly sliced dessert apples instead of the tomatoes. Omit the sherry.

Plus points

● Sweet potatoes have a delicious natural sweetness that intensifies during storage and cooking. Although they contain slightly more calories than ordinary white potatoes – sweet potatoes have 87 kcal per 100 g (3½ oz), white potatoes 75 kcal – they are low in fat.

● Sweet potatoes are also an excellent source of beta-carotene and they provide good amounts of vitamins C and E.

● Lean pork has a lower fat content than beef or lamb. It is a good source of zinc and provides useful amounts of iron.

Each serving provides

kcal 340, **protein** 34 g, **fat** 9 g (of which saturated fat 2 g), **carbohydrate** 32 g (of which sugars 16 g), **fibre** 4 g

✓✓✓	B₁, C
✓✓	A, B₆, B₁₂, E, iron, phosphorus, zinc
✓	B₂, folate, niacin, selenium

Main meals

181

Pork steaks with mustard sauce

This delectable dish is surprisingly easy to make. Steam the carrots over the pan of potatoes, with the cabbage added after a few minutes, to keep the nutrional value high. Serve with boiled potatoes sprinkled with chives, carrots and shredded Savoy cabbage.

Serves 4

1 tsp extra virgin olive oil

4 boneless pork loin steaks or chops,
    1.5–2 cm (⅝–¾ in) thick, about 550 g
    (1¼ lb) in total, trimmed of all fat

4 tbsp dry white wine or vermouth

1 garlic clove, finely chopped

170 ml (6 fl oz) chicken or vegetable stock

2 tsp cornflour mixed with 1 tbsp water

120 ml (4 fl oz) crème fraîche

1 tbsp Dijon mustard

1 tbsp chopped fresh tarragon

salt and pepper

fresh chives to garnish

Preparation and cooking time: 30 minutes

Each serving provides

kcal 325, **protein** 31 g, **fat** 20 g (of which saturated fat 7 g), **carbohydrate** 4 g (of which sugars 1 g), **fibre** 0 g

✓✓✓	B₁
✓✓	B₆, B₁₂, niacin, zinc
✓	B₂, iron, selenium

1 Heat the oil in a non-stick frying pan over a moderately high heat. Add the pork steaks and fry for 3 minutes on each side or until well browned. Put the pork steaks on a plate, and keep on one side.

2 Add the wine or vermouth to the frying pan with the garlic and let it bubble briefly, then pour in the stock and boil for 2 minutes. Stir together the cornflour mixture and crème fraîche until smooth. Add to the hot cooking liquid, stirring well. Simmer gently for 2 minutes, stirring constantly, until thickened and smooth. Stir in the mustard and tarragon, and season with salt and pepper to taste.

3 Return the pork steaks to the sauce. Reduce the heat to low, cover the pan and cook for 4–5 minutes or until the steaks are cooked through.

4 Arrange the pork steaks on warm plates and spoon the sauce over. Garnish with chives and serve at once.

Another idea

● Grill the steaks or chops and serve with a cabbage, apple and onion braise. Brush the steaks with a little extra virgin olive oil and cook under a preheated moderate grill for about 7 minutes on each side or until tender and well browned. Meanwhile, heat 1 tbsp extra virgin olive oil in a large, deep frying pan over a moderate heat and add 1 large red onion,

sliced, 2 apples, cored and cut in eighths, and 450 g (1 lb) shredded Savoy cabbage (about ½ head). Toss to mix well, then cover and cook for about 4 minutes or until lightly browned, stirring occasionally. Moisten with 3–4 tbsp apple juice and continue cooking, covered, until wilted and just tender, stirring frequently.

Plus points

● In the past, pork had a reputation for being rather fatty, but this is no longer the case. Over the last 20 years, in response to consumer demands for leaner meat, farmers have been breeding leaner pigs. While now containing considerably less fat, pork also contains higher levels of the 'good' polyunsaturated fats. The average fat content of lean pork is less than 3%, which is much the same as that of a chicken breast.

● Garlic was first used as a medicine at least 4000 years ago – the ancient Egyptians used it to treat infections and headaches, and Roman soldiers who marched across Europe to Britain wedged garlic cloves between their toes to help prevent athlete's foot. Allicin, the compound that gives garlic its characteristic smell and taste, acts as a powerful antibiotic and has anti-viral and anti-fungal properties.

Main meals

Sticky spare ribs

Here pork spare ribs are simmered to tenderise the meat and remove some of the fat, before being roasted in a delicious orange and mustard glaze. Choose the meatiest ribs you can find. Remember to put out finger bowls and napkins for cleaning sticky fingers.

Makes 12 spare ribs

12 meaty pork spare ribs, about 900 g (2 lb) in total
3 tbsp red wine vinegar
2 tsp sunflower oil
large strip of orange zest
150 ml (5 fl oz) orange juice
1 tbsp tomato purée
2 tbsp dark soft brown sugar
2 tbsp Worcestershire sauce
1 tbsp French mustard
½–1 tsp chilli powder, or to taste

Preparation time: 30 minutes
Cooking time: 40–45 minutes

1 Preheat the oven to 200°C (400°F, gas mark 6). Trim as much fat as possible off the spare ribs, then put them in a saucepan. Cover with cold water and add 2 tbsp of the vinegar. Bring to the boil, then simmer for 20 minutes, skimming the surface from time to time.

2 Meanwhile, combine the remaining 1 tbsp vinegar, the oil, orange zest and juice, tomato purée, brown sugar, Worcestershire sauce, mustard and chilli powder in a small pan and bring to the boil. Simmer for 4–5 minutes or until slightly reduced.

3 Drain the ribs and arrange them in a single layer in a large roasting tin. Pour over the orange mixture and turn the ribs to coat them evenly. Loosely cover with foil and roast for 20 minutes.

4 Remove the foil and roast for a further 20–25 minutes, turning and basting occasionally, until the ribs are dark brown and sticky. Transfer to a large serving dish and serve warm.

Some more ideas

● For Oriental spare ribs, make the glaze from 2 tsp grated fresh root ginger, 3 tbsp clear honey, 1 tbsp tomato purée, 2 tbsp dark soy sauce, 2 tbsp rice wine or dry sherry, 2 tbsp hoisin sauce, 2 tsp sherry vinegar and 1 tsp chilli sauce.

● Try a Cajun dry rub instead of a glaze. Mix together 2 tbsp paprika, 2 tsp ground cumin, 1 tsp dried thyme, ¼ tsp black pepper, ½ tsp cayenne pepper and 2 finely chopped garlic cloves. Simmer the ribs as in the main recipe, then drain, cool slightly and coat in the rub before roasting.

Plus points

● Pork is an excellent source of the B vitamins, particularly vitamin B_{12}, which is needed for all growth and the division of cells and for red-blood formation.

● Spare ribs are one of the fattier cuts of pork. Trimming off any visible fat, simmering in water and then roasting until crisp are clever ways to reduce their fat content.

Each spare rib provides

kcal 90, **protein** 7.5 g, **fat** 4 g (of which saturated fat 1 g), **carbohydrate** 6 g (of which sugars 6 g), **fibre** 0.1 g

✓ B_1, B_6, B_{12}, E, niacin, calcium, zinc

Main meals

Side dishes and breads

Whatever you add to a main course should both complement the food and supply extra nutrients. Vitamin-rich vegetables, which help protect against disease, can be served quite plain or combined to create delicious side dishes such as Sesame greens and bean sprouts or Roasted pepper salad. Rice and grains also play their part and warm home-made bread, whether basic or fancy, is sure to win praise.

Basil-scented sautéed vegetables

A large non-stick frying pan is ideal for sautéeing, the Western equivalent of stir-frying. Based on quick cooking over high heat, this method preserves colour while bringing out flavour. This vegetable dish goes very well with fish, poultry, meat and noodles.

Serves 4

500 g (1 lb 2 oz) broccoli
1 tbsp extra virgin olive oil
3–4 large garlic cloves, thinly sliced (optional)
1 large or 2 small red peppers, seeded and
   cut into chunks
1 turnip, about 150 g (5½ oz), cut into
   bite-sized chunks
pinch of sugar
8 sprigs of fresh basil, stalks discarded, then
   finely shredded
salt

Preparation time: 10 minutes
Cooking time: 7–8 minutes

1 Cut the broccoli into small florets; trim and thinly slice the stalks. Heat the olive oil in a large non-stick frying pan or wok. Add the garlic, if using, the red pepper, turnip and slices of broccoli stalk. Sprinkle in the sugar and salt to taste. Cook for 2–3 minutes, turning frequently.

2 Add the broccoli florets and stir. Pour in 6 tbsp of water to provide a thin covering on the bottom of the pan. Cover and cook over a fairly high heat for 3–4 minutes. The broccoli should be just tender and bright green.

3 Stir in the basil, replace the lid and leave on the heat for a few more seconds. Serve immediately.

Some more ideas

● For a Far-Eastern flavour, substitute 8 canned water chestnuts, drained and quartered or halved, for the turnips, and add 1 tsp chopped fresh root ginger and ½ fresh green or red chilli, seeded and finely chopped, with the broccoli florets. Increase the quantity of sugar to 1–2 tsp. At the end of cooking, add 1 tbsp chopped fresh coriander with the basil.

● Sugarsnap peas or mange-tout can be used instead of the broccoli. They will cook in 1–2 minutes and there is no need to add the water. Serve with lemon or lime wedges so that the juice can be squeezed over the vegetables.

● As well as replacing the broccoli with sugarsnap peas, use yellow peppers in place of red. Omit the garlic. Substitute tiny parboiled new potatoes, halved, for the turnip and sprinkle generously with fresh tarragon leaves rather than basil. This combination of sautéed vegetables is delicious with fish, especially grilled mackerel or salmon.

Plus points

● Broccoli, one of the brassicas, is a good source of the phytochemicals called glucosinolates. Red pepper is a rich source of the antioxidant beta-carotene which the body can convert into vitamin A. Both of these vegetables can help to fight cancer and prevent heart disease.

● In addition to providing fibre, turnips contain the B vitamins niacin and B_6, and are a surprisingly useful source of vitamin C.

Each serving provides Ⓥ

kcal 90, **protein** 6 g, **fat** 4 g (of which saturated fat 1 g), **carbohydrate** 7 g (of which sugars 7 g), **fibre** 5 g

✓✓✓	A, C
✓✓	E, folate
✓	niacin, iron

Side dishes and breads

New potatoes with nori

From the same botanical family known as laver in Wales, slouk in Scotland and sloke in Ireland, nori is a type of Japanese seaweed, sold dried in thin, dark-green sheets. The flavour is distinctive and savoury and goes well with potatoes.

Serves 4
500 g (1 lb 2 oz) new potatoes
30 g (1 oz) butter
grated zest and juice of ½ small lemon
1 sheet toasted sushi nori, about 20 x 18 cm (8 x 7 in)
2 tbsp snipped fresh chives
salt and pepper

Preparation time: 5 minutes
Cooking time: 15 minutes

1 Put the new potatoes in a saucepan, cover with boiling water and bring back to the boil. Cook for 12 minutes or until they are just tender.

2 Reserve 3 tbsp cooking water from the potatoes, then drain them and return them to the saucepan with the reserved water. Add the butter and lemon zest and juice. Turn the potatoes to coat them with the liquid.

3 Use scissors to snip the sushi nori into fine strips. Scatter the nori over the potatoes and cover the pan. Cook over a low heat for 1–2 minutes or until the nori has softened. Add seasoning to taste. Sprinkle with the chives and serve immediately.

Some more ideas
● Sushi nori is rather like parchment paper in texture. Toasted or roasted sushi nori has been toasted briefly and seasoned. It is shiny and almost black in colour – untoasted nori is slightly paler (more green) in colour. To toast nori, pass the sheet over the flame of a gas hob, once on each side of the sheet, or lay the sheet on a rack in a grill pan and place under a preheated grill for a few seconds. The sheet will darken and give off its aroma very quickly – take care not to overcook the nori or it will burn.
● Green beans go well with lemon and potatoes, and can be added to the dish or used to replace the nori. Snip 200 g (7 oz) French beans into short pieces and add them to the potatoes about halfway through the cooking: 4–5 minutes is sufficient time for cooking the beans. Drain and toss with the butter and lemon zest and juice.
● Look out for yard-long or asparagus beans, which, as their name suggests, grow to an amazing length. Their flavour is similar to that of runner beans and they are good with the potatoes and nori. Prepare them as for green beans (above).

Each serving provides Ⓥ
kcal 160, **protein** 6 g, **fat** 7 g (of which saturated fat 4 g), **carbohydrate** 20 g (of which sugars 2 g), **fibre** 7 g

✓✓✓	B₁₂
✓✓	A, B₆, C, E
✓	B₁, B₂, copper, iron, potassium, zinc

Plus points
● Nori is rich in vitamin A and minerals, including potassium, which helps to counteract the effects of sodium and keep blood pressure down. Nori also contains iron, zinc, copper and iodine.
● New potatoes and lemon juice contribute vitamin C, which promotes absorption of iron from the nori.

Side dishes and breads

191

Under
300 calories

Roast root vegetables with herbs

Use this recipe as a guide for roasting single vegetables, such as potatoes or parsnips, as well as for a superb dish of mixed roots. They are delicious with roast poultry or meat – or with vegetarian main dishes and lightly baked fish.

Serves 4

1 kg (2¼ lb) root vegetables, such as
    potatoes, sweet potatoes, carrots, parsnips,
    swede and kohlrabi
225 g (8 oz) shallots or pickling onions
2 tbsp extra virgin olive oil
1 tsp coarse sea salt
1 tsp cracked black peppercorns
few sprigs of fresh thyme
few sprigs of fresh rosemary
sprigs of fresh thyme or rosemary to garnish
    (optional)

Preparation time: 15–20 minutes
Cooking time: 30–35 minutes

1 Preheat the oven to 220°C (425°F, gas mark 7). Scrub or peel the vegetables, according to type and your taste. Halve or quarter large potatoes. Cut large carrots or parsnips in half lengthways, then cut the pieces across in half again. Cut swede or kohlrabi into large chunks (about the same size as the potatoes). Leave shallots or onions whole.

2 Place the vegetables in a saucepan and pour in enough boiling water to cover them. Bring back to the boil, then reduce the heat and simmer for 5–7 minutes or until the vegetables are lightly cooked, but not yet tender.

3 Drain the vegetables and place them in a roasting tin. Brush with the oil and sprinkle with the salt and peppercorns. Add the herb sprigs to the tin and place in the oven.

4 Roast for 30–35 minutes or until the vegetables are golden brown, crisp and tender. Turn the vegetables over halfway through the cooking. Serve hot, garnished with sprigs of thyme or rosemary, if liked.

Some more ideas

● The vegetables can be roasted at the same time as a joint of meat or poultry. Allow 45 minutes at 200°C (400°F, gas mark 6), or longer at a lower temperature, if necessary.

● Baby new vegetables can also be roasted. For example, try new potatoes, carrots, beetroot and turnips. As well as root vegetables, patty pan squash and asparagus are delicious roasted. Sprinkle with herbs and a little balsamic vinegar or lemon juice.

● Quartered acorn squash is good roasted with mixed root vegetables.

Plus points

● Combining different root vegetables instead of serving roast potatoes alone provides a good mix of flavours and nutrients: as well as vitamin C from the potatoes and beta-carotene from the carrots, swedes are part of the brassica family, which offer cancer-fighting phytochemicals.

● All these vegetables provide plenty of flavour and satisfying bulk, so portions of meat can be modest. They also contribute dietary fibre.

Each serving provides Ⓥ

kcal 200, **protein** 4 g, **fat** 7 g (of which saturated fat 1 g), **carbohydrate** 33 g (of which sugars 14 g), **fibre** 7 g

✓✓✓	A, C
✓✓	B₁, B₆, E, folate
✓	niacin, potassium

Side dishes and breads

193

Cauliflower with crispy crumbs

The crispy golden topping in this dish is usually made by frying the breadcrumbs in a generous quantity of butter. This low-fat version uses a modest portion of olive oil and fresh herbs to flavour a topping that contrasts particularly well with steamed cauliflower.

Serves 4

1 cauliflower, trimmed and broken into
   florets

Crispy crumb topping

2 tbsp extra virgin olive oil

100 g (3½ oz) fresh breadcrumbs

1 tbsp chopped fresh thyme

1 tbsp chopped fresh tarragon

2 tbsp chopped parsley

salt and pepper

sprigs of fresh herbs to garnish (optional)

Preparation time: 10 minutes
Cooking time: 15 minutes

1 Prepare a saucepan of boiling water with a steamer on top. Steam the cauliflower for about 15 minutes or until tender but not soft.

2 Meanwhile, heat the oil in a non-stick frying pan or saucepan. Add the breadcrumbs and stir well to coat the crumbs as evenly as possible with oil. Cook over a moderate heat, stirring often, for about 10 minutes or until the crumbs are well browned and crisp. As the crumbs cook, the oil will seep out of those that absorbed it initially, allowing the rest to become evenly crisp.

3 Transfer the cauliflower to a warm serving dish. Season the crumbs to taste and mix in the thyme, tarragon and parsley. Sprinkle the crumb mixture over the cauliflower. Garnish with sprigs of herbs, if using, and serve.

Some more ideas

● The crumb topping also goes well with lightly cooked Brussels sprouts (boiled or steamed). Use chopped fresh sage or marjoram instead of the tarragon and add the grated zest of 1 lemon to the crumb mixture. Serve lemon wedges with the sprouts so that the juice can be squeezed over.

● The crisp crumbs are delicious with hot beetroot. Use fresh sage instead of the tarragon and add the grated zest of 1orange to the crumb mixture. To serve, cut the freshly boiled beetroot into thick slices, arrange on a serving

platter, so that they overlap, and sprinkle with the crumb mixture. Garnish with orange slices. This goes well with roast or grilled pork, gammon or sausages.

● Celeriac is another vegetable that is enhanced by a crisp crumb topping. Cut the celeriac into small cubes, fingers or slices before cooking. For a delicate topping, instead of the herbs listed in the main recipe use 3 tbsp finely chopped fresh dill. Celeriac garnished in this way is super with grilled, poached or baked white fish.

Plus points

● Cauliflower is a member of the brassica family of cruciferous vegetables. It contains sulphurous compounds thought to help protect against cancer. It also provides vitamin C and fibre.

● Extra virgin olive oil is made from the first pressing of top grade olives from which the stones have been removed. It is green in colour, has a rich flavour and is high in monounsaturated fatty acids. These are the kinds of fat that are thought to help lower cholesterol levels in the blood.

Each serving provides Ⓥ

kcal 180, **protein** 7 g, **fat** 7 g (of which saturated fat 1 g), **carbohydrate** 23 g (of which sugars 4 g), **fibre** 3 g

✓✓✓	C
✓✓	folate
✓	B_1, B_6, niacin

Side dishes and breads

Sesame greens and bean sprouts

With a little inspiration, even the most humble vegetables can be elevated to feature in unusual, well-flavoured side dishes. This succulent and healthy stir-fry is full of flavour and crunch. It is equally delicious with plain grilled fish, poultry or meat.

Serves 4

30 g (1 oz) sesame seeds

2 tbsp sunflower oil

1 onion, chopped

2 garlic cloves, chopped

1 small Savoy cabbage, about 300 g
    (10½ oz), finely shredded

½ head of Chinese leaves, finely shredded

170 g (6 oz) bean sprouts

4 tbsp oyster sauce

salt and pepper

Preparation time: 10 minutes

Cooking time: 4–6 minutes

1 Heat a small saucepan and dry-fry the sesame seeds, shaking the pan frequently, until they are just beginning to brown. Turn the seeds out into a small bowl and set aside.

2 Heat the oil in a wok or large frying pan. Add the onion and garlic, and stir-fry for 2–3 minutes or until softened slightly. Add the cabbage and Chinese leaves and stir-fry over a fairly high heat for 2–3 minutes or until the vegetables are just beginning to soften. Add the bean sprouts and continue cooking for a few seconds.

3 Make a space in the centre of the pan. Pour in the oyster sauce and 2 tbsp of water, and stir until hot, then toss the vegetables into the sauce. Taste and add pepper, with salt if necessary (this will depend on the saltiness of the oyster sauce). Serve immediately, sprinkled with the toasted sesame seeds.

Some more ideas

• Use 250 g (9 oz) red cabbage, finely shredded, instead of the Savoy cabbage, and add 3 cooked beetroot, chopped, with the bean sprouts. Red cabbage will require 2 minutes additional stir-frying, so add to the wok before the Chinese leaves. Use 1 tbsp clear honey with 2 tbsp soy sauce instead of the oyster sauce.

• Finely shredded Brussels sprouts are crisp and full flavoured when stir-fried. Use them instead of the Savoy cabbage – slice the sprouts thinly, then shake the slices to loosen the shreds. Or use shredded spring greens. Toasted flaked almonds can be sprinkled over the vegetables instead of the sesame seeds.

Plus points

• As well as contributing distinctive flavour, sesame seeds are a good source of calcium and therefore useful for anyone who dislikes or does not eat dairy products, the main source of this mineral in the Western diet. A combination of good supplies of calcium and plenty of physical activity are particularly important for young girls so as to avoid osteoporosis later in life.

• Bean sprouts, along with other sprouted seeds, are rich in B vitamins and vitamin C. They also provide iron and potassium.

Each serving provides

kcal 150, **protein** 5 g, **fat** 11 g (of which saturated fat 1 g), **carbohydrate** 9 g (of which sugars 5 g), **fibre** 4 g

| ✓✓✓ C, folate |
| ✓✓ B₁₂ |
| ✓ B₁, calcium, iron, potassium |

Side dishes and breads

Fragrant basmati rice

Basmati cooks to perfect, separate, fluffy grains and is considered by many to be the finest rice. Here it is subtly scented and coloured with saffron, cinnamon and ginger. The sweet-sharp flavour of pomegranate adds a unique quality to this dish.

Serves 6

1 tbsp sunflower oil

55 g (2 oz) split blanched almonds, any tiny pieces discarded

250 g (8½ oz) basmati rice, rinsed

pinch of saffron strands

1 cinnamon stick

450 ml (15 fl oz) boiling vegetable stock

1 ripe pomegranate

2.5 cm (1 in) piece of fresh root ginger, grated

1 tsp clear honey

1 tbsp chopped fresh mint

2 tbsp chopped fresh coriander

salt and pepper

Preparation time: 15 minutes, plus standing
Cooking time: 15–20 minutes

Each serving provides ⓥ

kcal 249, **protein** 6 g, **fat** 7 g (of which saturated fat 0.5 g), **carbohydrate** 40 g (of which sugars 6 g), **fibre** 2 g

✓✓	E
✓	copper

1 Heat the oil in a large saucepan, add the almonds and cook gently for 2–3 minutes or until golden. Remove from the pan with a draining spoon and set aside.

2 Add the rice to the oil and cook, stirring, for 1 minute. Stir in the saffron strands and cinnamon stick, then add the stock and season with salt and pepper to taste. Bring to the boil. Stir, then cover and cook over a very low heat for 10–15 minutes or until the rice is tender and all of the stock has been absorbed.

3 Meanwhile, cut the pomegranate in half and remove all the seeds from the membranes. Reserve about one-third of the seeds for garnish. Put the rest of the seeds in a sieve placed over a mixing bowl and crush with a spoon to extract the juice.

4 Put the grated ginger into a garlic crusher, hold over the mixing bowl and squeeze out the ginger juice. Stir the honey into the juices.

5 When the rice is cooked, stir in the pomegranate juice mixture. Cover again and leave to stand for 2 minutes. Then remove the cinnamon stick, fork the mint and coriander through the rice, and transfer to a warmed serving dish. Scatter over the almonds and reserved pomegranate seeds, and serve.

Some more ideas

● For lemongrass-scented basmati rice, add a bruised stalk of lemongrass with the cinnamon stick. Instead of pomegranate and ginger juices, mix the juice of ½ lemon with the honey.

● Make a spiced basmati pilaf. Gently cook 55 g (2 oz) cashew nuts in 1 tbsp sunflower oil until golden. Remove from the pan with a draining spoon and set aside. Toast the basmati rice in the oil with 1 tsp cumin seeds and the crushed seeds of 3 cardamom pods for about 2 minutes. Stir in the stock, 3 tbsp coconut milk, 1 bay leaf and 3 cloves. Cover and cook as in the main recipe. Remove the bay leaf and cloves, then stir in 1 tbsp lemon juice and 2 tbsp chopped fresh coriander. Scatter over the cashew nuts and garnish with a sprig of fresh coriander before serving.

Plus points

● Pomegranate seeds not only add flavour to this dish, they also contribute vitamin C and some dietary fibre.

● Almonds, like other nuts, provide many of the nutrients usually found in meat, such as protein, many of the B vitamins and essential minerals such as phosphorus, iron, copper and potassium. They are also a good source of vitamin E, which helps to protect against heart disease.

Millet with spinach and pine nuts

Bright green spinach and golden apricots add rich colour and flavour to this easy grain and vegetable side dish. It is an ideal alternative to potatoes and rice, and is particularly suitable for serving with stews and casseroles that have plenty of sauce.

Serves 4

200 g (7 oz) millet

50 g (1¾ oz) ready-to eat dried apricots, roughly chopped

900 ml (1½ pints) vegetable stock

55 g (2 oz) pine nuts

250 g (8½ oz) baby spinach leaves

juice of ½ lemon

salt and pepper

Preparation time: 10 minutes

Cooking time: 20–25 minutes

1 Put the millet and dried apricots into a large saucepan and stir in the stock. Bring to the boil, then lower the heat. Simmer for 15–20 minutes or until all the stock has been absorbed and the millet is tender.

2 Meanwhile, toast the pine nuts in a small frying pan until they are golden brown and fragrant. Set aside.

3 Add the spinach and lemon juice to the millet, with salt and pepper to taste. Cover the pan and leave over a very low heat for 4–5 minutes to wilt the spinach.

4 Stir the millet and spinach mixture gently, then spoon into a serving bowl. Scatter the toasted pine nuts on top and serve immediately.

Another idea

● Try aubergine with millet and sesame seeds. Cut 2 medium-sized aubergines into dice. Heat 2 tbsp extra virgin olive oil in a large frying pan, add the aubergine and brown over a high heat, stirring constantly. Remove from the heat and stir in 200 g (7 oz) millet and 900 ml (1½ pints) vegetable stock. Return to the heat and bring to the boil. Stir, then reduce the heat and simmer for 15–20 minutes or until the stock has been absorbed and the millet is tender. Season with salt and pepper to taste. Transfer to a serving bowl and scatter over 2 tbsp chopped fresh coriander, 1 tbsp thinly sliced spring onions and 2 tbsp toasted sesame seeds.

Plus points

● Millet provides useful amounts of iron and B vitamins and, as it is not highly milled, it retains all its nutritional value. Being gluten-free, it can be an additional source of starchy carbohydrate for coeliacs.

● Pine nuts are a good source of vitamin E and potassium. They also contribute useful amounts of magnesium, zinc and iron.

● Dried apricots are one of the richest fruit sources of iron. They also contain beta-carotene, which the body can convert to vitamin A, and other minerals such as calcium, potassium and phosphorus.

Side dishes and breads

Each serving provides Ⓥ

kcal 307, **protein** 7 g, **fat** 11 g (of which saturated fat 1 g), **carbohydrate** 44 g (of which sugars 6 g), **fibre** 2 g

✓✓✓	A
✓✓	B₁, E
✓	C, folate, niacin, calcium, copper, iron, potassium, zinc

Mixed salad leaves with flowers and blueberries

Combining edible flowers, salad leaves, alfalfa sprouts and juicy blueberries, this is a pretty summer salad. Some supermarkets sell packs of edible flowers, or you can pick them from your garden – just be sure to choose those that have not been sprayed with pesticides.

Serves 4

1 small Oak Leaf lettuce, torn into bite-sized pieces

85 g (3 oz) rocket

85 g (3 oz) alfalfa sprouts

100 g (3½ oz) blueberries

30 g (1 oz) mixed edible flowers, including some or all of the following: nasturtiums, borage, violas or pansies, and herb flowers such as sage and rosemary

Honey mustard dressing

3 tbsp grapeseed oil

juice of 1 small lemon

1 tsp Dijon mustard

1 tsp clear honey

salt and pepper

Preparation time: 10–15 minutes

Each serving provides Ⓥ

kcal 107, **protein** 2 g, **fat** 9 g (of which saturated fat 1 g), **carbohydrate** 5 g (of which sugars 5 g), **fibre** 2 g

✓✓✓	B₁, B₆, C, niacin
✓✓	E
✓	A, folate

1 To make the dressing, whisk the oil with the lemon juice, mustard, honey, and salt and pepper to taste in a large shallow salad bowl.

2 Add the lettuce and rocket and toss to coat with the dressing. Sprinkle the salad with the alfalfa sprouts and blueberries. Arrange the flowers on top and serve at once.

Some more ideas for flowery salads

• Make a flowery carrot salad. Tear 1 batavia or Oak Leaf lettuce into bite-sized pieces and put into a shallow salad bowl. Add 2 carrots, cut into long thin ribbons with a swivel vegetable peeler, 2 oranges, peeled and divided into segments, and 75 g (2½ oz) blueberries. Make the honey mustard dressing as in the main recipe, but replace the lemon juice with fresh orange juice. Drizzle it over the salad and garnish with mixed orange and yellow nasturtium flowers.

• For a refreshingly lemony leaf and raspberry salad, mix 15 g (½ oz) sweet cicely leaves and a few lemon geranium leaves with 1 small Webb's Wonder or cos lettuce, torn into pieces. Scatter over 100 g (3½ oz) raspberries. For the dressing, whisk 2 tbsp extra virgin olive oil with the juice of 1 lemon and seasoning to taste. Garnish the salad with 30 g (1 oz) mixed chive, sweet cicely and mint or viola flowers.

• Try a peppery salad with pears and wild garlic. Separate 2 Little Gem lettuces into leaves and mix with 85 g (3 oz) rocket in a salad bowl. For the dressing whisk 3 tbsp extra virgin olive oil with the juice of 1 lemon and 3 tbsp chopped fresh chives. Add 1 ripe red Williams pear, cored and thinly sliced, and turn to coat with the dressing, then add the pear and dressing to the salad leaves and toss gently. Garnish with 30 g (1 oz) mixed wild garlic, chive and borage flowers.

Plus points

• Naturally sweet blueberries are rich in vitamin C and also contain antibacterial compounds thought to be effective against some gastro-intestinal disorders and urinary infections such as cystitis.

• The nutritional value of petals and flower heads is very small as they are used in such tiny quantities, but you will get some essential oils and phytochemicals, particularly antioxidants, from some flowers, especially herb flowers.

Side dishes and breads

Roasted pepper salad

This colourful salad makes a tasty accompaniment to seafood, chicken or lamb, and the added benefit is that it is low in calories. Peppers are an excellent source of vitamin C, and even when roasted they still retain substantial amounts of this important vitamin.

Serves 6

2 large red peppers

2 large yellow or orange peppers

2 large green peppers

2½ tbsp extra virgin olive oil

2 tsp balsamic vinegar

1 small garlic clove, very finely chopped or
    crushed

salt and pepper

To garnish

12 black olives, stoned

a handful of small fresh basil leaves

Preparation time: 45 minutes, plus cooling

Each serving provides Ⓥ

kcal 97, **protein** 2 g, **fat** 6 g (of which
saturated fat 1 g), **carbohydrate** 10 g (of
which sugars 9 g), **fibre** 3 g

✓✓✓ A, B₁, B₆, C, E, niacin

✓✓ folate

1 Preheat the oven to 200°C (400°F, gas mark 6). Brush the peppers with 1 tbsp of the olive oil and arrange them in a shallow roasting tin. Roast for about 35 minutes or until the pepper skins are evenly darkened, turning them 3 or 4 times. Place the peppers in a polythene bag and leave until they are cool enough to handle.

2 Working over a bowl to catch the juice, peel the peppers. Cut them in half and discard the cores and seeds (strain out any seeds that fall into the juice), then cut into thick slices.

3 Measure 1½ tbsp of the pepper juice into a small bowl (discard the remainder). Add the vinegar, garlic and salt and pepper to taste, and whisk in the remaining 1½ tbsp olive oil.

4 Arrange the peppers on a serving platter or on individual salad plates. Drizzle over the dressing and garnish with the olives and basil leaves.

Some more ideas for pepper salads

• For a roasted red pepper and onion salad to serve 4, quarter and seed 4 red peppers and put them in a baking dish with 4 small red onions, quartered. Drizzle over 1½ tbsp extra virgin olive oil and season to taste. Roast in a preheated 200°C (400°F, gas mark 6) oven for about 35 minutes, turning once, until the vegetables are tender and browned around the edges. Cool, then peel the peppers, if wished,

holding them over the baking dish. Whisk 2 tsp lemon juice with 1½ tbsp extra virgin olive oil in a salad bowl and season to taste. Add 115 g (4 oz) rocket or mixed red salad leaves and toss to coat. Pile the peppers and onions on top and drizzle over their cooking juices.

• For an Oriental-style pepper and Chinese leaf salad to serve 4, seed and thinly slice 2 red peppers (or 1 red and 1 yellow pepper) and 1 fresh red chilli. Mix in a salad bowl with 150 g (5½ oz) shredded Chinese leaves. For the dressing, whisk together 1 tbsp rice vinegar, 1 tsp toasted sesame oil, 2 tsp groundnut oil and 1 tsp soy sauce. Drizzle over the vegetables and toss to coat. Sprinkle with 2 tbsp toasted sesame seeds and serve.

Plus points

• Herbalists recommend basil as a natural tranquiliser. It is also believed to aid digestion, ease stomach cramps and help relieve the headaches associated with colds.

• Olives are a source of vitamin E, although they are usually not eaten in large enough quantities to make a significant contribution to the diet.

Side dishes and breads

204

Crunchy nut coleslaw

Everyone loves coleslaw, and this fresh-tasting version is sure to appeal. Made with white cabbage, carrot and radishes, it is flecked with spring onions, sweet sultanas and roasted peanuts, and tossed with a creamy dressing that is healthily low in fat.

Serves 4

200 g (7 oz) white cabbage, finely shredded

1 large carrot, about 150 g (5½ oz), coarsely grated

50 g (1¾ oz) sultanas

4 spring onions, finely chopped, with the white and green parts kept separate

2 tbsp mayonnaise

150 g (5½ oz) plain low-fat yogurt

30 g (1 oz) radishes, sliced

50 g (1¾ oz) unsalted roasted peanuts

3 tbsp chopped parsley or snipped fresh chives, or a mixture of the two (optional)

salt and pepper

Preparation time: 15 minutes

1 Mix together the cabbage, carrot, sultanas and white parts of the spring onion in a large bowl.

2 Stir the mayonnaise and yogurt together and season with salt and pepper to taste. Stir this dressing into the cabbage mixture and toss to coat all the ingredients.

3 Just before serving, stir in the radishes and peanuts, and sprinkle with the chopped green parts of the spring onions and the parsley or chives.

Some more ideas for coleslaw

• Toss 1 cored and diced red-skinned dessert apple with 2 tbsp lemon juice, then stir into the coleslaw with 1 tsp caraway seeds.

• Add 100 g (3½ oz) of either canned or thawed frozen sweetcorn.

• Lightly toast 1 tbsp pumpkin seeds and 2 tbsp sunflower seeds under the grill and use to garnish the coleslaw in place of the herbs.

• For a celeriac coleslaw, use 250 g (8½ oz) peeled celeriac, cut into matchstick strips, instead of white cabbage. Flavour the yogurt and mayonnaise dressing with 2 tsp wholegrain mustard, or 1 tsp Dijon mustard and 1 tbsp mango chutney.

• For a red cabbage and blue cheese coleslaw to serve 4–6, mix together 200 g (7 oz) finely shredded red cabbage with 150 g (5½ oz) tiny cauliflower florets, 150 g (5½ oz) grated carrot, ½ finely chopped red onion and 50 g (1¾ oz) dried cranberries or cherries. Make the dressing by mashing 150 g (5½ oz) plain low-fat yogurt with 115 g (4 oz) crumbled St Agur cheese and seasoning to taste. Garnish with 2 rashers of lean back bacon, derinded, grilled until crisp and cut into thin strips.

Plus points

• Roasted peanuts are a delicious and nutritious addition to this recipe. Research suggests that a daily intake of peanuts, peanut butter or peanut (groundnut) oil may help to lower total cholesterol, harmful LDL cholesterol and triglyceride levels and thus help to protect against coronary heart disease.

• Home-made coleslaw not only looks and tastes far superior to shop-bought coleslaw, but it will be much lower in fat.

Each serving provides

kcal 209, **protein** 7 g, **fat** 12 g (of which saturated fat 2 g), **carbohydrate** 19 g (of which sugars 18 g), **fibre** 3 g

✓✓✓	A, B₁, B₆, C, E, niacin
✓✓	folate
✓	calcium, copper, potassium

Side dishes and breads

Garlicky tomato salad

When tomatoes are at their sweetest, this salad is particularly delicious. It can also be eye-catching if you make it with a mixture of different-coloured tomatoes – look for yellow cherry tomatoes as well as small red or yellow pear-shaped plum tomatoes.

Serves 4

1 large soft lettuce, large leaves torn into smaller pieces

4 large or 6 small ripe plum tomatoes, about 500 g (1 lb 2 oz) in total, sliced

20 cherry tomatoes, about 225 g (8 oz) in total, halved

16 fresh basil leaves

1½ tbsp toasted pumpkin seeds

1½ tbsp toasted sunflower seeds

Garlic vinaigrette

1 small garlic clove, very finely chopped

1½ tsp red wine vinegar

2 tbsp extra virgin olive oil

salt and pepper

Preparation time: 15 minutes

1 To make the garlic vinaigrette, whisk together the garlic, vinegar, oil, and salt and pepper to taste in a small mixing bowl.

2 Place a layer of lettuce leaves on a serving platter or on 4 plates and arrange the sliced tomatoes and then the cherry tomatoes on top. Drizzle over the vinaigrette.

3 Scatter the basil leaves and the pumpkin and sunflower seeds over the tomatoes, and serve at once.

Some more ideas for tomato salads

● For a tomato and black olive salad, slice about 550 g (1¼ lb) ripe tomatoes, preferably beefsteak, and arrange on a serving platter. Top with 100 g (3½ oz) thinly sliced spring onions and drizzle over 1 tbsp extra virgin olive oil and the juice of ¼ lemon. Arrange 8 black olives, halved and stoned, on top and sprinkle with 2 tbsp chopped parsley.

● Make a salad of fresh and sun-dried tomatoes. Cut 6 ripe plum tomatoes into thin wedges and put them in a mixing bowl. Thinly slice 3 sun-dried tomatoes and add to the bowl. Make a vinaigrette by whisking 1½ tbsp of the oil from the jar of sun-dried tomatoes with 1½ tsp wine vinegar and seasoning to taste. Drizzle the dressing over the tomatoes and marinate briefly. Arrange 100 g (3½ oz) rocket on 4 plates and divide the tomatoes among them, or arrange on a serving platter. Sprinkle with 2 tbsp toasted pine nuts and serve.

● Try a salad of cherry tomatoes and sugarsnap peas. Trim 250 g (8½ oz) sugarsnap peas and steam for about 3 minutes or until tender but still crisp. Refresh under cold running water, then cool. Mix with 375 g (13 oz) cherry tomatoes, halved if large, and 6 thinly sliced spring onions. Make the garlic vinaigrette as in the main recipe and drizzle it over the tomatoes and peas. Add 3 tbsp chopped fresh mint, or 1 tbsp each chopped fresh tarragon and parsley, and toss to mix.

Plus points

● Pumpkin seeds are one of the richest vegetarian sources of zinc, a mineral that is essential for the functioning of the immune system and for growth and wound healing. They are also a good source of protein and unsaturated fat and a useful source of iron, magnesium and fibre.

● Tomatoes are a rich source of vitamin C, an important nutrient for maintaining immunity and healthy skin. The vitamin C is concentrated in the jellylike substance surrounding the seeds.

Each serving provides Ⓥ

kcal 160, **protein** 5 g, **fat** 12 g (of which saturated fat 2 g), **carbohydrate** 9 g (of which sugars 7 g), **fibre** 3 g

✓✓✓	A, B₁, B₆, C, E, niacin
✓✓	folate, copper
✓	iron, zinc

Basic loaf

This recipe makes a very good basic loaf, and it is infinitely flexible. You can make any number of breads by using different types of flour or adding extra ingredients – you don't even need a loaf tin as the bread is baked on a baking tray.

Makes 1 large round loaf (cuts into about 12 slices)

340 g (12 oz) strong white (bread) flour

340 g (12 oz) strong wholemeal (bread) flour, preferably stoneground, plus a little extra to sprinkle

1 tsp salt

1 sachet easy-blend dried yeast, about 7 g

450 ml (15 fl oz) tepid water

Preparation time: 25 minutes, plus about 2 hours rising

Cooking time: 35 minutes

Each slice provides

kcal 180, protein 6 g, fat 1 g (of which saturated fat 0 g), carbohydrate 40 g (of which sugars 1 g), fibre 3 g

✓✓	B$_1$, B$_6$, selenium
✓	niacin, copper, iron, zinc

1 Sift the white and wholemeal flours and salt into a large bowl, tipping in any bran left in the sieve. Stir in the dried yeast, then make a well in the centre and pour in the tepid water. Using your hands, gradually draw the flour into the water, mixing well to make a dough.

2 Gather the dough into a ball that feels firm and leaves the sides of the bowl clean; if necessary, add a little more flour or a little more water.

3 Turn the dough out onto a lightly floured work surface and knead for about 10 minutes or until smooth and elastic. Put the dough into a large, lightly greased bowl and cover with cling film. Leave to rise in a warm place for about 1 hour or until the dough has doubled in size.

4 Turn out the risen dough onto a floured work surface and knock it back with your knuckles. Gently knead the dough into a neat ball shape, then set it on a large greased baking sheet. Cover with a damp tea-towel and leave to rise in a warm place for 1 hour or until doubled in size again.

5 Towards the end of the rising time, preheat the oven to 220ºC (425ºF, gas mark 7). Uncover the loaf and sprinkle with a little flour, then make 4 slashes across the top using a small serrated knife. Bake for 35 minutes or until the bread sounds hollow when tapped on the base.

6 Transfer the loaf to a wire rack and cool completely before slicing. It can be kept for up to 5 days.

Plus points

- The positive features of bread have often been overlooked, as it has quite unfairly gained a reputation for being fattening: it is what you put on the bread, not the bread itself, that can be fattening. Even white bread provides good amounts of dietary fibre, and by law it is fortified with vitamins and minerals, including B$_1$ and calcium.
- This is a fat-free loaf with plenty of fibre from the wholemeal flour. The wholemeal flour also provides B vitamins, magnesium, zinc, selenium, iron, copper and phosphorus.
- Stoneground flour is milled by traditional methods, which keep the wheat grains cool and thus preserve almost all the nutrients in the whole grain.

Some more ideas

● For a white loaf, use 675 g (1½ lb) strong white (bread) flour and omit the wholemeal flour. For a loaf with plenty of texture, use 675 g (1½ lb) strong wholemeal (bread) flour and omit the white flour.

● For extra calcium, mix the dough with tepid semi-skimmed milk instead of water, or use a mixture of milk and water.

● To make a tin loaf, after the first rising, knock back the dough, knead it for 2-3 minutes, then shape it and place in a greased 900 g (2 lb) loaf tin. Leave to rise until doubled in size, then bake as in the main recipe.

● To make rolls, after the first rising divide the dough into 20 pieces. For round rolls, shape each piece into a rough ball, then roll it under your cupped hand on the work surface. For an oval roll, shape each piece into a ball, flatten slightly, mould to an oval, then make a crease down the centre with side of your little finger.

Focaccia

This light Italian flat bread is prepared from a soft dough enriched with olive oil. Traditionally extra olive oil is sprinkled over the dough before baking – sometimes quite generously – but this recipe uses just enough to give a good texture and flavour.

Makes 1 round, flat bread (serves 8)
450 g (1 lb) strong white (bread) flour
1 tsp salt
1 sachet easy-blend dried yeast, about 7 g
4 tbsp extra virgin olive oil
300 ml (10 fl oz) tepid water
½ tsp coarse sea salt

Preparation time: 15 minutes, plus about 45 minutes rising
Cooking time: 15 minutes

Each serving provides
kcal 240, **protein** 5 g, **fat** 6 g (of which saturated fat 1 g), **carbohydrate** 44 g (of which sugars 1 g), **fibre** 2 g

✓ B₁, calcium

1 Put the flour into a large bowl and stir in the salt and yeast. Make a well in the centre and pour in 3 tbsp of the olive oil and the tepid water. Gradually mix the flour into the oil and water, using a wooden spoon at first, then by hand, to make a soft, slightly sticky dough.

2 Turn the dough out onto a floured surface and knead for about 10 minutes or until smooth and elastic. Keep the dough moving by turning, punching and folding it to prevent it from sticking. Sprinkle the surface with a little extra flour if necessary, but try not to add too much as this will make the dough dry.

3 Shape the dough into a ball and slap it onto a greased baking sheet, then roll it out (or push it out with your hands) into a round about 21 cm (8½ in) in diameter and 2 cm (¾ in) thick. Cover loosely with a clean tea-towel, tucking the ends under the baking sheet, and leave in a warm place for about 45 minutes or until the dough has doubled in thickness.

4 Towards the end of the rising time, preheat the oven to 230ºC (450ºF, gas mark 8). Uncover the bread. Pour a little hand-hot water into a cup, then dip your fingers into the water and press into the risen dough to make deep dents all over the top; wet your fingers each time, to leave the top of the loaf moist. Brush the remaining 1 tbsp olive oil over the bread and sprinkle with the coarse salt.

5 Bake the focaccia for about 15 minutes or until golden brown. Transfer to a wire rack to cool for 15 minutes, then wrap it in a clean tea-towel to soften the crust. Serve warm or allow to cool completely. The bread can be kept in a polythene bag for up to 2 days.

Plus points
• Olive oil is high in monounsaturated fat, which may help to lower blood cholesterol levels.
• Although focaccia has slightly more fat than other types of bread, it has a moist texture and so can be eaten plain, without spreading with butter or other fat.

Side dishes and breads

Some more ideas

• To make individual focaccia, divide the dough into 8 portions. Press each portion out into a round about 10 cm (4 in) in diameter. These small breads will rise in 30–45 minutes and bake in 10–15 minutes.

• A variety of ingredients can be sprinkled over the focaccia before baking. Try fennel or dill seeds, chopped fresh or dried oregano, finely chopped onion and/or garlic, or chopped black or green olives.

• For olive focaccia, stone and chop 8 black olives and add to the dough with the olive oil and water. Sprinkle 1 tsp finely chopped fresh rosemary over the focaccia before making the dents on the surface with your fingers.

• For thyme and garlic focaccia, add 1 tbsp chopped fresh thyme to the dough with the oil and water, and sprinkle over 2 finely chopped garlic cloves before making the dents.

• For sun-dried tomato focaccia, add 4 finely chopped sun-dried tomatoes to the dough with the oil and water. Before serving, sprinkle with some shredded fresh basil.

Pitta breads

These pitta breads are delicious served warm from the oven. They make a good accompaniment to soups and dips or they can be left to cool, then split and filled: try goat's cheese with roasted vegetables or hummus and a crunchy mixed salad.

Makes 10 breads

450 g (1 lb) strong white (bread) flour

1 tsp salt

½ tsp caster sugar

1 sachet easy-blend dried yeast, about 7 g

300 ml (10 fl oz) tepid water, or as needed

Preparation time: 30 minutes, plus 1½–2 hours rising

Cooking time: 8–10 minutes

1 Sift the flour and salt into a bowl, then stir in the sugar and yeast. Make a well in the centre and mix in enough water to make a soft dough.

2 Turn the dough out onto a lightly floured surface and knead for about 10 minutes or until it is smooth and elastic. Place in a lightly greased bowl, cover with a tea-towel and leave to rise in a warm place for 1–1½ hours or until the dough has doubled in size.

3 Turn the risen dough onto the lightly floured surface and knock it back, then knead for 2–3 minutes. Divide it into 10 pieces and shape each one into a ball. Roll out each ball to an oval about 5 mm (¼ in) thick. Leave on the floured surface to rise at room temperature for about 30 minutes.

4 Towards the end of the rising time, preheat the oven to 230ºC (450ºF, gas mark 8). Place 3 non-stick baking sheets (or 3 floured baking sheets) in the oven to heat for about 5 minutes. Place the pitta breads on the hot baking sheets and bake for 8–10 minutes or until firm and golden brown.

5 Transfer to a wire rack to cool. Serve warm or reheat under the grill, or in the toaster, as required. Pitta breads are best eaten on the day they are made, but they can be kept, wrapped in foil, for 1–2 days.

Some more ideas

● Substitute wholemeal flour for half the white flour.

● For seeded pitta breads, brush the dough ovals with water, then sprinkle with sesame or other seeds before baking. Alternatively, knead 2 tbsp seeds into the dough in step 2.

● For herb pitta breads, knead 1 tbsp chopped fresh rosemary or 2 tbsp chopped fresh basil into the dough in step 2.

Plus points

● White flour provides calcium, a mineral that is essential for healthy bones and teeth. Calcium is also important for normal functioning of nerve impulses and it aids blood clotting.

● These pitta breads contain no saturated fat and almost no fat of any kind, making them an excellent healthy choice for a bread to serve with cheese, meat or other foods that are higher in fat.

Each bread provides Ⓥ

kcal 155, **protein** 4 g, **fat** 0.5 g (of which saturated fat 0 g), **carbohydrate** 35 g (of which sugars 1 g), **fibre** 1.5 g

✓ B₁, folate, calcium

Bagels

These little bread rings, Jewish in origin, are delicious teamed with savoury fillings.
The double cooking method – first by briefly poaching in boiling water, then baking –
gives bagels their unique texture and slightly chewy crust.

Makes 12 bagels

450 g (1 lb) strong white (bread) flour
1½ tsp salt
1 sachet easy-blend dried yeast, about 7 g
3 eggs
1 tsp clear honey
2 tsp sunflower oil
200 ml (7 fl oz) tepid water

Preparation time: 35 minutes, plus about
  1 hour rising
Cooking time: 15 minutes

Each bagel provides

kcal 160, **protein** 6 g, **fat** 3 g (of which
saturated fat 0.5 g), **carbohydrate** 29 g (of
which sugars 1 g), **fibre** 1 g

✓✓	selenium
✓	B₁, B₁₂

1 Put the flour into a large mixing bowl and stir in the salt and yeast. Make a well in the centre.

2 Lightly whisk 2 of the eggs with the honey and oil, and pour into the well in the flour. Add the water and mix to a soft dough.

3 Turn out onto a lightly floured surface and knead for 10 minutes or until smooth and elastic. Place the dough in a large greased bowl, cover with a damp tea-towel and leave to rise in a warm place for 40 minutes or until doubled in size.

4 Turn out the dough onto the floured work surface and knead it lightly, then divide it into 12 equal pieces. Form each into a 20 cm (8 in) long sausage, then shape it into a ring. Dampen the two ends with a little water, slightly overlap them and gently pinch them together to seal.

5 Arrange the bagels on a lightly oiled baking sheet, cover with oiled cling film and leave to rise in a warm place for 20 minutes or until they are slightly puffy.

6 Preheat the oven to 200°C (400°F, gas mark 6). Bring a large pan of lightly salted water to the boil. Drop the bagels into the water, one at a time, and poach for 20 seconds. Lift out with a large draining spoon and return to the baking sheet.

7 Lightly beat the remaining egg and brush it over the bagels to glaze. Bake for 14–15 minutes or until well risen and golden brown. Transfer to a wire rack to cool. The bagels can be kept in an airtight container for up to 3 days.

Plus points

• Enriching the bagel dough with eggs increases the protein, iron and zinc content, as well as adding vitamins A, D and E and some of those in the B group.

• Serving the bagels with a vitamin C-rich fruit, or including a vitamin C-rich salad in the bagel filling, will help the body to absorb the iron provided by the bagels.

Some more ideas

- For cinnamon and raisin bagels, soak 85 g (3 oz) raisins in 3 tbsp orange juice for about 2 hours or until the juice has been absorbed. Make the dough as in the main recipe, but reduce the salt to 1 tsp and add 30 g (1 oz)

caster sugar and 1 tsp ground cinnamon with the flour. Mix in the raisins with the water.

- For rye bagels, substitute 170 g (6 oz) rye flour for 170 g (6 oz) of the white flour. Stir in 1 tsp caraway seeds with the yeast, and use molasses instead of honey.

- The bagels can be finished with a variety of toppings. After brushing them with the egg glaze, sprinkle with sesame, poppy, nigella or caraway seeds, or try sprinkling them with 1 finely chopped small onion tossed in 1 tbsp extra virgin olive oil.

Desserts

The wonderful thing about counting calories while also enjoying a balanced diet is that everything is permitted – in moderation – including luscious desserts. In this mouthwatering chapter are recipes such as Fresh figs with raspberries and rose cream, Pistachio floating islands, Blackberry ripple frozen yogurt, Hot apricot soufflés or even Rich chocolate torte. Refreshingly fruity, creamy or light, these attractive desserts are a perfect finale to a meal.

Little custard pots

Delicately flavoured with vanilla, these creamy baked custards are easy to make and sure to be popular. Take care not to overcook the custards – they should be just set when you take them out of the oven. This dessert can be prepared well ahead of serving.

Serves 6

600 ml (1 pint) semi-skimmed milk

½ vanilla pod, split

2 eggs

2 egg yolks

40 g (1¼ oz) caster sugar

½ tsp cornflour

Cherry compote

30 g (1 oz) demerara sugar

450 g (1 lb) fresh cherries, stoned

2 tsp arrowroot

Preparation time: 15 minutes

Cooking time: 25–30 minutes

Each serving provides   Ⓥ

kcal 188, **protein** 7 g, **fat** 6 g (of which saturated fat 2 g), **carbohydrate** 29 g (of which sugars 26 g), **fibre** 1 g

✓✓	B₁₂
✓	A, B₂, C, calcium, zinc

1 Place the milk and vanilla pod in a saucepan and heat until almost boiling. Remove from the heat, cover and set aside to infuse for 15 minutes.

2 Preheat the oven to 160°C (325°F, gas mark 3). Put the whole eggs, egg yolks, caster sugar and cornflour into a bowl and lightly whisk together.

3 Bring the milk back to boiling point, then remove the vanilla pod and pour the hot milk over the egg mixture, whisking all the time. Strain the mixture into a jug, then divide among 6 lightly buttered 120 ml (4 fl oz) ramekin dishes.

4 Set the ramekins in a roasting tin and pour enough hot water into the tin to come halfway up the sides of the ramekins. Bake for 30–35 minutes or until lightly set – the custards should still be slightly wobbly, as they will continue cooking for a few minutes after being removed from the oven. Lift them out of the tin of hot water and place on a wire rack to cool. Once cold, chill until ready to serve.

5 For the cherry compote, put the demerara sugar and 6 tbsp water in a saucepan and heat gently until the sugar has dissolved. Bring to the boil, then reduce the heat and add the cherries. Cover and simmer gently for 4–5 minutes, stirring occasionally, until tender. Lift out the cherries with a draining spoon and put them into a serving bowl.

6 Mix the arrowroot with 1 tbsp cold water. Stir into the cherry juices in the saucepan and simmer for 1 minute, stirring, until thickened and clear. Allow to cool for a few minutes, then pour over the cherries. (The compote can be served warm or at room temperature.)

7 Spoon a little of the cherry compote over the top of each custard pot, and serve the rest of the compote in a bowl.

Plus points

● The nutrients found in eggs are concentrated in the yolk rather than the white. Adding extra egg yolks in this recipe therefore boosts the content of vitamins A and D and most of the B vitamins.

● Cherries are rich in potassium and provide useful amounts of vitamin C.

Some more ideas

• If you want to turn out the custards for serving, line the bottom of each ramekin with a circle of baking parchment, and add an extra egg yolk to the mixture. After baking, chill for at least 4 hours or, preferably, overnight. To turn out, lightly press the edge of each custard with your fingertips to pull it away from the dish, then run a knife around the edge. Put an inverted serving plate on top of the ramekin,

then turn them both over, holding them firmly together, and lift off the ramekin.

• For chocolate custard pots with poached pears, flavour the milk with a thin strip of pared orange zest instead of the vanilla pod. In step 2, replace the caster sugar with light soft brown sugar, and add 1 tbsp sifted cocoa powder. Continue making the custards as in the main recipe. For the pears, heat 300 ml (10 fl oz) water with 85 g (3 oz) caster sugar and a split

vanilla pod until the sugar dissolves, then bring to the boil and simmer for 2–3 minutes. Add 4 small, firm dessert pears, peeled, cored and thickly sliced. Cover and simmer gently for 12–15 minutes or until just tender, turning the pear slices in the syrup occasionally. Lift out the pears with a draining spoon and transfer to a serving dish. Simmer the syrup for 5 minutes to reduce slightly, then cool for 5 minutes. Remove the vanilla pod and pour over the pears.

Fresh figs with raspberries and rose cream

As well as being a superb end to a meal, this simple fruit dessert is packed with fibre from both the figs and raspberries. Rosewater is a popular flavouring in the Middle East and in parts of the Mediterranean. It is made from distilled rose petals and has an intense aroma.

Serves 4

8 small, ripe juicy figs
4 large fresh fig leaves (optional)
200 g (7 oz) fresh raspberries
fresh mint leaves to decorate
Rose cream
100 g (3½ oz) crème fraîche
2 tsp raspberry jam
finely grated zest of 1 lime
1–2 tbsp rosewater, or to taste

Preparation time: about 15 minutes

1 To make the rose cream, place the crème fraîche in a bowl and beat in the raspberry jam and lime zest until the jam is well distributed. Add the rosewater and stir to mix in. Transfer to a pretty serving bowl.

2 Cut each of the figs vertically into quarters without cutting all the way through, so they each remain whole. Arrange the fig leaves, if using, on 4 plates and place 2 figs on each plate.

3 Spoon a dollop of the rose cream into the centre of each fig; serve the remaining cream separately. Scatter the raspberries over the plates, decorate with the mint leaves and serve.

Some more ideas

● Stir 350 g (12 oz) sliced ripe strawberries into the rose cream.

● On the same theme, serve fresh peaches with an orange cream. To make the cream, flavour 100 g (3½ oz) crème fraîche with 2 tsp orange-blossom honey, the finely grated zest of ½ orange and 1–2 tbsp orange-flower water, to taste. For a special occasion, sprinkle in 1–2 tsp almond liqueur. Cut 4 large peaches in half and remove the stones. Place 2 halves on each plate and fill with the orange cream. Arrange fresh orange slices on the plates and grate a little nutmeg over both the peaches and the orange slices.

● For a quick dessert that is rich in vitamin C, fold 500 g (1 lb 2 oz) raspberries, blackberries, blueberries or halved strawberries into the rose or orange cream and spoon into dessert glasses (omit the figs).

● For a lower-fat dessert use reduced-fat crème fraîche.

Plus points

● Raspberries not only provide plenty of vitamin C, but they also contain an important antioxidant, fat-soluble vitamin E. The effects of vitamin E are enhanced by the presence of other antioxidants, such as vitamin C.

● In addition to fibre, fresh figs offer small but not negligible amounts of many vitamins and minerals.

Each serving provides Ⓥ
kcal 150, **protein** 2 g, **fat** 10 g (of which saturated fat 6 g), **carbohydrate** 12 g (of which sugars 12 g), **fibre** 3 g

✓✓✓	C
✓	B$_6$

Desserts

Pistachio floating islands

In this version of the classic French pudding *îles flottantes* fluffy poached meringues studded with pistachio nuts float on a creamy vanilla custard. A flourish of fresh blueberry coulis is the finishing touch.

Serves 4

Vanilla custard

600 ml (1 pint) semi-skimmed milk

1 vanilla pod

25 g (scant 1 oz) caster sugar

4 large egg yolks

1 tsp cornflour

Pistachio meringues

1 large egg white

45 g (1½ oz) caster sugar

30 g (1 oz) unsalted pistachio nuts, chopped

Blueberry coulis

250 g (8½ oz) blueberries

15 g (½ oz) icing sugar, sifted

Preparation and cooking time: about
50 minutes, plus at least 30 minutes chilling

Each serving provides ⓥ

kcal 283, **protein** 10 g, **fat** 12 g (of which saturated fat 4 g), **carbohydrate** 38 g (of which sugars 34 g), **fibre** 2 g

✓✓✓	B₁₂
✓✓	calcium
✓	A, B₁, B₂, C, folate, niacin, copper, iron, potassium, selenium, zinc

1 Pour the milk into a medium-sized frying pan. Split the vanilla pod down its length with a sharp knife and scrape out the tiny black seeds into the milk. Cut the pod in half and add to the pan with the sugar. Bring to a gentle simmer, stirring occasionally.

2 Meanwhile, in a clean bowl whisk the egg white for the meringues to soft peaks. Gradually whisk in the caster sugar, then continue whisking for about 1 minute or until the meringue is stiff and glossy. Gently fold in the pistachio nuts.

3 When the milk is just simmering, spoon on the meringue in 4 neat mounds. Poach gently for 5 minutes, turning once, until the meringues feel set. Remove with a draining spoon onto kitchen paper and set aside.

4 Strain the milk into a heavy-based saucepan. Mix together the egg yolks and cornflour, then whisk into the milk. Cook over a very low heat for 5–7 minutes, stirring all the time, until smooth and thickened. Do not allow the custard to boil or it will curdle. If it does start to curdle, immediately strain it through a fine sieve into a clean pan.

5 Remove the custard from the heat and pour it into a large, shallow serving bowl or onto 4 individual plates or dishes. Cover and chill for at least 30 minutes or up to 1 hour.

6 Meanwhile, make the blueberry coulis. Put the blueberries and icing sugar in a small saucepan with 2 tsp water. Simmer over a low heat, stirring occasionally, for 4–5 minutes or until the blueberries burst and release their juices. Press the mixture through a sieve and leave to cool.

7 Float the meringues on the custard and drizzle a little blueberry coulis over them. Serve immediately, with the rest of the coulis separately.

Plus points

• As long as eggs are not overcooked, there is no protein loss and they retain all their content of vitamins A, D and niacin. But if cooked for a long time there can be some loss of vitamins B₁ and B₂.

• Pistachios are a good source of vitamin B₁ and contain a small amount of carotene. Like other nuts, they are rich in potassium and low in sodium (unless salt is added during roasting).

• Blueberries, like all berries, are rich in vitamin C and also provide some beta-carotene. Both of these nutrients are important antioxidants.

Desserts

Some more ideas

- Use frozen and thawed blueberries for the coulis.
- Omit the pistachios, if you prefer, or replace them with chopped pecan nuts.

- For lime and passion fruit floating islands, flavour the milk with the grated zest of 1 lime instead of vanilla. Make the meringues as in the main recipe, but without the pistachio nuts. Replace the blueberry coulis with a passion fruit

coulis: halve 6 large, ripe passion fruits and scoop out the pulp into a small saucepan. Stir in 15 g (½ oz) caster sugar and cook over a low heat for 1–2 minutes, stirring, until the sugar has dissolved. Leave to cool.

Pimm's melon cup

This slimline dessert is inspired by the classic summer drink, which can often be almost a fruit salad in itself. Sweet melon, berries, pear and cucumber are marinated in Pimm's and then served in melon shells. A decoration of pretty borage flowers is a traditional finish.

Serves 4

1 small Ogen melon
1 small cantaloupe or Charentais melon
200 g (7 oz) strawberries, sliced
1 pear, cut into 2.5 cm (1 in) chunks
¼ cucumber, cut into 1 cm (½ in) dice
1 carambola, cut into 5 mm (¼ in) slices
6 tbsp Pimm's
2 tbsp shredded fresh mint or lemon balm
    leaves
borage flowers to decorate (optional)

Preparation time: 20–25 minutes,
    plus 20 minutes' marinating

1 Cut the melons in half horizontally and scoop out the seeds from the centre. Using a melon baller or a small spoon, scoop out the flesh into a large bowl. Reserve the melon shells.

2 Add the sliced strawberries, pear chunks and cucumber dice to the melon in the bowl. Reserve some slices of carambola for decoration and chop the rest. Add to the bowl.

3 Sprinkle the Pimm's over the fruit. Add the shredded mint or lemon balm and stir gently to mix together. Cover with cling film and set aside in a cool place or the fridge to marinate for 20 minutes.

4 With a tablespoon scoop any odd pieces of melon flesh from the shells to make them smooth. Pile the fruit mixture into the shells and decorate with the reserved slices of carambola and borage flowers, if using.

Some more ideas

● For a non-alcoholic version, omit the Pimm's and flavour with 1–2 tsp of a cordial such as elderflower.

● Turn this into a luncheon fruit and vegetable salad, using just 1 melon (either Ogen or cantaloupe), the strawberries and cucumber plus an apple instead of the pear and 100 g (3½ oz) seedless green grapes. Omit the Pimm's. Make a bed of salad leaves, including some watercress and chopped spring onion, on each plate and pile the fruit on top. Add a scoop of plain cottage cheese and sprinkle with chopped fresh mint and toasted pine nuts.

Plus points

● This delicious combination of fresh fruit provides plenty of fibre and vitamins, especially vitamin C and beta-carotene (which is found in orange-fleshed melon varieties), both important antioxidants.

● While the latest research shows that women should avoid alcohol altogether during pregnancy, in the population as a whole moderate alcohol consumption is now associated with a lower risk of death from coronary heart disease. Moderate means avoiding binges and taking no more than 3–4 units a day for men and 2–3 units a day for women.

Each serving provides Ⓥ
kcal 101, **protein** 1.5 g, **fat** 0 g, **carbohydrate** 12 g (of which sugars 12 g), **fibre** 2 g

✓✓✓	C
✓✓	A
✓	folate

Desserts

227

Blackberry ripple frozen yogurt

Here creamy custard-based ice cream is lightened with Greek-style yogurt, instead of the usual rich cream, and flavoured with a hint of orange. A fresh blackberry purée is stirred through for a pretty purple ripple effect.

Serves 4

300 ml (10 fl oz) full-fat milk

finely grated zest of 1 orange

1 large egg

2 large egg yolks

55 g (2 oz) caster sugar

1 tsp cornflour

1 tsp pure vanilla extract

250 g (8½ oz) Greek-style yogurt

125 g (4½ oz) blackberries to decorate

Blackberry purée

115 g (4 oz) blackberries

30 g (1 oz) caster sugar

Preparation time: about 35 minutes, plus cooling and freezing

---

Each serving provides Ⓥ

kcal 276, **protein** 9 g, **fat** 12.5 g (of which saturated fat 6 g), **carbohydrate** 34 g (of which sugars 32 g), **fibre** 2 g

✓✓✓	B₁₂
✓✓	A, calcium
✓	B₂, C, E, folate, niacin, copper, potassium, zinc

1 Warm the milk in a heavy-based saucepan with the orange zest until scalding hot. Meanwhile, put the whole egg, egg yolks, sugar, cornflour and vanilla extract in a mixing bowl, and whisk together until pale and creamy.

2 Stir the milk into the egg mixture, then return to the pan and cook over a low heat, stirring constantly, until thickened. Do not allow the custard to boil. Remove from the heat and set aside to cool.

3 When the custard is cold, beat in the yogurt. Pour the mixture into an ice-cream machine and churn according to the manufacturer's instructions until the mixture is thick and slushy.

4 Alternatively, pour the mixture into a freezerproof container and freeze for 2 hours or until the mixture begins to set around the edges. Tip out into a bowl and whisk well with a balloon whisk or electric mixer to break down the ice crystals that have formed, then return to the container. Freeze for a further 1½ hours.

5 Meanwhile, make the purée. Put the blackberries in a saucepan with the sugar and 1 tbsp water. Heat until the berries are soft and juicy, then bring to the boil and boil for 1–2 minutes to reduce slightly. Remove from the heat and cool. Press the blackberries through a nylon sieve to make a smooth purée.

6 If using an ice-cream machine, transfer the frozen yogurt to a rigid plastic container, then lightly stir in the blackberry purée to make a ripple effect. If frozen in a container, tip out into a bowl and whisk well until softened, then swirl in the blackberry purée and return to the container. Freeze for a further 3 hours, or overnight, until firm. (The frozen yogurt can be kept, covered, in the freezer for 3 months.)

7 About 45 minutes before serving, remove the frozen yogurt from the freezer so it can soften a little. Scoop into glasses and decorate with berries.

Plus points

• Cornflour is a good source of both starch and protein. It also supplies useful amounts of potassium, iron, phosphorus and thiamin.

• This delicious frozen yogurt is much lower in sugar and calories than most commercial frozen yogurts.

Desserts

Some more ideas

● Make blueberry ripple frozen yogurt, using fresh or frozen and thawed blueberries instead of blackberries.

● Instead of vanilla extract, add 1 tsp ground cinnamon to the egg mixture in step 1.

● For strawberry frozen yogurt, make the custard as in the main recipe, but omit the vanilla extract. Cool, then add the yogurt. Gently cook 500 g (1 lb 2 oz) strawberries with the juice of ½ lemon and 55 g (2 oz) caster sugar until soft. Leave to cool, then press through a sieve. Beat the strawberry purée evenly into the custard and yogurt mixture, then freeze as in the main recipe.

Strawberry yogurt mousse

This lovely strawberry dessert captures the taste of summer. Mild bio yogurt is used in place of cream for a lighter, lower fat mousse, which is chilled until set and then served with a raspberry and currant sauce.

Serves 4

1 tbsp powdered gelatine

450 g (1 lb) strawberries

25 g (scant 1 oz) caster sugar

500 g (1 lb 2 oz) plain low-fat bio yogurt

Raspberry and currant sauce

115 g (4 oz) red or black currants, plus a few extra on stalks to decorate

25 g (scant 1 oz) caster sugar

115 g (4 oz) raspberries

1 tbsp framboise (raspberry liqueur) or kirsch

Preparation and cooking time: 20 minutes, plus at least 2 hours chilling

Each serving provides

kcal 185, **protein** 11 g, **fat** 1 g (of which saturated fat 0.5 g), **carbohydrate** 33 g (of which sugars 33 g), **fibre** 3 g

✓✓✓	C
✓✓	calcium
✓	B₂, folate, niacin, copper, potassium, zinc

1 Sprinkle the gelatine over 3 tbsp cold water in a small mixing bowl and leave to soak for 5 minutes or until spongy. Set the bowl over a pan of hot water and stir until the gelatine has dissolved. Remove from the heat and leave to cool.

2 Meanwhile, put the strawberries and sugar in a bowl and mash with a fork. Add the dissolved gelatine and then the yogurt, mixing well. Divide among 4 glasses or serving dishes of 200 ml (7 fl oz) capacity. Cover and chill for at least 2 hours or until set.

3 Meanwhile, make the sauce. Put the currants, sugar and 2 tsp water in a small saucepan and bring to the boil, stirring to dissolve the sugar. Simmer for 1 minute, then remove from the heat and add the raspberries. Purée in the pan with a hand-held blender, or crush with a fork, then press through a sieve.

4 Pour a little of the sauce over the top of each mousse and decorate with a stalk of currants. Serve the remaining sauce separately.

Another idea

● For a plum and yogurt bavarois, sprinkle 1 tbsp powdered gelatine over 3 tbsp apple juice and leave to soak for 5 minutes. Bring 200 ml (7 fl oz) semi-skimmed milk to boiling point. Meanwhile, whisk together 1 whole egg,

2 egg yolks, 1 tsp cornflour and 45 g (1½ oz) caster sugar in a bowl. Pour in the hot milk, whisking. Return the mixture to the rinsed-out pan and stir over a low heat for 3–4 minutes or until thickened. Remove from the heat and stir in the gelatine until dissolved. Pour the custard into a bowl and cool, stirring occasionally. Meanwhile, halve and stone 4 firm, ripe plums and put in a pan with 45 g (1½ oz) caster sugar and 170 ml (6 fl oz) apple juice. Poach for 8–10 minutes or until the plums are just soft. Remove them with a draining spoon. Simmer the poaching liquid for 5 minutes or until syrupy. Leave to cool. Stir 150 g (5½ oz) plain low-fat bio yogurt into the cooled custard, then fold in 150 ml (5 fl oz) lightly whipped whipping cream. Spoon a thin layer of the custard mixture into a chilled 1 litre (1¾ pint) ring mould, and arrange the cooled plums on top. Spoon in the remaining custard mixture. Chill for at least 2 hours or until set. Turn out and serve with the plum syrup.

Plus point

● Bio yogurts contain live bacteria that have a beneficial effect on the digestive system. These yogurts also have a milder, creamier flavour than normal yogurt.

Desserts

Fragrant mango cream in brandy-snap baskets

What could be more delicious than luscious fresh fruit blended with Greek-style yogurt and lemon curd, and spooned into ready-made brandy-snap baskets? This is a really special treat, wonderfully creamy without being too high in calories.

Serves 6
1 large ripe mango
2 passion fruit
2 tbsp good-quality lemon curd
300 g (10½ oz) Greek-style yogurt
6 brandy-snap baskets
1 tbsp chopped pistachio nuts
fresh mint leaves to decorate

Preparation time: 15 minutes

Each serving provides ⓥ
kcal 220, **protein** 5 g, **fat** 11 g (of which saturated fat 3 g), **carbohydrate** 26 g (of which sugars 22 g), **fibre** 2 g

✓✓✓	C
✓✓	A
✓	B₂, B₁₂, calcium

1 Cut the peel from the mango and slice the flesh from the flat stone. Place half the mango flesh in a food processor or blender and process briefly until smooth. Spoon into a bowl. Chop the remaining mango flesh into pieces and set aside.

2 Cut the passion fruit in half and scoop out the seeds and pulp into the mango purée. Stir in the lemon curd. Add the yogurt and fold everything together until well combined.

3 Spoon the fruit and yogurt cream into the brandy-snap baskets and top with the chopped mango. Scatter a few chopped pistachio nuts over the top of each serving and decorate with fresh mint leaves. Serve immediately.

Some more ideas
● Orange curd, which is becoming more widely available, makes a delicious alternative to lemon curd.
● Substitute a papaya for the mango.
● For a raspberry and chocolate cream on panettone, add 2 tbsp chopped toasted hazelnuts and 4 tbsp chocolate ice cream sauce to 300 g (10½ oz) Greek-style yogurt, and swirl together until the chocolate sauce has marbled the yogurt. Cut 3 long slices of dried fruit panettone in half and toast under the grill

until golden. Spoon the chocolate cream over the panettone and scatter on 125 g (4½ oz) fresh raspberries. Dust lightly with icing sugar and serve decorated with fresh mint leaves.
● Slice 2 bananas and divide them among the brandy-snap baskets. Top with the chocolate and hazelnut cream above and finish with a fine drizzle of warm chocolate sauce.

Plus points
● Greek-style yogurt tastes luxurious, but has a fraction of the fat and calories of double cream: double cream contains 449 kcal and 48 g fat per 100 g (3½ oz), while the same weight of Greek-style yogurt has just 115 kcal and 9 g fat.
● The ancient Indians believed that mangoes helped to increase sexual desire and prolong love-making. Whether or not this is true, mangoes are rich in beta carotene. This antioxidant is easily absorbed by the body, because of the digestible mango flesh, and is then converted into vitamin A, which is essential for growth. Mangoes also provide useful amounts of fibre and copper.

Desserts

233

Cinnamon banana caramels

Any fruit – fresh, canned or frozen – can be used to make this instant version of crème brûlée. The fruit is simply topped with Greek-style yogurt – a lower-fat alternative to double cream – then sprinkled with demerara sugar and grilled to a rich caramel.

Serves 4

4 bananas

¼ tsp ground cinnamon

300 g (10½ oz) Greek-style yogurt

4 tbsp demerara sugar

Preparation time: 8 minutes

Cooking time: 1 minute

1 Preheat the grill. Peel and slice the bananas, cutting each one into about 16 slices. Divide the slices among four 250 ml (8½ fl oz) ramekin dishes and sprinkle with the ground cinnamon. Spoon the yogurt over the banana slices to cover them completely. Sprinkle 1 tbsp of sugar evenly over each dessert.

2 Place the dishes on a baking sheet and put them under the grill. Cook for about 1 minute or until the sugar melts into the yogurt – keep watch to make sure that it does not burn. Remove from the grill and leave to cool for a few minutes before serving.

into the yogurt along with 2 tbsp clear honey. Spoon the yogurt mixture over the raspberries and sprinkle the top with 25 g (scant 1 oz) toasted flaked almonds.

Some more ideas

• For a very low-fat dessert, use 0%-fat Greek-style yogurt.

• Instead of yogurt, you can use low-fat soft cheese, thick fromage frais or crème fraîche.

• Try chopped peaches or nectarines, or a mixture of summer fruits, instead. Prepare the fruit in the same way as the main recipe. Plums, rhubarb, blackcurrants and gooseberries can also be used, but these fruits are best lightly stewed in the minimum amount of water until tender, then cooled before the yogurt topping goes on.

• To make a crunchy raspberry dessert, use 200 g (7 oz) fresh raspberries. Toast 2 tbsp medium oatmeal in a frying pan over a moderately high heat for 2–3 minutes, watching to make sure it does not burn. Stir the oatmeal

Plus points

• Bananas are great energy providers and one of the best sources of potassium (in terms of fruit), a mineral we need to keep a stable balance of water in our bodies. Apart from pure carbohydrate, bananas also provide fibre plus useful amounts of vitamins B_6 and C, magnesium and copper.

• Yogurt is a useful source of calcium and phosphorus for strong bones and teeth, as well as vitamins B_2, needed for releasing energy from food, and B_{12}, essential for a healthy nervous system. Yogurt can help to regulate the balance of the bacteria in the large bowel, which may help to protect against cancer of the colon.

Each serving provides Ⓥ

kcal 240, **protein** 6 g, **fat** 7 g (of which saturated fat 4 g), **carbohydrate** 40 g (of which sugars 38 g), **fibre** 1 g

✓ B_6, B_{12}

Desserts

234

Hot apricot soufflés

Keep cans of apricots packed in fruit juice in your storecupboard and you will be able to make these light and fluffy dessert soufflés in minutes. They look impressive and do not contain the large amounts of sugar and eggs found in most sweet soufflé recipes.

Serves 4

1½ tsp ground almonds or caster sugar

1 can apricot halves in natural juice, about 400 g, well drained

2 eggs, separated

2 tbsp double cream

1 tbsp caster sugar

½ tsp pure vanilla extract

½ tsp lemon juice

½ tsp cream of tartar

To finish

icing sugar

cocoa powder (optional)

Preparation time: about 10 minutes

Cooking time: 15 minutes

1 Preheat the oven to 200°C (400°F, gas mark 6) and place a baking tray inside to heat. Lightly butter four 175 ml (6 fl oz) ramekins and dust the sides with the ground almonds or caster sugar, shaking out the excess.

2 Put the apricot halves, egg yolks, cream, sugar, vanilla extract and lemon juice in a food processor or blender and process until smooth.

3 Place the egg whites in a clean bowl and whisk until soft peaks form. Sift over the cream of tartar and continue whisking until stiff peaks form. Spoon the apricot mixture over the egg whites and use a large metal spoon to fold together, taking care not to overmix and deflate the egg whites.

4 Divide the apricot mixture among the prepared ramekins. Use a round-bladed knife to mark a circle in the centre of each soufflé; this helps the tops to rise evenly.

5 Place the ramekins on the heated baking sheet and bake in the centre of the oven for 15 minutes or until the soufflés are well risen and golden brown on top. Immediately dust with icing sugar, or a mixture of icing sugar and cocoa powder, sifted through a sieve, and serve at once.

Plus points

- Using fruit canned in natural juice, rather than in syrup, cuts the sugar and thus the amount of calories.
- Eggs are a first-class source of protein – an essential nutrient for good health and well-being.

Some more ideas

- For double-fruit soufflés, drain a second can of apricot halves and finely chop the fruit. Flavour the apricots with a little very finely chopped preserved stem ginger or ground mixed spice. Prepare 6 ramekins, instead of 4. Make the soufflé mixture as above. Divide the chopped fruit among the ramekins, then top with the soufflé mixture and bake.
- Substitute pears canned in natural juice and add a pinch of ground cardamom to the mixture. Other fruits to try are blackcurrants and peaches.
- Save the fruit juice to add to a fruit salad or make into a fruit drink.

Each serving provides Ⓥ

kcal 155, **protein** 5 g, **fat** 9 g (of which saturated fat 4 g), **carbohydrate** 13 g (of which sugars 13 g), **fibre** 1 g

| ✓✓ | B$_{12}$, C |
| ✓ | A, E |

Desserts

Summer pudding

What an amazing dish the British summer pudding is – simplicity itself. The peaches or nectarines add a slightly different dimension to this version, a marvellous way of eating a large portion of ripe fresh fruit, not cooked at all so as to retain all its nutrients.

Serves 6

600 g (1 lb 5 oz) mixed summer fruit (raspberries, blueberries, redcurrants, sliced strawberries)

2 ripe peaches or nectarines, stoned and diced

3 tbsp sugar, or to taste

150 ml (5 fl oz) cranberry juice

8 thin slices white bread, about 200 g (7 oz) in total, preferably 1–2 days old

To serve (optional)

reduced-fat crème fraîche

Preparation time: 20 minutes, plus 2 hours macerating and 8 hours chilling

1 Crush the different types of fruit individually, to be sure all the skins are broken and the fruit is pulpy. Put all the fruit in a large bowl with the sugar and cranberry juice and stir to mix. Leave to macerate for 2 hours.

2 Cut the crusts from the bread and cut the slices into strips or triangles. Fit the bread into a 1 litre (2 pint) pudding basin to line the bottom and sides, reserving enough bread to cover the top. Fill in any gaps with small bits of bread.

3 Reserve 3–4 tbsp of juice from the mixed fruit, then gently pour the fruit mixture into the bread-lined pudding basin. Top with the remaining bread. Cover with a plate that just fits inside the rim of the basin, setting it directly on top of the bread, and then place a heavy weight such as a can of food on top. Place the basin in the fridge to chill for 8 hours or overnight.

4 To serve, turn the pudding out onto a serving dish. Use the reserved fruit juice to brush or pour over any parts of the bread that have not been coloured. Serve with crème fraîche, if liked.

Some more ideas

● Use an enriched bread such as Jewish challah or brioche instead of white bread.

● For an autumn pudding, substitute raisin bread for white bread, and instead of the summer fruits and peaches, use 2 large dessert apples, diced, 2 pears, diced, 30 g (1 oz) sultanas, 30 g (1 oz) dried cranberries and 50 g (1¾ oz) dried apricots, chopped. Put the fruit in a saucepan with 300 ml (10 fl oz) apple juice and ½ tsp ground cinnamon. Bring to the boil, then poach gently for 5–7 minutes or until the apples are tender. Pour into the bread-lined mould and weight as in step 3. Serve decorated with diced sharon fruit and/or a scattering of pomegranate seeds, if you like.

Plus points

● Cranberries and cranberry juice are good sources of vitamin C. They also contain a compound that prevents E. coli bacteria from causing urinary tract infections.

● Low in fat and high in carbohydrate and fibre, this is a delicious dessert in a diet for a healthy heart.

Each serving (pudding alone) provides Ⓥ

kcal 160, **protein** 4 g, **fat** 1 g, **carbohydrate** 36 g (of which sugars 20 g), **fibre** 3 g

✓✓✓ C

✓   folate, niacin

Desserts

Sultana lemon cheesecake

Here is a delicious Italian-style cheesecake with a fresh lemon flavour. Cheesecakes are usually high in fat, but this recipe isn't baked with a butter-rich crust, and it uses lower-fat ricotta cheese rather than rich cream cheese, so the fat content is much reduced.

Serves 8

45 g (1½ oz) sultanas

3 tbsp brandy

3 tbsp semolina

340 g (12 oz) ricotta cheese

3 large egg yolks

85 g (3 oz) caster sugar

3 tbsp lemon juice

1½ tsp pure vanilla extract

finely grated zest of 2 large lemons

Topping

2 oranges

2 satsumas

1 lemon

4 tbsp lemon jelly marmalade

Preparation time: 20 minutes, plus 30 minutes soaking and 2–3 hours cooling

Cooking time: 35–40 minutes

Each serving provides

kcal 220, **protein** 7 g, **fat** 7 g (of which saturated fat 4 g), **carbohydrate** 32 g (of which sugars 26 g), **fibre** 1 g

✓✓	C
✓	A, B₁₂, calcium

1 Place the sultanas in a small bowl, add the brandy and leave to soak for at least 30 minutes or until most of the brandy has been absorbed.

2 Preheat the oven to 180°C (350°F, gas mark 4). Line the bottom of a non-stick, 20 cm (8 in) loose-bottomed sandwich tin with buttered baking parchment. Lightly butter the side of the tin. Sprinkle 1 tbsp of the semolina into the tin, turn and tilt the tin to coat the bottom and sides, then tap out any excess semolina. Set the tin aside.

3 Put the ricotta cheese into a fine sieve and press it through into a mixing bowl. Beat in the egg yolks, sugar, lemon juice, vanilla extract and remaining semolina. Stir in the lemon zest and the sultanas with any remaining brandy.

4 Spoon the mixture into the prepared tin and smooth the surface. Bake for 35–40 minutes or until the top is browned and the sides are shrinking from the tin. Leave to cool in the switched-off oven for 2–3 hours with the door ajar.

5 For the topping, peel the oranges, satsumas and lemon, removing all the white pith, then cut out the segments from between the membranes. Warm the marmalade very gently in a small saucepan until it has melted.

6 Carefully remove the cooled cheesecake from the tin and set on a serving platter. Brush with a layer of the melted marmalade. Arrange the citrus segments on top and glaze with the rest of the marmalade. Leave to set before serving.

Some more ideas

● Replace the sultanas with finely chopped dried apricots or sour cherries.

● For a mixed citrus flavour, add grated lime and orange zests, and soak the sultanas in orange juice. Replace the lemon juice with orange juice.

● Alternative fruit toppings include halved strawberries, blueberries and raspberries.

Plus points

● Many cheesecake recipes include finely ground nuts to help to bind the ingredients together. In this recipe the nuts have been replaced by semolina, which is finely ground durum wheat, thus omitting the fat that nuts would have supplied.

● The fresh citrus fruit topping provides lots of vitamin C.

Desserts

Rich chocolate torte

A generous amount of good-quality dark chocolate makes this Continental-style cake moist and rich – just a small slice will satisfy any sweet tooth. It's perfect as a warm dessert, with a spoonful of soured cream or Greek-style yogurt and some fresh berries.

Serves 10

170 g (6 oz) good dark chocolate (at least 70% cocoa solids)

75 g (2½ oz) unsalted butter

4 eggs

100 g (3½ oz) light muscovado sugar

30 g (1 oz) plain flour

To decorate

cape gooseberries, papery skins folded back (optional)

icing sugar

cocoa powder

Preparation time: 20 minutes

Cooking time: 15–20 minutes

Each serving provides Ⓥ

kcal 230, **protein** 4 g, **fat** 14 g (of which saturated fat 8 g), **carbohydrate** 24 g (of which sugars 21 g), **fibre** 0 g

✓✓	B₁₂
✓	A, copper

1 Preheat the oven to 180°C (350°F, gas mark 4). Grease a 23 cm (9 in) springform cake tin and line it with greased greaseproof paper.

2 Break up the chocolate and put it in a heatproof bowl with the butter. Set the bowl over a pan of almost boiling water, making sure that the water is not touching the base of the bowl. Leave the chocolate and butter to melt, then remove from the heat and stir the mixture until smooth.

3 Meanwhile, put the eggs and sugar in a large bowl and beat with an electric mixer until the mixture has increased considerably in volume and leaves a trail on the surface when the beaters are lifted out. (If using a hand whisk or rotary beater, set the bowl over a pan of almost boiling water, making sure the water is not touching the base of the bowl.)

4 Add the chocolate mixture to the whisked mixture and fold it in with a large metal spoon. Gradually sift the flour over the top of the egg and chocolate mixture, folding in until it is just combined.

5 Turn the mixture into the prepared cake tin, gently spreading it to the edges to level the surface. Bake for 15–20 minutes or until the top of the cake feels just firm to the touch. Leave to cool in the tin.

6 Remove the cake from the tin and peel away the lining paper. Cut into thin wedges for serving, decorating each with a cape gooseberry, if liked, and dusting the plates with sifted icing sugar and cocoa powder. The cake can be kept in the fridge for 2–3 days.

Some more ideas

● Use ground almonds instead of flour.

● If you're making the torte for a special dessert, drizzle 3 tbsp brandy or an orange liqueur such as Cointreau over the top after baking, then leave the cake to cool.

Plus points

● Scientists at the University of California have discovered that chocolate, particularly dark chocolate, contains significant amounts of phenols. These substances work as an antioxidant, helping to prevent the oxidation of harmful LDL cholesterol, which is the cholesterol responsible for clogging the arteries. A 1¼ oz piece of chocolate contains about the same amount of phenols as a glass of red wine.

● Cape gooseberries contain useful amounts of beta-carotene, vitamin C and potassium.

Pannacotta

The traditional recipe for this 'cooked cream', from the Piedmont region of Italy, is made with rich double cream. This lighter version, served with a pretty fruit compote, is still smooth and creamy yet much lower in fat. Prepare it the day before serving, if possible.

Serves 4

500 ml (17 fl oz) semi-skimmed milk

1 tbsp powdered gelatine

75 g (2½ oz) caster sugar

100 ml (3½ fl oz) single cream

strip of pared orange zest

1 vanilla pod, split

Rhubarb and strawberry compote

400 g (14 oz) pink rhubarb, trimmed and cut
   into 5 cm (2 in) lengths

juice of 1 orange

30 g (1 oz) caster sugar

450 g (1 lb) ripe strawberries, sliced

Preparation and cooking time: 30 minutes, plus
   at least 3 hours chilling

Each serving provides

kcal 265, **protein** 10 g, **fat** 7 g (of which
saturated fat 4 g), **carbohydrate** 43 g (of
which sugars 43 g), **fibre** 3 g

✓✓✓	C
✓✓	calcium
✓	A, B$_2$, B$_{12}$, folate, copper, potassium, zinc

1 Pour 150 ml (5 fl oz) of the milk into a saucepan. Sprinkle over the gelatine and leave to soak, without stirring, for 5 minutes or until the gelatine has become spongy.

2 Stir in the sugar, then set the pan over a low heat. Warm gently, without boiling, until the sugar and gelatine have completely dissolved, stirring frequently.

3 Remove the pan from the heat and add the remaining milk, the cream and orange zest. Scrape the seeds from the vanilla pod into the milk mixture, then add the pod too. Leave to infuse for 10 minutes while preparing the compote.

4 Place the rhubarb in a saucepan with the orange juice and sugar. Bring just to a simmer, then cook gently for 3–4 minutes or until the rhubarb is tender but still holding its shape. Spoon the rhubarb into a serving dish using a draining spoon. Boil the juice remaining in the pan to reduce it slightly until syrupy. Pour the juice over the rhubarb and gently stir in the sliced strawberries. Leave to cool.

5 Strain the milk mixture through a fine sieve into a jug, then pour into 4 moulds, cups or ramekins of 170 ml (6 fl oz) capacity. Allow to cool, then cover and chill for at least 3 hours or until set.

6 To serve, run the tip of a knife around the edge of each pannacotta. Place an inverted serving plate over the top of the ramekin and turn them upside down, holding the two firmly together. Lift off the ramekin. Spoon some of the compote on the side of the pannacotta. Serve the remaining compote separately.

Plus points

● A fruit compote complements a creamy dessert in taste and colour, and also adds nutritional benefits.

● Although used as a fruit, rhubarb is actually a vegetable. It contains vitamin C and is a good source of potassium.

● The red colouring of strawberries comes from antioxidant anthocyanin flavonoids, which may help to strengthen the walls of small blood vessels.

Desserts

244

Some more ideas

• If you do not have a vanilla pod, use a few drops of pure vanilla extract.

• Serve the pannacotta with a fresh raspberry sauce. Push 450 g (1 lb) raspberries through a fine sieve, then mix the purée with 1 tbsp sifted icing sugar.

• For rosewater pannacotta, instead of orange zest and vanilla, add 1 tsp rosewater and the seeds from 8 cardamom pods to the milk and cream mixture in step 2, then leave to infuse. Serve with a fresh raspberry and passion fruit sauce. To make the sauce, add the juice of ½ orange and the pulp scooped from 2 passion fruits to a basic raspberry sauce.

Fruit and pistachio baklava

Here is an update of the traditional Greek pastries, made with a cinnamon-spiced filling of dried dates, dried mango and pistachio nuts, layered with filo pastry. Although this version uses less fat and honey than usual, it is sure to be a winner.

Makes 20 squares

55 g (2 oz) butter

2 tbsp sunflower oil

85 g (3 oz) dried mango, finely chopped

85 g (3 oz) stoned dried dates, finely chopped

115 g (4 oz) pistachio nuts, finely chopped

1½ tsp ground cinnamon

8 tbsp clear honey

20 sheets filo pastry, about 18 x 30 cm
    (7 x 12 in) each

4 tbsp orange juice

Preparation time: 40 minutes

Cooking time: 20–25 minutes

1 Gently heat the butter and oil in a small saucepan until melted and blended. Remove the pan from the heat and set aside. Mix together the dried mango, dates, pistachios, cinnamon and 4 tbsp of the honey in a bowl. Set aside.

2 Preheat the oven to 220ºC (425ºF, gas mark 7). Lightly grease a shallow 18 x 28 cm (7 x 11 in) baking tin with a little of the melted butter and oil mixture.

3 Place one sheet of filo pastry in the bottom of the tin, allowing the pastry to come up the sides of the tin if necessary, and brush sparingly with the butter and oil mixture. Layer in 4 more sheets of filo, brushing each one lightly with the mix of oil and butter. Spread with one-third of the fruit mixture.

4 Repeat the layering of filo sheets and fruit mixture 2 more times. Top this final layer of fruit filling with the remaining 5 sheets of filo, brushing each with a little of the melted butter and oil. Trim the edges of the pastry to fit the tin.

5 Mark the surface of the top pastry layer into 20 squares using the tip of a sharp knife. Bake for 15 minutes, then reduce the oven temperature to 180ºC (350ºF, gas mark 4). Bake for a further 10–15 minutes or until the pastry is crisp and golden brown.

6 Meanwhile, gently warm the remaining 4 tbsp honey with the orange juice in a small saucepan until blended, stirring constantly.

7 When the pastry has finished baking, remove it from the oven and pour the honey and orange mixture evenly over the surface. Leave it to cool in the tin. When cold, cut into the marked squares for serving.

Each square provides Ⓥ

kcals 196, **protein** 4 g, **fat** 10 g (of which saturated fat 2 g), **carbohydrate** 24 g (of which sugars 15 g), **fibre** 2 g

✓✓	E
✓	copper

Plus points

• Filo pastry is a lower-fat alternative to shortcrust and puff pastries. In 100 g (3½ oz) of filo pastry there are 2 g fat and 275 kcals, whereas the same weight of shortcrust pastry contains 29 g fat and 449 kcals.

• The sweetness of fruit is concentrated in its dried form, so no additional sugar is needed in the filling for this pastry. Dried fruit is also a significant source of dietary fibre.

Desserts

Some more ideas

• To make peach or apricot and pecan baklava, use 170 g (6 oz) chopped ready-to-eat dried peaches or apricots in place of the dates and mango, and chopped pecan nuts (or hazelnuts)

in place of some or all of the pistachios. Spice with ground ginger, nutmeg or mixed spice instead of cinnamon.

• For pear, hazelnut and almond baklava, make the filling by mixing together 55 g (2 oz) finely

chopped hazelnuts, 55 g (2 oz) finely chopped almonds, 85 g (3 oz) chopped ready-to-eat dried pears, 85 g (3 oz) sultanas, 1½ tsp ground mixed spice and the finely grated zest of 1 small lemon.

Steamed kumquat honey pudding

A pleasingly light yet traditional pudding for wintry days, this offers all the pleasure of a steamed pudding without the unhealthy saturated fat in suet. Layers of sliced kumquats add a deliciously tangy citrus flavour.

Serves 6

2 tbsp clear honey

150 g (5½ oz) fresh fine white breadcrumbs

100 g (3½ oz) demerara sugar

50 g (1¾ oz) self-raising flour

1 tsp baking powder

1 egg, beaten

2 tbsp semi-skimmed milk

30 g (1 oz) unsalted butter, at room temperature

225 g (8 oz) kumquats, sliced (with skin)

Custard

2 eggs

1 tbsp sugar

300 ml (10 fl oz) semi-skimmed milk

1 tsp pure vanilla extract

Preparation time: 15 minutes

Cooking time: 1¾ hours

Each serving provides Ⓥ

kcal 275, **protein** 6 g, **fat** 6 g (of which saturated fat 3 g), **carbohydrate** 53 g (of which sugars 28 g), **fibre** 2 g

✓✓ B₁₂, C, calcium

1 Put the honey in the bottom of a 900 ml (1½ pint) pudding basin and turn it so that the honey coats the bottom half of the basin. Set aside.

2 Put the breadcrumbs in a large mixing bowl. Stir in the sugar, flour and baking powder. Add the egg, milk and softened butter and mix together to form a stiff cake-like mixture.

3 Place a quarter of the pudding mixture in the bottom of the honey-lined pudding basin and arrange half of the kumquat slices on top. Add half the remaining mixture to the basin and top with the remaining kumquat slices. Finish with the last of the pudding mixture and press down lightly to smooth the surface.

4 Bring a steamer or deep pan of water to the boil. Cover the top of the pudding basin with cooking foil and secure it firmly with string tied round under the rim. Use some more string to make a handle. Place the pudding in the steamer. The water should come no more than halfway up the side of the basin. Cover and steam for 1¾ hours, topping up the water as necessary.

5 About 20 minutes before serving, make the custard. In a bowl, beat the eggs with the sugar and 3 tbsp of the milk. Put the rest of the milk in a heavy-based saucepan and heat until bubbles appear round the edge. Pour the hot milk onto the eggs, stirring, then strain the mixture back into the pan. Cook over a low heat, stirring constantly, until the custard thickens enough to coat the back of the spoon in a thin layer. Do not allow to boil. Stir in the vanilla extract.

6 When the pudding is cooked, carefully remove it from the steamer, lifting it by the string handle. Remove the foil covering, place a plate over the top of the basin and invert it. With a gentle shake, the pudding will fall out of the basin onto the plate. Serve hot, with the custard.

Another idea

• Use sliced oranges instead of kumquats.

Plus points

• Kumquats are not a true citrus fruit, but are closely related and so, not surprisingly, they are an excellent source of vitamin C. Although this vitamin is no longer believed to have a direct effect in preventing the common cold, it does help to maintain the immune system and may well modify the severity and duration of infections.

• Milk provides calcium and phosphorus – both important for strong bones and teeth – as well as protein and many B vitamins.

Desserts

Strawberry shortcake

This streamlined version of an American classic makes an impressive summer dessert. Based on a quick, light scone mixture and filled with Greek-style yogurt, whipped cream and lots of juicy fresh strawberries, it is easy to make and simply irresistible.

Serves 8

250 g (8½ oz) self-raising flour

1 tsp baking powder

75 g (2½ oz) unsalted butter, cut into small
    pieces

3 tbsp caster sugar

1 egg, beaten

4 tbsp semi-skimmed milk

½ tsp pure vanilla extract

1 tsp icing sugar

Strawberry filling

340 g (12 oz) strawberries

90 ml (3 fl oz) whipping cream

85 g (3 oz) Greek-style yogurt

Preparation time: 15 minutes
Cooking time: 10–15 minutes

1 Preheat the oven to 220°C (425°F, gas mark 7). Sift the flour and baking powder into a bowl. Rub in the butter with your fingertips until the mixture resembles fine breadcrumbs. Stir in the caster sugar and make a well in the centre.

2 Mix together the egg, milk and vanilla extract, and pour into the dry ingredients. Gradually stir the dry ingredients into the liquid, then bring the mixture together with your hand to form a soft dough. Gently pat the dough into a smooth ball and turn it out onto a floured surface.

3 Roll out the dough into a 19 cm (7½ in) round. Transfer it to a greased baking sheet and bake for 10–15 minutes or until well risen, firm and browned on top. Slide the shortcake onto a wire rack and leave to cool.

4 Using a large serrated knife, slice the shortcake horizontally in half. With a large fish slice, lift the top layer off and place it on a board. Cut into 8 equal wedges, leaving them in place. (If you like, for an attractive finish, trim a fraction off each cut so that the wedges are slightly smaller.) Place the bottom layer on a serving plate.

5 For the filling, reserve 8 whole strawberries, then hull and thickly slice the remainder. Whip the cream until it forms soft peaks. Stir the yogurt until smooth, then gently fold it into the cream until evenly blended.

6 Spread the cream mixture thickly over the bottom shortcake layer and cover with the sliced strawberries, pressing them into the cream.

7 Sift the icing sugar over the top of the shortcake wedges. Carefully put the wedges into place on top of the shortcake. Slice each reserved strawberry lengthways, leaving the slices attached at the stalk end, then open the slices slightly to fan them out. Place a strawberry fan on each wedge of shortcake. Eat within a few hours of assembling.

Each serving provides

kcal 275, **protein** 5 g, **fat** 14 g (of which saturated fat 8 g), **carbohydrate** 34 g (of which sugars 10 g), **fibre** 1 g

✓✓✓	C
✓✓	A
✓	B₁, B₂, B₆, B₁₂, calcium

Plus points

• Strawberries contain a phytochemical called ellagic acid, which is believed to help protect against cancer. In traditional medicine, strawberries are believed to purify the digestive system and act as a mild tonic for the liver.

• The action of whipping incorporates air into cream and increases its volume, thus making a modest amount go a long way.

Desserts

Some more ideas

• Raspberries, blueberries and stoned cherries can all be substituted for the strawberries.

• To make a spiced shortcake with autumn fruit, add 1 tsp ground cinnamon to the scone mixture with the caster sugar. Halve, stone and slice 225 g (8 oz) ripe plums. Reserve 8 neat slices for decoration, then use the rest to top the cream in place of the strawberries. Reserve 8 blackberries from 225 g (8 oz) and press the remainder into the cream with the plums. Finish as in the main recipe, decorating the top of the shortcake wedges with the reserved plum slices and blackberries.

• Instead of whipped cream and yogurt, fill the shortcake with 300 g (10½ oz) fromage frais flavoured with 2 tsp icing sugar and ½ tsp pure vanilla extract.

Index

Titles in *italics* are for recipes in 'Some more ideas'.

A

Alcohol 9
Almonds: *Almond polenta biscuits* 44
   Cherry and almond cookies 48
Anchovies: Pissaladière 56-57
Antioxidants 7
Apples: Apple and blackberry brioches 28
   Apple and hazelnut drop scones 25
   Apple and mincemeat rock cakes 42
   Apple and muesli rock cakes 42
   Apple sauce 176
   Fruity ginger biscuits 40
   Gingered roast pork 176-7
Apricots: *Apricot and walnut or pecan drop scones* 25
   Berry salad with a peach and apricot sauce 18
   Chicken with apricots and cumin 121
   Hot apricot soufflés 236
   Mango, peach and apricot fizz 17
Artichoke risotto 148
Asparagus: *Chicken with fennel seeds and* 127
   Summer salmon and asparagus 110
Aubergines: *Aubergine with millet and sesame seeds* 200
   Baked aubergines with yogurt 146-7
   Hotpot with golden parsnips 172
   Vegetarian goulash 178
Autumn pudding 238
Avocados: *Baked potato skins with guacamole topping* 59

B

Bacon: Herbed French toast 34
Bagels 216-17
   Cinnamon and raisin 217
   Rye 217
Baklava, Fruit and pistachio 246-7
Balanced diet 6
Bananas: Banana and mango shake 12
   Banana and raspberry toasts 28
   Cereal bars 38
   Cinnamon banana caramels 234
Barley, Slow-braised beef and 164-5
Basil: Basil-scented sautéed vegetables 188
   Basil-stuffed chicken breasts 118

Pesto-yogurt dip 52
Bavarois, Plum and yogurt 230
Bean sprouts, Sesame greens and 197
Beans: Hotpot with golden parsnips 172
   Italian cannellini bean and tuna salad 100
   Moroccan-style pumpkin and butter beans 156-7
   Tuscan bean crostini 60
   Vegetarian goulash 178
Beef: Beef and mushroom Stroganoff 158
   Keema curry 163
   Perfect pot roast 160-1
   Slow-braised beef and barley 164-5
   Thai-style stir-fried beef with mango 166
   Vietnamese broth with noodles 76
Beetroot: *Beetroot with crispy crumbs* 194
   Borscht with crunchy mash 74-75
Berry salad with passion fruit 18
Beta-carotene 7
Biscuits: Double chocolate chunk and nut cookies 48
   Ginger nuts 40
   Orange and pecan biscuits 44
   Sesame cheese twists 50
Black-eyed beans: Hotpot with golden parsnips 172
Blackberries: Apple and blackberry brioches 28
   Blackberry ripple frozen yogurt 228-9
   Fresh berry drop scones 25
   Spiced shortcake with autumn fruit 251
Blood pressure 9
Blueberries: Blueberry and cranberry granola 22
   Blueberry and walnut muffins 31
   Blueberry popovers 26
   Blueberry ripple frozen yogurt 229
   Mixed salad leaves with flowers and 203
   Pistachio floating islands 224
Borscht 74-75
Bowel disease 7
Bread: Bagels 216-17
   Basic loaf 210-11
   Focaccia 212-13
   Goat's cheese toasts 81
   Herbed French toast 34
   Pitta breads 214
   Scrambled eggs with smoked salmon and dill 32
   Summer pudding 238
   Tuscan bean crostini 60
Breads 210-217
Breakfast 10-35

Breakfast muffins 31
Brioches, Apple and blackberry 28
Broccoli: Basil-scented sautéed vegetables 188
   Beef and mushroom Stroganoff 158
   Broccoli and red pepper quiche 150-1
   Creamy broccoli and pea sauce 139
Brussels sprouts with crispy crumbs 194
Bulghur wheat: *Bulghur wheat and feta salad* 98
   Bulghur wheat and ham salad 98
   Bulghur wheat and prawn salad 98
Buns, Spicy fruit 46
Burgers, lamb 170
Butter beans, Moroccan-style pumpkin and 156-7

C

Cabbage: Crunchy nut coleslaw 206
   Pheasant casserole with chestnuts and 135
   Sesame greens and bean sprouts 197
   Stuffed cabbage rolls 89
   see also Red cabbage
Cajun dry rub 185
Cakes: Apple and muesli rock cakes 42
   Rich chocolate torte 242
Calcium 7
Calories 6
Cancer 7
Cannellini beans: *Italian cannellini bean and tuna salad* 100
   Tuscan bean crostini 60
Caramels, Cinnamon banana 234
Carbohydrates 6, 7
Cardiovascular disease 7
Carrots: *Carrot and celeriac purée* 136
   Carrot and poppy seed scones 54
   Carrot and spice muffins 31
   Flowery carrot salad 203
   French-style chicken in wine 124-5
   Golden lentil soup 70
Casseroles: Fragrant lamb with spinach 169
   Goulash in a hurry 178
   Hotpot with golden parsnips 172
   Keema curry 163
   Moroccan-style pumpkin and butter beans 156-7
   Perfect pot roast 160-1
   Pheasant casseroled with ginger 135

Slow-braised beef and barley 164-5
Cauliflower with crispy crumbs 194
Celeriac: *Carrot and celeriac purée* 136
   Celeriac and spinach soup 66
   Celeriac coleslaw 206
   Celeriac with crispy crumbs 194
Celery: *Cheese and celery scones* 54
Cereal bars 38
Cheese 7
   Basil-stuffed chicken breasts 118
   Blue cheese and walnut biscuits 50
   Bulghur wheat and feta salad 98
   Cheese and celery scones 54
   Cheese and watercress scones 54
   Cheese and watercress soufflé 155
   Cottage cheese and vegetable curry 141
   Feta and couscous salad 153
   Fruity goat's cheese toasts 81
   Goat's cheese toasts 81
   Greek-style feta and watercress soufflé 155
   Halloumi and lentil salad 153
   Italian-style tomato dip 52
   Parmesan-topped mussels 94
   Pea curry with Indian paneer 140-1
   Pears grilled with pecorino 92
   Red cabbage and blue cheese coleslaw 206
   Red Leicester and onion clafoutis 142
   Sesame cheese twists 50
   Sweetcorn and blue cheese chowder 73
   Tapenade goat's cheese toasts 81
   Tomato and pecorino clafoutis 142
Cheesecake, Sultana lemon 241
Cherries: *Cherry and almond cookies* 48
   Cherry compote 220
Chestnuts, Pheasant casserole with cabbage and 135
Chicken: Basil-stuffed chicken breasts 118
   Chicken and vegetable filo rolls 82-83
   Chicken kebabs with fresh citrus salsa 84
   Chicken, spinach and yogurt layered bake 147
   Chicken with apricots and cumin 121
   Chicken with asparagus and fennel seeds 127
   Chicken with Riesling 125
   French-style chicken in wine 124-5

Greek-style chicken parcels 83
Indian-style grilled chicken
breasts 122-3
Indian-style kebabs 123
Marsala chicken with fennel
126-7
Chicken liver mousse 87
Chickpeas: *Vegetarian goulash*
178
Chillies: Chilli dressing 153
Lime and chilli dressing 98
Chinese leaves: *Oriental-style
pepper and Chinese leaf salad*
204
Sesame greens and bean sprouts
197
Chocolate: *Chocolate custard pots
with poached pears* 221
Double chocolate chunk and nut
cookies 48
*Raspberry and chocolate cream
on panettone* 233
Rich chocolate torte 242
Chowder, Salmon and tomato
72-73
Chutney 169
Cinnamon and raisin bagels 217
Cinnamon banana caramels 234
Clafoutis, Tomato and pecorino
142
Clams: *Clam and tomato pizzas*
116
Quick clam chowder 73
Cod: *Cod with mustard lentils* 104
Cod with spicy Puy lentils 104
Oriental fish casserole 110
Thai-style crab cakes 102
Welsh cod crumble 108
Coleslaw, Crunchy nut 206
Cookies *see* Biscuits
Cottage cheese and vegetable curry
141
Courgettes: Baked aubergines with
yogurt 146-7
Fresh green soup 65
Couscous 157
Feta and couscous salad 153
Crab cakes, Thai-style 102
Cranberries: Blueberry and
cranberry granola 22
Cranberry relish 82-83
Fruity goat's cheese toasts 81
Crostini, Tuscan bean 60
Crudités with three dips 52
Crumble, Herbed fish 108
Cucumber: Raita 122
Curries: Fragrant lamb with spinach
169
Keema curry 163
Pea curry with Indian paneer
140-1
Custard 248
Little custard pots 220-1
Pistachio floating islands 224-5

D
Dairy foods 6, 7
Dates: Cereal bars 38
Desserts 218-51
Dips, Crudités with 52
Dolmades 88-89
Dried fruit: Fruit and nut bread 46
Fruit and pistachio baklava 246-7
Spicy fruit buns 46
Drinks: Banana and mango shake
12
Mango, peach and apricot fizz
17
Strawberry yogurt smoothie 14
Drop scones, Apple and hazelnut
25
Duck: *Duck stir-fry with a citrus
flavour* 132
Spiced stir-fried duck 132

E
Eggs 8
Ham and egg scramble 32
Herbed French toast 34
Parsee scrambled eggs 32
Scrambled eggs with smoked
salmon and dill 32
Energy requirements 6
Essential fatty acids 8

F
Fat, in diet 8
Fennel: Marsala chicken with fennel
126-7
Turkey kebabs with fennel and red
pepper relish 130-1
Feta and couscous salad 153
Fibre 7
Figs with raspberries and rose
cream 222
Fish 8
Floating islands, Pistachio 224-5
Flowers, Mixed salad leaves with
blueberries and 203
Focaccia 212-13
Folate 7
Free radicals 7
French beans: Pan-fried turkey
escalopes with citrus honey
sauce 129
French-style chicken in wine 124-5
French toast, Herbed 34
Fromage frais: Fresh herb dip 52
Lemon mackerel pâté 91
Fruit 6, 7, 9
Autumn pudding 238
Berry salad with passion fruit
18
Mixed berry salad 26
Pimm's melon cup 227
Summer pudding 238
see also individual types of fruit

Fruit and nut bread 46
Fruit and pistachio baklava 246-7
Fruity Bircher muesli 21
Fruity ginger biscuits 40
Fruity goat's cheese toasts 81

G
Gammon: *Perfect pot roast* 161
Gazpacho, Classic 65
Ginger: Ginger and honey dressing
166
Ginger nuts 40
Gingered roast pork 176-7
Pheasant casseroled with ginger
135
Ginger ale: Mango, peach and
apricot fizz 17
Goat's cheese *see* Cheese
Goulash in a hurry 178
Granola, Blueberry and cranberry
22
Greek-style chicken parcels 83
*Greek-style feta and watercress
soufflé* 155
*Guacamole topping, Baked potato
skins with* 59
Gumbo, Prawn 112

H
Haddock *see* Smoked haddock
Halibut: Griddled halibut steaks
with tomato and red pepper
salsa 106
Halloumi and lentil salad 153
Ham: *Bulghur wheat and ham salad*
98
Ham and egg scramble 32
Hazelnuts: Apple and hazelnut drop
scones 25
Heart disease 7, 9
Herb and saffron risotto 148
Herb dip 52
Herb pitta breads 214
Herbed fish crumble 108
Herbed French toast 34
Hotpot with golden parsnips 172

I, K
Indian-style grilled chicken breasts
122-3
Indian-style kebabs 123
Iron 8
*Italian cannellini bean and tuna
salad* 100
Italian-style tomato dip 52
Keema curry 163
King prawn bisque 68-69
Kumquats: *Duck stir-fry with a
citrus flavour* 132
Steamed kumquat honey pudding
248

L
Lamb: Fragrant lamb with spinach
169
Hotpot with golden parsnips 172
Lamb burgers with fruity relish
170
Mediterranean stuffed vegetables
174-5
*Middle Eastern-style stuffed
vegetables* 175
Slow-braised lamb and barley 165
Leeks: Leek and spring green filo
pie 144
Golden lentil soup 70
Halloumi and lentil salad 153
Lime: Lime and chilli dressing 98
*Lime and passion fruit floating
islands* 225
Liver: Chicken liver mousse 87

M
Macadamia nuts: Double chocolate
chunk and nut cookies 48
Mackerel *see* Smoked mackerel
Main meals 96-185
Mangoes: Banana and mango shake
12
Fragrant mango cream in brandy-
snap baskets 233
Mango, peach and apricot fizz 17
Thai-style stir-fried beef with
mango 166
Marsala chicken with fennel 126-7
Meat 8
Mediterranean stuffed vegetables
174-5
Mediterranean-style pastry 151
Melon cup, Pimm's 227
Meringues, Pistachio floating
islands 224-5
*Middle Eastern-style stuffed
vegetables* 175
Milk 7
Banana and mango shake 12
Millet: *Aubergine with millet and
sesame seeds* 200
Millet with spinach and pine nuts
200
Mincemeat: *Apple and mincemeat
rock cakes* 42
Minerals 6, 7
Moroccan-style pumpkin and butter
beans 156-7
Mousses: Chicken liver 87
Strawberry yogurt 230
Muesli: Apple and muesli rock
cakes 42
Blueberry and cranberry granola
22
Fruity Bircher muesli 21
Muffins, Breakfast 31
Mushrooms: Beef and mushroom
Stroganoff 158

Herbed French toast 34
Partridge pot-roasted with mushrooms 136
Vegetarian Stroganoff 158
Mussels: Hearty mussel soup 79
Parmesan-topped mussels 94
Mustard sauce, Pork steaks with 183

N

Noodles, Vietnamese broth with 76
Nori, New potatoes with 191
Nuts: Fruit and nut bread 46
see also individual types of nut

O

Oats: Blueberry and cranberry granola 22
Cereal bars 38
Crunchy raspberry dessert 234
Fruity Bircher muesli 21
Oat and orange ginger biscuits 40
Okra: Prawn gumbo 112
Olives: *Olive focaccia* 213
Pissaladière 56-57
Tapenade goat's cheese toasts 81
Tomato and black olive salad 208
Onions: *Onion and herb raita* 123
Onion and pancetta pissaladière 57
Pissaladière 56-57
Orange: Orange and pecan biscuits 44
Orange and raspberry relish 170
Orange and strawberry-topped muffins 28
Orange and tomato salsa 115
Peaches with an orange cream 222
Sultana lemon cheesecake 241
Sweet orange French toast 34
Turbot with sauce maltaise 114-15
Oriental fish casserole 110
Oriental spare ribs 185
Oriental-style pepper and Chinese leaf salad 204
Osteoporosis 7

P

Pancetta: *Onion and pancetta pissaladière* 57
Paneer, Pea curry with 140-1
Pannacotta 244-5
Parmesan-topped mussels 94
Parsee scrambled eggs 32
Parsnips: Gingered roast pork 176-7
Golden lentil soup 70
Hotpot with golden parsnips 172
Partridge: *Partridge pot-roasted with mushrooms* 136

Pot-roasted partridge with sage 136
Passion fruit: Berry salad with passion fruit 18
Fragrant mango cream in brandy-snap baskets 233
Lime and passion fruit floating islands 225
Pastries: Chicken and vegetable filo rolls 82-83
Fruit and pistachio baklava 246-7
Greek-style chicken parcels 83
Peach and pecan baklava 247
Pear, hazelnut and almond baklava 247
Pastry, Mediterranean-style 151
Pâté, Lemon mackerel 91
Peaches: *Berry salad with a peach and apricot sauce* 18
Mango, peach and apricot fizz 17
Peach and pecan baklava 247
Peaches with an orange cream 222
Pears: *Chocolate custard pots with poached pears* 221
Pear, hazelnut and almond baklava 247
Pears grilled with pecorino 92
Peppery salad with pears and wild garlic 203
Peas: *Creamy broccoli and pea sauce* 139
Leek and spring green filo pie 144
Pea curry with Indian paneer 140-1
Pecan nuts: *Apricot and pecan drop scones* 25
Orange and pecan biscuits 44
Peach and pecan baklava 247
Peppers: Basil-scented sautéed vegetables 188
Broccoli and red pepper quiche 150-1
Goulash in a hurry 178
Griddled halibut steaks with tomato and red pepper salsa 106
Oriental-style pepper and Chinese leaf salad 204
Provençal tuna and pepper salad 100
Roasted pepper salad 204
Roasted red pepper and onion salad 204
Tiger prawns with pepper salsa 84
Tomato and red pepper pissaladière 57
Turkey kebabs with fennel and red pepper relish 130-1
Pesto-yogurt dip 52
Pheasant: *Pheasant casserole with chestnuts and cabbage* 135

Pheasant casseroled with ginger 135
Phytochemicals 6, 7
Pies: Leek and spring green filo pie 144
Pilaf, Spiced basmati 198
Pimm's melon cup 227
Pine nuts, Millet with spinach and 200
Pissaladière 56-57
Pistachio nuts: Fruit and pistachio baklava 246-7
Pistachio floating islands 224-5
Pitta breads 214
Pizza, Tuna and tomato 116
Plums: *Plum and yogurt bavarois* 230
Spiced shortcake with autumn fruit 251
Polenta biscuits, almond 44
Pork: Gingered roast pork 176-7
Goulash in a hurry 178
Oriental spare ribs 185
Pork steaks with mustard sauce 183
Rich fruit casserole 181
Spiced pork with sweet potatoes 181
Sticky spare ribs 185
Potassium 9
Potatoes: Baked potato skins with smoked salmon and fresh dill 58-59
Borscht with crunchy mash 74-75
Cottage cheese and vegetable curry 141
Keema curry 163
New potatoes with nori 191
Perfect pot roast 160-1
Potato and watercress soup 66
Provençal tuna and pepper salad 100
Salmon and tomato chowder 72-73
Prawns: Bulghur wheat and prawn salad 98
King prawn bisque 68-69
Prawn gumbo 112
Thai-style prawn cakes 102
Tiger prawns with pepper salsa 84
Pregnancy 7
Processed foods 8, 9
Protein 6, 8
Provençal tuna and pepper salad 100
Prunes: *Rich fruit casserole* 181
Pumpkin: Moroccan-style pumpkin and butter beans 156-7

Q, R

Quiche, Broccoli and red pepper 150-1
Raisins: Breakfast muffins 31

Raita 122, 123, 163
Raspberries: *Banana and raspberry toasts* 28
Crunchy raspberry dessert 234
Fresh berry drop scones 25
Fresh figs with raspberries and rose cream 222
Lemony leaf and raspberry salad 203
Mixed berry salad 26
Orange and raspberry relish 170
Raspberry and chocolate cream on panettone 233
Raspberry and currant sauce 230
Sweet orange French toast 34
Red cabbage: Goulash in a hurry 178
Red cabbage and blue cheese coleslaw 206
Red currants: Raspberry and currant sauce 230
Red kidney beans: *Vegetarian goulash* 178
Red Leicester and onion clafoutis 142
Rhubarb and strawberry compote 244-5
Rice: *Artichoke risotto* 148
Dolmades 88-89
Fragrant basmati rice 198
Herb and saffron risotto 148
Lemongrass-scented basmati rice 198
Mediterranean stuffed vegetables 174-5
Middle Eastern-style stuffed vegetables 175
Spiced basmati pilaf 198
Stuffed cabbage rolls 89
Tomato rice 181
Risotto *see* Rice
Rock cakes, Apple and muesli 42
Rolls 211
Rose cream 222
Rosewater pannacotta 245
Rye bagels 217

S

Saffron: Herb and saffron risotto 148
Salads: Bulghur wheat and prawn 98
Crunchy nut coleslaw 206
Feta and couscous 153
Garlicky tomato 208
Mixed salad leaves with flowers and blueberries 203
Provençal tuna and pepper 100
Roasted pepper 204
Thai-style stir-fried beef with mango 166
Salmon: *Baked potato skins with salmon and tomato topping* 59

Salmon and tomato chowder 72-73
Summer salmon and asparagus 110
see also Smoked salmon
Salsas: *Orange and tomato* 115
  Pepper 84
  Tomato and olive 106
  Tomato and red pepper 106
Salt 9
Saturated fat 8
Scones, Cheese and watercress 54
  see also Drop scones
Seeds: Cereal bars 38
Sesame seeds: *Seeded pitta breads* 214
  Sesame cheese twists 50
  Sesame greens and bean sprouts 197
Shortcake, Strawberry 250-1
Side dishes 186-209
Smoked haddock: Herbed fish crumble 108
  Smoked haddock and spinach soufflé 155
Smoked mackerel: Lemon mackerel pâté 91
Smoked salmon: Baked potato skins with 58-59
  Scrambled eggs with 32
Smoothie, Strawberry yogurt 14
Snacks 36-61
Soufflés: Cheese and watercress 155
  Hot apricot 236
Soups 63-79
  Borscht with crunchy mash 74-75
  Celeriac and spinach soup 66
  Classic gazpacho 65
  Golden lentil soup 70
  Hearty mussel soup 79
  King prawn bisque 68-69
  Salmon and tomato chowder 72-73
  Vietnamese broth with noodles 76
Spinach: Celeriac and spinach soup 66
  Chicken, spinach and yogurt layered bake 147
  Fragrant lamb with spinach 169
  Keema curry 163
  Millet with spinach and pine nuts 200
  Smoked haddock and spinach soufflé 155
  Tagliatelle with green sauce 139
Spring greens: Leek and spring green filo pie 144
Starchy carbohydrate foods 6, 7
Starters 80-95
Strawberries: Berry salad with passion fruit 18
  Mixed berry salad 26

Orange and strawberry-topped muffins 28
Rhubarb and strawberry compote 244-5
Strawberry frozen yogurt 229
Strawberry shortcake 250-1
Strawberry yogurt mousse 230
Strawberry yogurt smoothie 14
Stroke 9
Sugar 8
Sugarsnap peas, Salad of cherry tomatoes and 208
Sultanas: Fruity Bircher muesli 21
  Sultana lemon cheesecake 241
Summer pudding 238
Swede: Slow-braised beef and barley 164-5
Sweet and sour dipping sauce 102
Sweet potatoes, Spiced pork with 181
Sweetcorn and blue cheese chowder 73

T
Tagliatelle with green sauce 139
Tapenade goat's cheese toasts 81
Teabreads: Fruit and nut bread 46
Thai-style crab cakes 102
Thai-style stir-fried beef with mango 166
Thyme and garlic focaccia 213
Tiger prawns with pepper salsa 84
Toast *see* Bread
Tomatoes: *Baked potato skins with salmon and tomato topping* 59
  Chutney 169
  Clam and tomato pizzas 116
  Classic gazpacho 65
  Garlicky tomato salad 208
  Griddled halibut steaks with tomato and red pepper salsa 106
  Italian-style tomato dip 52
  Orange and tomato salsa 115
  Pea curry with Indian paneer 140-1
  Pissaladière 56-57
  Salad of cherry tomatoes and sugarsnap peas 208
  Salad of fresh and sun-dried tomatoes 208
  Salmon and tomato chowder 72-73
  Stuffed cabbage rolls 89
  Sun-dried tomato focaccia 213
  Tiger prawns with pepper salsa 84
  Tomato and black olive salad 208
  Tomato and olive salsa 106
  Tomato and pecorino clafoutis 142

Tomato and red pepper pissaladière 57
Tomato rice 181
Tuna and tomato pizzas 116
Tropical rock cakes 42
Trout: *Smoked trout pâté* 91
Tuna: *Italian cannellini bean and tuna salad* 100
  Provençal tuna and pepper salad 100
  Tuna and tomato pizzas 116
  Tuna crostini 60
Turbot with sauce maltaise 114-15
Turkey: Pan-fried turkey escalopes with citrus honey sauce 129
  Turkey kebabs with fennel and red pepper relish 130-1
  Turkey burgers 170
Tuscan bean crostini 60

V
Vegetables 6, 7, 9
  Basil-scented sautéed vegetables 188
  Chicken and vegetable filo rolls 82-83
  Crudités with three dips 52
  Mediterranean stuffed vegetables 174-5
  Middle Eastern-style stuffed vegetables 175
  Roast root vegetables with herbs 193
  see also individual types of vegetable
Vegetarian goulash 178
Vegetarian Stroganoff 158
Vietnamese broth with noodles 76
Vine leaves: Dolmades 88-89
Vitamins 6
  Vitamin A 7
  Vitamin B group 7, 8
  Vitamin C 7
  Vitamin E 7

W
Walnuts: *Apricot and walnut drop scones* 25
  Blue cheese and walnut biscuits 50
Water, drinking 9
Watercress: Cheese and watercress scones 54
  Cheese and watercress soufflé 155
  Greek-style feta and watercress soufflé 155
  Pears grilled with pecorino 92
  Potato and watercress soup 66
Welsh cod crumble 108
White loaf 211
Whiting: Herbed fish crumble 108

Y,Z
Yogurt 7
  Baked aubergines with yogurt 146-7
  Blackberry ripple frozen yogurt 228-9
  Blueberry ripple frozen yogurt 229
  Cinnamon banana caramels 234
  Fragrant mango cream in brandy-snap baskets 233
  Indian-style grilled chicken breasts 122-3
  Onion and herb raita 123
  Pesto-yogurt dip 52
  Plum and yogurt bavarois 230
  Raita 122, 163
  Strawberry frozen yogurt 229
  Strawberry yogurt mousse 230
  Strawberry yogurt smoothie 14
Zinc 8

Low Calorie Cookbook was published by
The Reader's Digest Association Limited, London
from material first published in the Reader's Digest Eat Well, Live Well series

Project Editor
Rachel Warren Chadd

Art Editor
Jane McKenna

Assistant Editor
Rachel Weaver

Reader's Digest, General Books, London

Editorial Director
Cortina Butler

Art Director
Nick Clark

Executive Editor
Julian Browne

Development Editor
Ruth Binney

Managing Editor
Alastair Holmes

Picture Resource Manager
Martin Smith

Style Editor
Ron Pankhurst

First edition Copyright © 2002
The Reader's Digest Association Limited,
11 Westferry Circus, Canary Wharf, London E14 4HE

We are committed to both the quality of our products and the service
we provide to our customers. We value your comments, so please feel
free to contact us on 08705 113366 or via our web site at:
www.readersdigest.co.uk
If you have any comments or suggestions about the content of our books,
email us at **gbeditorial@readersdigest.co.uk**

Copyright © 2002 Reader's Digest Association Far East Limited
Philippines Copyright © 2002 Reader's Digest Association Far East Limited

Reader's Digest production
Book production manager: Fiona McIntosh
Pre-press accounts manager: Penelope Grose
Senior production controller: Sarah Fox

Origination: Colour Systems Limited, London
Printing and Binding: Toppan Printing Company, Hong Kong

ISBN 0 276 42740 8
Book code 400-151-01

Visit our web site at www.readersdigest.co.uk